THE AGONY OF
VICTORY

ALSO BY STEVE FRIEDMAN

The Gentleman's Guide to Life:
What Every Guy Should Know
About Living Large, Loving Well,
Feeling Strong, and Looking Good

Loose Balls:
Easy Money, Hard Fouls, Cheap Laughs
& True Love in the NBA

(with Jayson Williams)

Lost on Treasure Island:
A Memoir of Longing, Love, and
Lousy Choices in New York City

STEVE FRIEDMAN

THE AGONY OF
VICTORY

When Winning Isn't Enough

Arcade Publishing • New York

Arcade Publishing books may be purchased in bulk at special discounts for sales promotion, corporate gifts, fund-raising, or educational purposes. Special editions can also be created to specifications. For details, contact the Special Sales Department, Arcade Publishing, 307 West 36th Street, 11th Floor, New York, NY 10018 or arcade@skyhorsepublishing.com.

Arcade Publishing® is a registered trademark of Skyhorse Publishing, Inc.®, a Delaware corporation.

Visit our website at www.arcadepub.com.

10 9 8 7 6 5 4 3 2 1

Library of Congress Cataloging-in-Publication Data is available on file.

ISBN: 978-1-61145-492-5

Printed in the United States of America

For my mother and father,
Janet Hupert Friedman and Barry Morton Friedman

And in memory of
David Wallace Hupert and Irwin "Sonny" Friedman

"The real glory is being knocked to your knees and then coming back. That's real glory."

—Vince Lombardi

CONTENTS

ACKNOWLEDGMENTS

I'm grateful to the athletes who exhibited such generosity and patience with me, even when they had no way of knowing whether they would like the resulting stories. (Some didn't.) Also, thanks to their friends, families, fans, teammates, coaches, competitors, detractors, and everyone else who put up with my questions and presence.

Thank you to the editors who assigned, edited, improved, and—in some cases—conceived of these stories: John Atwood, Charlie Butler, the late Art Cooper, Jonathan Dorn, Hal Espen, Peter Flax, David Granger, Jon Gluck, Eric Hagerman, Jay Heinrichs, Lisa Henricksson, Stephen Madden, Adam Moss, Barry Murov, Scott Omelianuk, Bill Strickland, Brad Wieners, and David Willey. Thank you to Steve Murphy, majordomo at Rodale, Inc., the publishing juggernaut that owns the magazines in which many of these stories first appeared.

I am indebted to those who read draft after draft of one, many, or all of these stories, offering suggestions and wise counsel when there was absolutely nothing in it for them. Thank you for your kindness, Joe Bargmann, Jeff Colt, Rachael Combe, Carolyn Craig, Scott Dickensheets, Nancy Donaghue, Chris Ducker, Mary Duffy, Mary Kate Frank, Ann Friedman, Don Friedman, Christina Frohock, Ken Fuson, Robbin Gourley, Helen Henry, Anne Kelsh, Kristen Kemp, Lynn Medford,

Katharine Medina, Miranda Ryshawy, Nicholas Ryshawy, Jennifer Scruby, Jonathan Thompson, Mary Wible, and Leslie Yazel.

I'm grateful to Megan Williams and Emily Getchell for their translation work, reporting help, and indefatigable good cheer in Italy and Cuba respectively.

Thank you to agent Faye Bender and publisher/editor/book lovers Jeannette Seaver and Dick Seaver. Thank you, Eddie, Isaac, and Iris, for reminding me what's important and what's not.

I am especially grateful to Jeff Leen, who for twenty-seven years has helped and inspired me more than he imagines. Thank you, friend.

INTRODUCTION

The cycling champion couldn't decide what to order for dinner. He had invented a new kind of bike. He had created a new way of riding. He had revolutionized the sport, inspired millions, and ridden faster than any human ever had. And now, just a few years later, he couldn't choose between chicken korma and chicken rogan josh.

He blinked. He squinted. He mused aloud about the chicken dishes. He took great gulps from his pint of Diet Coke. Sweat dripped from his nose onto the tablecloth as his wife and two small boys studied the floor.

We were at an Indian restaurant in the northwest of Scotland, hard on the Irish Sea, near where the champion was born, in the country that once named him its "most intriguing sports personality." I knew about his subsequent failures and debt, his bitter and public feuds with cycling's sanctioning bodies. I knew he had recently quit drinking. I knew he had tried to kill himself four times. And I knew that, as much as he hungered to achieve athletic greatness again, *he* knew the disfiguring costs of his ambition. When he chose rogan josh, his wife and boys seemed to start breathing.

Graeme Obree was one of the most tortured men I had ever met. And one of the most heroic. I thought there might be a connection.

Obree's is just one of the stories included in this book. There's also the hard-drinking professional bowler who has spent his life trying to exorcise the ghost of his legendary father; the leading scorer in Division I college basketball who blamed his chronic unemployment and arrest for shoplifting on the voices in his head and an "animation machine"; another cyclist, who saved the Tour de France, restored cycling glory to Italy, enraged Lance Armstrong, then, just a few years later, checked into a hotel room in a seedy coastal village south of Venice and on Valentine's Day, killed himself. There's the greatest Orthodox Jewish boxer in the world, if not in history, whom I watched fall twice in the first round of an Atlantic City bout — to an unknown — and transform instantly from an avatar of cultural and religious strength into a young, confused, and motherless immigrant, even as his fans screamed his name and waved Israeli flags. Here also is the eagle scout, astronaut, and cross-country runner whose most stirring feats of heroism live on — contrary to what most people think — not in what he did but how. And here is the most celebrated high school distance runner who ever lived, a man who accomplished long-distance running feats almost half a century ago that still astound, then abandoned his wife and three children in Washington, adopted a false identity, and started selling water-filled insoles from a pushcart on the beaches of Waikiki. He called them "Happy Feet."

Here are men (and two women) who despite their inner torment ascended to the absolute peaks of their sports. Or did their success come *because* of their despair? That's just one question I tried to answer as I watched them work, and rest, and — as much as they could — play. That's what I tried to understand as I talked to the others whose lives had been bent — often cruelly — by the fierce need that seemed to drive so many of these men to greatness and just as often destroyed them.

I spent a week in Tucson at a tournament with another bowler, a professional "hustler" who had made a career out of cheating officially sanctioned pros out of their hard-earned tournament winnings and was now trying to go legit for reasons he couldn't quite articulate. I pored over maps and photos in Northern California with a convenience-store clerk and tree climber who decided that his life wouldn't be complete unless he hiked from Mexico to Canada — and back — in one season. I sat bleary-eyed in the chilly predawn darkness at a pancake hut at ninety-three hundred feet with scores of recovering drug addicts, bulimics, and garden-variety obsessives who set out each midsummer to travel 101 miles over six thirteen-thousand-foot mountain peaks and through countless melt-swollen alpine rivers as they competed in the most forbidding ultra marathon in the world; I retraced the doomed Italian cyclist's final desperate weeks in Cuba, and then, in Italy, found fans who still refused to face the truth about their hero. I gazed into the empty autumn sky with the dutiful company man who for much of his adult life had risen at 4 A.M., run his four miles, showered, and then caught an early morning commuter train into Manhattan . . . until September 11, 2001. I traveled to the Midwest, to my hometown, so that my father could teach me to play golf. That's what he thought, anyway. What I wanted was to discover exactly what he had found as a young man on the links those many Wednesday afternoons, and Saturday mornings, and Sunday summer evenings, and why he couldn't find it at home, where my mother and brother and sister and I waited for him. I wanted to learn whether his passion for golf was a cause or consequence of our family's falling apart.

These were serious athletes (my father included), engaged in matters of life and death, but just as often they were involved with characters and in — there's no other word — hijinks as hilarious as they were surreal. There were professional-bowling karaoke nights. There were long-distance hikers known only as Mr. Beer and Hobo Joe and Real Fat (who was really fat). There was Gatorade and kosher cake in the boxer's hotel room, with his

Hasidic handlers and my miniskirted, cross-wearing Catholic girlfriend. There was the excitable cycling writer who once described a particular race as so daunting that it "chopped through the ranks of great cyclists like a tsunami across a coconut festooned atoll." There was the Hawaiian "magic pillow" and the near-miraculous feats the schoolboy-legend-turned-deadbeat-dad inspired in people whom he persuaded to believe in what they could not see. There were, memorably, bowling groupies.

Mostly, though, there were men who were knocked down and who got back up.

These are not stories primarily about fame, or glory, though fame and glory are fiercely sought. They are neither celebrations of today's glib and smiling professional gladiators and corporate pitchmen, nor screeds against the toxic braggarts whose combination of villainy and strength attract even as it repels. These are tales of athletes who seek mastery over one thing without realizing that what they're really trying to master is something deep and unrecognizable within themselves.

Here are lonely people in lonely pursuits. Champions and would-be champions who work at their solitary crafts — cycling and running, boxing and bowling, hiking and golfing — away from the comfort and safety of teammates and agents and public-relations managers, far outside the protective and distorting circle of the spotlight.

Here are men and women driven neither by the will to win nor by the love of competition but by an existential terror most can't even acknowledge — a burning need to prove themselves and all too often a corrosive certainty that they are beyond redemption. Consequently, no amount of victory or athletic achievement brings them lasting happiness, and their only moments of real peace occur at those instants when they realize the futility of their struggles. The human experience, in other words. Counted in seconds and miles, scrawled on scorecards, etched in the ravaged souls of ruined champions.

1

GOING NOWHERE FAST:
GRAEME OBREE, CYCLIST

CHOOSING IS AN ORDEAL. CHICKEN KORMA VERSUS CHICKEN rogan josh should not matter so much. To the ravaged cyclist, though, it is a matter of life and death. He needs to be vigilant. How can he afford not to be? Ten years ago, just a short bike ride from here, the racer peered through a chilly, driving rain and glimpsed the future of his sport in a blinding instant, and what he saw brought him fame and riches and love. And then, for ten years, the mad vision tortured him.

He can't afford such prescience anymore. He can't survive the agonies it exacts. His doctors have warned him. His wife has pleaded with him. Even his former competitors and detractors, the ones he spent years challenging and vanquishing and mocking, with the hubris only a Prometheus on pedals could summon, even they wish him nothing but peace because they have witnessed the disfiguring price of revelation.

He was an inventor and visionary and champion who twice stood atop the cycling world by riding farther in one hour than anyone ever had, and today he needs to forget all that. He needs to concentrate on the moment. The doctors have told him that. Otherwise, what happened last Christmas might happen again. He couldn't bear doing that to his family. He needs to calm down, to take care of himself. He needs to order dinner.

But how can he? Korma versus rogan josh is just one of the agonizing choices facing him tonight. His eight-year-old son wants Kashmiri naan, and, though there will be plenty to share with his ten-year-old brother, the eight-year-old isn't much of a sharer. The older boy deserves his own bread, and it should be a different flavor, to make him feel special. Garlic bread! That might be the answer. How does the older boy feel about garlic bread? He doesn't feel so great about it, but he *really* doesn't feel great about sharing with his little brother. The older boy is dyslexic, like the cyclist was when he was a child, and he is clumsy, too, just like his father. The cyclist wants to protect his firstborn. He wishes someone had protected him when he was young. He will take a chance. Garlic bread.

The decision has cost the cyclist. He is blinking, squinting, grinding his jaw. It is September, chilly and damp in this coastal Scottish village, even inside the restaurant. But he is sweating. First his brow moistens, then beads appear on his broad forehead, and before long — even as he gulps at his pint of Diet Coke — the sweat is dripping down his aquiline nose and onto the table.

His eyes are grayish blue, and he squints and blinks and clenches his jaw during times of stress, like ordering dinner, or when he hears a question that causes him pain, like one about last Christmas. He is olive-skinned, dark-haired, six feet tall and 190 pounds, with broad shoulders and heavy, muscled thighs. In racing close-ups, his high cheekbones and angular jaw combine with an unusually full lower lip to exude lupine menace. He has gained six pounds in the past few months, though, taking the edges from his face, softening him. Combined with the nervous tics, the effect is prey rather than predator. He is self-conscious about his recent paunch.

The bread arrives and the boys are squabbling and the first pint of Diet Coke is gone and the sweat continues to drip from the racer's nose onto his appetizers, which he has ordered with enormous, excruciating difficulty.

"Oh, for God's sake," his wife says, doing a brave imitation of a laugh. "Wipe your brow."

The racer laughs, too, a small, helpless sound.

"It's a mark of health, you know," he says. "Sweating like that."

Bicycling's giants strap on heart-rate monitors and hire coaches who measure maximal oxygen uptakes and calibrate recovery times to the millisecond. They travel with nutritionists. Graeme Obree ate sardines and chili con carne, vegetables and marmalade sandwiches ("A pretty good diet, I'd say"), and boasted that he trained by the "feel factor," which involved "riding when I feel like it." The heroes of the sport — Lemond and Armstrong notwithstanding — grow up in biking strongholds like Italy and Switzerland and France, and they ride state-of-the-art machines that cost as much as $500,000, products of sophisticated engineering and corporate investments.

Obree lived in Irvine, Scotland, a grim little town in a green, hilly district hard on the Irish Sea, a spot so provincial that even other Scots deride it as a backwater. When he was twenty-eight years old, broke, in debt, and on welfare, he announced that he was going to break one of bicycling's most prestigious and time-honored races. He said he would do it on a bicycle he had built himself, for two hundred dollars ("not including the man hours, naturally.")

What followed over the next few years — world hour records in 1993 and 1994, world pursuit championships in 1993 and 1995, domination of time trialing in the midnineties — infuriated bicycling's image-conscious racing aristocracy as much as it inspired the sport's assorted couch potatoes, dreamers, and wheel-happy Walter Mittys. Obree's bike was as ungainly as it was original, his riding style as awkward as it was effective. He was funny and, on it, funny looking. He was also something of a loudmouth, often complaining about rampant blood doping in professional biking years before the highly publicized French and Italian drug investigations of 1998 and beyond proved him right.

After his first and most shocking world championship, in 1993, the British Broadcasting Company (BBC) conducted a telephone poll and named Obree "Scotland's most intriguing sports personality." That's when bicycling's bureaucrats set out to destroy him. Or he began to destroy himself. He's still not sure.

He was a clumsy child, falling into streams, knocking into walls, cracking his head open so often that "the blood poured out every other week." He broke his nose more times than he can remember.

His brother, Gordon, older by fourteen months, was the smart one. His little sister, Yvonne, not as gifted academically as Gordon, was tougher than either brother. Graeme was dyslexic, and sensitive, a less-than-ideal combination for a middle child and the son of a cop. The Obrees lived in Newmilns, population five thousand, just down the road from Irvine. As the cop's kid, Obree was "filth," or "son of the filth." Every day he'd be in a fight. And when he got hauled into the principal's office, "I'd get the belt, because I was the common factor."

He was terrible at sports, terrible in the classroom. He liked building things, though, and would have enjoyed metalwork class if it hadn't provided the central gathering place for his huskiest tormentors. He stood with his back against a wall, a chisel in his hand, and he fashioned a trowel and half a plant-holder bracket. It took him a year.

"I hated school," he says. "I hated Newmilns, I hated most of my childhood."

His parents didn't believe in pampering.

"Yvonne started working at sixteen," his mother, Marcia says, "and *she* cried and said she didn't want to go to school because of the bullying. . . . Even me, as a policeman's wife, I was ostracized. So it wasn't just Graeme."

"As far as we're concerned, he was just a normal boy," says John, his father. "He had trouble reading, yes, but I wouldn't go so far as to say he was dyslexic. . . . We just thought he was lazy about reading."

He wished his parents loved him more. Sometimes he wished he were dead.

"I have no idea how I managed to pass as normal in school," writes Kay Redfield Jamison in *An Unquiet Mind*, her memoir of manic depression, "except that other people are generally caught up in their own lives and seldom notice despair in others if those despairing make an effort to disguise the pain. I made not just an effort, but an enormous effort not to be noticed. I knew something was dreadfully wrong, but I had no idea what, and I had been brought up to believe that you kept your problems to yourself."

Graeme discovered bicycling as an adolescent, was racing by fifteen, on a burgundy prewar Gianelli. Pedaling as hard as he could, he could almost forget that he didn't have any friends, that his parents always seemed disappointed with him. At seventeen he won his first race, the eighteen-mile Ayr-to-Girvan time trial. He won the junior prize and the overall prize and, because he had never won before, the handicap prize. His total haul: fifty pounds, (approximately one hundred dollars). Why wasn't he happy?

This was Scotland, and this was Newmilns, and his father was a cop, so no one talked too much about loneliness, or self-esteem, or emotional problems. It was adolescent angst. Teenage moodiness. He was high-strung. Maybe the knocks on the head? So he pedaled harder and faster. He got a job in the local bike shop in Irvine. He went on longer training rides (always alone — he never liked riding with others), and he entered more races. He went faster, won more races, but he could never go fast enough, could never win what he wanted.

In 1985, when he was twenty years old, three years after Obree won his first race, after considerable success on the local racing circuit, after he'd managed to parlay his winnings into ownership of the bike shop, his father came home from work early one afternoon and found his son sucking on the pipe to a canister of welding gas.

"He assured us it was an accident," John Obree says, "and he seemed to be perfectly all right afterwards. I tried to get him to seek medical attention, but he seemed to be all right. I did talk to my own GP about it, though. What did he say? There's nothing much he could say. He said to keep an eye on things. But everything seemed to be normal."

This was normalcy: hopelessness, terror, a crushing fatigue that sent Obree to his bedroom, where he would wait — sometimes weeks and months — for the miraculous moment when the blackness lifted to be replaced with a delight and otherworldly energy that made the horror show almost worth it. During the bad times, he couldn't get out from under the covers. In the good times, though, he never slept more than two or three hours a night. He hatched business schemes then. He figured out a new position in which to race, a modified ski tuck. He started reading Victorian novels — he was fond of Anne Brontë — biology texts, essays, dozens of books at a time (he never finished any). He met a local girl, got married, won scores of time trials with his weird crouch position. He twice set the British record for distance in an hour. He also sold his bike shop and joined with an investor to start his own bike business.

For seven years he endured the bad times and reveled in the

good. By 1992, when he was twenty-six years old, it was mostly bad. His investor had pulled out and the business had failed. Obree was broke, in debt, and his wife was pregnant. Many weeks he and his wife, Anne, now living in Irvine, had to scrabble through the kitchen drawers looking for coins with which to buy bread. He was taking government-sponsored typing and filing lessons — welfare — so he could become a receptionist.

He watched on television that summer as an Englishman named Chris Boardman rode his bike to a first-place finish in the four-kilometer pursuit at the Barcelona Olympics. Obree knew Boardman, had raced him many times (Boardman was one of the few who usually defeated Obree, but not always, and not by much). And now Boardman had a gold medal. What did Obree have? Debt. Disappointed parents. An obscure place in local biking history, reserved for provincial oddballs who crouched when they pedaled.

"Everything was bleak," he says. "Pointless."

He didn't want to spend his life in his bedroom. How would he ever find peace? A new business scheme? Another riding position? Or was the answer within? The vision came to him on a chilly Saturday afternoon when he was sitting in the Irvine bike shop, where he still occasionally worked, alone. A cold, horizontal rain was blowing in from the Irish Sea, beating against the storefront window.

A slow reader, a lazy student, Obree nevertheless possessed an instinctive grasp of physics. He knew there were only two ways to increase his speed. He could boost his power output or he could reduce resistance. But he was already pedaling as hard as he could. And nothing was more aerodynamic than his ski tuck. He stared into space, then at his bike. He kept staring at the bike.

What if he adjusted the handlebars? And what if he moved the seat closer to the front of the frame? And what if he rode with his arms not just tucked but completely folded in to his body, so that air flowed more easily around his torso? He would have to learn to keep his entire body rigid, but that would increase his pedal power. And he would have to train his muscles, and he would need . . . but what if . . . ? In a flash, he could see the outlines of salvation. The answer *wasn't* within. It was there, in front of him.

It took him three months to build the thing. He used pieces of scrap metal from the bike shop, bearings he dug out of a washing machine.

In one of his first races, a ten-miler in Port Glasgow, he circled the roundabout at the halfway mark, where the race marshal stood with a local cop.

The cop had never seen anything like it before. He thought he was watching a handicapped racer trying to keep up with the others. "Look at that poor guy," the cop said. "Somebody's gone and built a special bike for him."

"Don't worry about that boy," the marshal said. "I think he's going to win this thing."

The marshal knew more than the cop. He didn't know nearly as much as Obree.

It had been late afternoon when he finished building the frame, and he had planned to carry it home, where he would paint it and tinker with it and think about how he was going to ride it. Instead, on a whim, he slapped some wheels on, carried it outside, and took off on a familiar ten-mile training route. First, out of curiosity, he punched his stop watch.

It was dusk. He didn't carry a spare tube. He wore a long-sleeved shirt with pockets in back and long tights, not racing gear.

When he finished the ride, he looked at his watch. Nineteen minutes, thirty seconds. It was the fastest he'd ever covered the route.

"I thought, 'Man, this feels so right.'

"I thought, 'This is magic.'"

*   *   *

Few agreed. To the gentlemen of the sport who even noticed him, he was a freak show, a lucky tinkerer, not a real athlete. The bike was a monstrosity. The professionals referred to Obree as the Praying Mantis because of his position on the bike. And the blackness had returned. In his mind, he was still the dyslexic, clumsy kid with no friends, with classmates who beat him, authority figures who blamed him, parents who didn't love him.

"It was never enough," he says. "*I* wasn't enough. 'What's the point?' I thought. 'What's the point? What's the point?'"

Only one thing made him feel better. Speed. More speed.

So he kept pushing himself harder, and harder, and one night the black mood lifted, and *that* was magic. "Everything made sense. It made more sense than it had ever made before. I was invincible. I could do anything. I could take on the world."

He would come home from his receptionist training at dusk, wheel out his odd duck of a bike at dark, ride as hard as he could, over the biggest hills, in the biggest gears, in the pitch black. At night he lay in bed, awake, thinking about the next evening's training.

He saw the point. He would ride his strange bicycle farther in an hour than any human being had ever ridden before. Graeme Obree — clumsy, dyslexic, a cop's kid and receptionist-in-training on the dole — he would seek triumph in an event so forbidding that many of bicycling's greatest professionals had avoided it for a hundred years, so ravenous that it consumed even its champions. He would seek the world hour record (WHR).

The record was first set in 1893, by a Frenchman named Henri Desrange, ten years before he founded the Tour de France. The Tour, of course, is bicycling's Super Bowl, World Series, NBA Finals, and World Cup rolled into one, a midsummer odyssey of guile and courage, strength and strategy. The WHR, the race that Obree hoped would save him, is merely a sixty-minute sprint around a banked track. In its utter simplicity lies its irreducible brutality. There are no gentle slipstreams, no opportunities to draft, no coasting strategies, no tactical slowdowns. A man simply gets on his bike and pedals as fast as he can.

"The absence of wind, the regularity of terrain, and the depth of self-knowledge necessary to maintain a near peak effort for sixty minutes have chopped through the ranks of great cyclists like a tsunami across a coconut festooned atoll," wrote Owen Mulholland, a prolific and apparently island-loving bike scribe.

The WHR poses two fundamental questions: Who is the strongest sprinter in the world? And who can best endure unimaginable pain?

"How much hubris do you have to have to say, 'I can ride a bike faster in an hour than any person who has ever walked the face of the earth, and I'm going to do it in this place, on this day, at this time?'" says longtime cyclist and sports physiologist Andrew Coggan, a research associate at St. Louis's Washington University. "That's why so many champions haven't even attempted it, because they've figured out the ratio of benefit to reputation risk."

The Tour de France brings its champions worldwide acclaim, deep and flowing income streams, the yellow jersey. But it is the WHR, not the Tour, that is known among biking cognoscenti, simply and starkly, as the Race of Truth.

It is not an event for the young or brash. Eddy "the Cannibal" Merckx, the legendary Belgian cyclist whom many still consider the sport's greatest competitor, entered his first WHR only after winning four consecutive Tours de France (he is one of only five men in history to win five).

It is not an event for the unprepared or the nonchalant. The Cannibal (so dubbed because his hunger to annihilate opponents was so voracious and insatiable) chose Mexico City to take advantage of the thinner air, which would allow for greater speed. Having made that strategic decision, he focused on tactics; he trained on a stationary cycle hooked up to a respirator with air that approximated the oxygen content at Mexico City's elevation.

Obree was neither unprepared nor nonchalant. He took precautions. He called Mike Burrows, the premier bicycle designer who had built Boardman's gold-medal-winning bike, and asked him to improve on his vision. Burrows fabricated a replica of Obree's peculiar machine, but instead of titanium Burrows used steel tubes filled with carbon. The new bike was twice as wide in the front as Obree's invention, two kilograms heavier, but aerodynamically more effective, mechanically more efficient. Burrows painted it a luminous, pearly white.

Anne urged her husband to ride the bike he'd built himself. It was a touching sentiment inspired by love and faith. In the Race of Truth, though, sentiment holds the same approximate value as that of a thatch hut on a coconut-festooned atoll, immediately pretsunami. So at 1:50 P.M. on a Friday afternoon in July, on a wooden track in Hamar, Norway, Obree mounted his Burrows-built machine.

People had been calling him the night before, telling him how much the race meant. As if he didn't know. Friends had warned him that the WHR, nine years old at the time, was unbreakable, not least because the Italian Francesco Moser, like Merckx, had set it in Mexico City, where the air was thinner and speed more attainable. (In fact, the past *four* WHRs had been set in Mexico City, dating back to 1968). Callers to the hotel, biking fans on the street, they all told the Scotsman the same thing — that what he was attempting was impossible, that, if he could do it, he would be doing the unthinkable. Didn't they realize? That was the point.

"Now take a deep breath," the starter said. "This is a very big deal, this is Moser's record, now get hold of yourself."

He pedaled as hard as he could, and it wasn't enough, so he

pedaled harder. And when he had finished pedaling and the hour was used up, Obree had traveled 50.8 kilometers (31.56 miles), farther than anyone had ever biked at sea level. A French television crew rushed him as he crossed the finish line, presenting him with a huge bouquet of yellow roses.

It was a great achievement. But not great enough. He had fallen short of Moser's mark by three-tenths of a kilometer. Less than two-tenths of a mile.

When Merckx finished his WHR in 1972, he could barely speak. As two thousand people cheered, including fifty-three reporters and the former king of Belgium, Leopold, his wife, Princess Liliane, and their daughters Esmeralda and Maria Christina, Merckx was asked about what he had done. To gaze upon a photograph of the Cannibal in that moment is to see a portrait of a man enlarged and diminished at the same time. Even after he was able to summon his voice, he said that the past sixty minutes were "the longest of my career . . . The hour record demands a total effort, permanent and intense, one that's not possible to compare to any other. I will never try it again."

And now the race had claimed another. Or had it?

Obree told the French television crew he wouldn't accept their flowers.

Then he told the track officials something else. "I'm going again," he said.

Even Merckx, one of the greatest bikers to ever live, endured only one Race of Truth. To race two? Consecutively? Out of the question. Obree insisted. Race officials relented, but only to a point. He could go back to his hotel. If he still wanted to race the next morning, if he could even *walk*, they would open the track.

He was there at 9:50 A.M., but without the state-of-the-art racer that Burrows had specially built. The Scotsman mounted the machine he had put together from scrap tubing and washing-machine parts. Burrows's machine had gleamed. Obree's was dull, smudged with oil.

"Are you sure you're ready?" the starter asked. It was the same pep talk from the day before. "This is Moser's record now. Now take a deep breath . . ."

He had tried it cautious and prudent. He had tried it on a carbon-filled, artisan-built bike. He had tried it respectful and calculating. But as hard as he ever pedaled, as desperately as he ever pushed, he would never be able to escape who he was. *This* is who he was.

"Are *you* ready?" Obree spat out from atop his old and faithful contraption. "Yeah," the starter said, "but —" The Praying Mantis was off and churning.

To ride for an hour at faster than thirty miles per hour, as Merckx and Moser had done, and as Obree was attempting to do, puts strain on the body that very few people ever experience. Most of us, when we're pushing ourselves to what we think are our absolute limits, are nowhere near them. A human heart can beat only so rapidly before it fails; most of us can get within ten beats or so of that rate for a few minutes before we have to cease whatever we're doing. Obree would spend an hour there. Pumping furiously up a hill, most of us arrive rather quickly at 60 percent of our maximal oxygen uptake, or the most efficient rate at which our blood delivers oxygen to our lungs. Competitive cyclists can go for some time at 75 to 80 percent. Obree would spend sixty minutes at 95 percent.

He would produce an enormous amount of pure energy as he sped around the track, but fully three-quarters of it would go to heating his own body. At rest, while the core of the human body thrums along at 98.6 degrees, skin temperature stays at about 95. Even with intense exercise it usually doesn't get above 100. During the Race of Truth, Obree's skin would burn at close to 107. Normally a quarter of our blood pumps to the liver, kidneys, and other internal organs. Nearly all of Obree's blood would course toward his muscles, for strength, and to his skin, in a desperate attempt at cooling. (The ideal situation for winning the Race of his, then, would seem to be a cold room, except cold air has higher density, which creates greater resistance.)

Obree would create enough raw power to light sixteen hundred-watt lightbulbs. "I could produce one-tenth to one-twentieth of that," Coggan says.

He would burn about eighteen hundred calories. That's about three-quarters of a human's average *daily* caloric expenditure.

"You can't go any faster, and you also can't go much longer," Coggan says. "It's like you're flying a jet, and you've hit your afterburners, and you're going through your jet fuel at a profligate rate. At some point, you have to slow down."

"I felt as if I'd reached the stage of death," Obree says. "I think I rode right through it."

He kept riding until he had gone 51.596 kilometers, more than thirty-two miles. He broke Moser's nine-year-old record by almost half a kilometer.

A Parisian newspaper reporter wrote, "There are no words in the English or French language to do justice to this story."

Another reporter counted the crowd that greeted Obree. Most had gone home the night before. The reporter counted eighty-nine people, including the janitor.

A third journalist had a question for the man on the funny machine.

"What is the name of your bicycle?"

"Name?" Obree said. "It doesn't have a name. It's just a bicycle."

"It must have a name. What is its name?"

Obree looked at his oil-stained frame, born on a rainy afternoon in the Scottish hinterlands, born again in the land of the midnight sun.

"I guess I'll call it 'Old Faithful.'"

*   *   *

No one knew his secret.

He didn't want them to know. So, as the reporters came calling, he created someone to greet them. Cycling's wild child who drank only curdled yak's milk and trained when the spirit moved him. Biking's bad boy who decorated his homemade creations (Old Faithful begat Old Faithful II, which begat Old Faithful III) with fingernail polish. The poor kid forced to scavenge scrap metal from ditches, and bearings from his mother's old washing machine. They were half-truths, embellishments, and outright lies. He used spray paint for some models, slopped paint out of a can for others. He trained hard, albeit on a schedule no one could figure out. The scrap metal came from the bike shop. And it was *his* washing machine. He might have been wacky, but he was an athlete; in training he guzzled liter after liter of water. He just loved the sound of "yak's milk."

The Praying Mantis had died in Hamar. Now he was "the Flying Scotsman." Or "the Ayr Man." The French referred to him as *L'homme de l'heure* ("the Man of the Hour"). When he had returned to Scotland after his triumph, "I got fifty messages on my answering machine, many of them saying, 'We want to pay you thousands of pounds to come to a track meet.' Before I'd make thirty to fourty pounds a week if I won. Now I'd make thousands just to show up."

He was adored, never more so than when another cyclist broke the WHR only six days after Obree's magnificent ride, and Obree vowed revenge. That the cyclist was Chris Boardman made the situation even more delicious.

Like Obree, Boardman was a sprinter. Like Obree, he was obsessive. There, the similarities ended. Boardman was a professional, a team member, a regular Tour de France entrant who had a coach, a manager, an Olympic gold medal, and a host of sponsors. Obree had trained in the dark after his typing lessons.

Boardman often worked out in a laboratory, hooked up to monitors. Boardman's warm-ups were scripted to the second. "Graeme," says Joe Beer, a friend of Obree, "would roll up to a race with his kit over his shoulder, in jeans, and he'd take his fleece off, roll up and down the road a couple times, chatting the people up, asking how they were doing, and the next minute he'd be on the track, going for it."

Boardman's trainer wrote academic treatises on aerobic capacity and lactate thresholds. Before races, Obree nibbled on marmalade sandwiches. "I reckoned they were about as good as energy drinks."

Boardman lavished as much attention on clothing and equipment maintenance as he did on his work-out regimen. (Some racers speculated that Boardman's obsession with sartorial style and burnished hardware had as much to do with his attention to sponsors' interests as it did with any constitutional disposition toward cleanliness.) Obree was a slob.

Boardman's roadwork involved hours of interval training and scrupulously crafted sprints. Obree, though he worked harder (and suffered more) than anyone imagined, pedaled to a drummer — or a wild-eyed, frazzle-haired jazz trumpeter — no other soul had ever heard. A reporter once asked him to describe his preparation. "Ride lots," he replied.

The Flying Scotsman crushed his opponents. Or, when he didn't, he gave up. "I've either zeroed out on a race," he says, "or I've won."

Boardman was more predictable. "He was like a robot," says Beer, "and I don't mean that as a putdown."

Boardman, a gold medalist, rode a Burrows-built machine, and it never failed to shimmer. The Ayr Man stuck with dull, clumsy Old Faithful.

Ali had Frazier, Russell had Chamberlain. Seabiscuit, stubby-legged and forever doughty, never drew closer to equine immortality than when he was thundering down the backstretch, flank-to-flank with the majestic and indomitable War Admiral.

Obree had Boardman.

"I was art," Obree says, "where he was science."

That fall, at the 1993 World Track Championships, again at the wooden track in Hamar, the men raced each other in the semifinals of the four-kilometer pursuit. They started at opposite ends of the track. Obree beat his "archrival" (as Boardman was now inevitably called) handily, setting a new world record.

That's the moment when adoration changed to something more primitive, more powerful. That a man who trained when he felt like it and ate what he wanted . . . that such a man could vanquish the most highly trained, scrupulously analyzed, laboratory-designed athlete in the world . . . that he could do it with a smile, with such careless panache . . . it wasn't just a world's record, it was a victory for the human soul, a triumph for scrappy underdogs and free spirits everywhere. It was a stunning display of what unalloyed joy and unbridled faith could accomplish, wondrous proof that, with belief in yourself, anything was possible.

If only people had known the truth.

For three months after the race, unbeknownst to everyone but Anne, he spit up blood every day.

"I've never heard of that happening in a human being," says Coggan, the sports physiologist. "It's quite common in thoroughbreds, though. What happens is the pulmonary blood pressure rises so much that capillaries burst and blood gets into the lungs. That's why you see horses frothing blood-flecked foam at the end of races."

People possess pain thresholds, built-in regulators to keep us from pushing our bodies to the point where they start self-destructing. Could Obree be so driven that he ignored exploding capillaries?

Coggan is reluctant to speculate. "But yes, it's possible."

In April 1994, nine months after he'd dispatched his archrival, Obree traveled to Bordeaux to reclaim the honor Boardman had stolen, to take back the world hour record.

Obree's wife and his mother were walking with him when they saw a crowd of four thousand people surging toward the stadium.

"My mother turned to me and she asked, 'What are all those people here to see?' I said, 'They're here to see me, Mum.' She said, 'Ah, no. That can't be. Ah, no.'"

He set a new record that spring afternoon: 52,713 kilometers.

Again, cycling fans celebrated their new hero. If only they had known the truth.

This is what pushed him: "It was pure fear. It was a feeling of 'This isn't good enough, I'm not good enough.'"

The Union Cycliste Internationale (UCI), the worldwide governing body that sets the rules for competitive cycling, didn't like Old Faithful. Maybe it's because Obree was a working-class loudmouth in a sport of ostensible gentlemen. Perhaps UCI president Hein Verbruggen had taken Obree's drug gibes personally. Or was the officer, as his supporters claim, merely protecting the purity of the sport, trying to keep bicycling's most venerable events (especially the Race of Truth) from being cheapened by clever cheats and tinkerers like Obree?

Just weeks before the 1994 World Track Championships, the organization issued new regulations. Henceforth, it said, saddle position had to be X. The top of the frame had to have angles Y and Z. There were other rules, too, all absurd, all clearly aimed at Old Faithful.

He had raced till he'd spit blood. He'd built the fastest bike in the world out of a washing machine. Did Verbruggen think a piece of paper would stop him?

He tinkered with the bike until it was in compliance with the new rules, and in April he brought it to Palermo, Sicily, to defend his world pursuit title.

On the ninth lap, after two and a half kilometers, Verbruggen, in a blue blazer, rushed onto the track flailing his arms. He couldn't object to the bike. Now he was objecting to the *way* Obree was riding it.

Obree aimed. He pedaled harder. "I thought, if this guy stands here, I'm gonna kill him. I'm gonna run smack into him and I'm gonna kill him. I didn't give a shit. I would have smacked him if he hadn't jumped out of the way."

Verbruggen jumped.

Even swerving, unnerved, Obree finished with the third fastest time in the event. It didn't matter. He was disqualified. Verbruggen and the UCI would hear no appeals.

"I asked for the written version of the rule and they said it's unwritten, it's not a written rule," Obree says. "To this day, I don't know the rule I was breaking."

Shaun Wallace, silver medalist at two world championships and a former holder of the Flying Kilometer record, says, "At the time, the two main problems in cycling were the escalating costs of bicycles, and drugs in sports. Graeme should have been the UCI's poster child. What they did to him was arrogance, plain and simple. That an 'everyday rider,' which is how they thought of Graeme, should hold the blue riband of cycling, they just couldn't take that."

Sentiments like that were common, but they wouldn't help Obree. He knew that. So six months later, in September 1995, he showed up at Bogotá, Colombia, at the World Track Championships with a new bike. Old Faithful was history. This contraption had an ultra-extended handlebar that put him almost prone over the frame. He called his new position "the Superman."

In Bogotá the Ayr Man took back his world pursuit title.

Again he bested Boardman. Worse, as far as the UCI was concerned, the Superman could more easily be copied than the Praying Mantis. Before long the design dominated velodrome races all over Europe. In 1996 Boardman used the Superman to retake the hour record.

The ruling body had learned its lesson. No more tricks! Both of Obree's inventions, the UCI declared, were banned forever. No one could ride the Superman, or Old Faithful, or any other insolent heap of cannibalized washing-machine metal in a UCI-sanctioned event again.

Obree fared little better than his inventions. He joined a French cycling team, Le Groupement, but lasted only weeks. Team officials said they sacked him because he didn't show up to training camp on time. He claimed the team wanted him to use drugs, that team officials had demanded he agree to have money for blood doping deducted from his weekly paycheck and fired him when he refused. (Subsequent criminal investigations and journalistic probes make his version credible to most cycling fans.)

He was thirty-one, poor again, with two young children now and little in the way of marketable skills. He could design machines, but where had that gotten him? He could endure pain, but what had that produced but more pain?

He traveled to the Atlanta Olympics in 1996 to represent Great Britain. His parents stayed home.

"My father said, 'Well, that's a six-day wonder, when are you getting a job?'"

"They didn't even come to the Olympics to watch their son," Anne says. "His mom said, 'It's too hot in Atlanta.' So instead they went on holiday to Egypt!"

"Crap," says John Obree. "That's total crap that he's talking. I rather think this is his imagination working overtime. It sounds like someone is pointing the finger at us. It's total shite. He said that just to prove a point."

Yes, they didn't go to the Olympics, Obree's mother says, partly because "we can't stand too much heat" but also because John couldn't get away from work. And, yes, they traveled to Egypt, but it was *before* the Olympics, and "I don't know if you're aware of it, but Egypt around Christmastime is dry and it's not an oppressive, sultry heat like Atlanta."

Obree didn't place. Afterward a teammate had to coax him from a fifth-floor windowsill, from which he was about to jump.

The next few years he won some local races, but nothing like the WHR or the world pursuit championship. "That," says Joe Beer, "was where Graeme started to disappear." It was injuries, newspapers said. Or a viral infection. "Mental strain," one publication reported. He didn't get along with others, some whispered. Or it was just bad luck. In 1998, walking through an airport in Geneva, he entered a pharmacy, bought 112 aspirin ("That's all they would sell me"), washed them down with water. He was hospitalized in critical condition, diagnosed with bipolar disorder.

Sports fans could grasp the agony of defeat, the tawdry shame of being thwarted by bureaucrats in blue blazers. But could they comprehend Obree's predicament? Could they understand that by 1998, when he was only thirty-three years old, money was tight, that he was still unskilled at anything but tinkering and racing, that he despaired of ever pleasing his parents, that the one constant in his life, his wife, forever-loving Anne, was asking Obree if they could please move to a small farm, so she could do something *she* loved every day, which was to ride her horse, a half Thoroughbred, half Appaloosa named Broxy, and that even though she said it would entail only a "wee mortgage," the notion scared him to death, made him feel more worthless than ever, that the biking riches were gone, frittered away, but he didn't know how to tell her that, so he didn't say anything? Biking fans and hero-worshipers had no trouble at all picturing Obree on his glorious two-wheeled gimcrack, but could they envision him silent, unshaven, huddled under the covers in his bed hour after hour, day after day?

In the fall of 2000, he showed up at the World Track Championships. He had been hospitalized for fifteen months, on and off, since the suicide attempt. He was swallowing a gram of lithium a day. He told reporters he was training hard and "probably fitter than at any time in my life." He announced his impending assault on the hour record.

People so wanted to believe. When he was first challenging the cycling establishment, it had been easier for the world to see a man-child who drank yak's milk and trained by whim, a fierce and loveable idiot savant of the sport, rather than someone driven by shame and self-loathing, an unloved son, a frightened child. Now that he was a fallen star, it was more convenient to see a cheated champion rather than a man with mental illness. People had invested Obree with their hopes, their dreams. He *had* to get better.

Miraculously, he did. It was impossible, what he was doing. But he was doing it. Training again, on a conventional bike this time, in yet another position and at speeds he'd never obtained before. He took better care of himself this time. He worked with a coach. And he got faster. He added glucose polymer drinks. And he got faster. He was only half a kilometer per hour off the pace he needed for a new WHR. If he set a third record, no one would ever doubt him again. He would never doubt himself. Speed. He needed more speed. But, no matter what he did, he couldn't find it. There was only one thing left to try.

He stopped taking the lithium. "I thought, 'It'll be just the way it was before.'"

*   *   *

It was Monday, December 17, 2001, eight days before Christmas. He spoke with his psychiatrist that morning, assured him that he was feeling fine. He told Anne at midday he was going out for a ride. Late in the afternoon, when he hadn't returned, she worried that he'd had a flat tire.

He had cycled eight miles through a steady rain to the farm where Anne boarded Broxy, parked his bike outside the horse's stall. He fashioned a noose from a long piece of plastic, tied one end to a rafter and the other to his neck.

The farmer's daughter wasn't supposed to check on the horse that day, but for some reason she did. The teenage girl's little brother usually tagged along when his sister ran her errands, but that day, for some reason, he didn't. That day, for some reason, the girl's father accompanied her. He had once practiced forensic law. He knew about saving lives.

At the hospital doctors told Anne that even if Obree recovered, he might be paralyzed or brain damaged, that if his lungs hadn't held 6.5 liters of oxygen instead of the normal human capacity of 2.5, he'd already be dead. Anne asked if she should get a priest to perform last rites. The doctor said that would be a good idea.

It is midnight in Irvine and we are sitting in the Obree kitchen, Graeme and Anne and I. The dinner had gone well (he chose rogan josh and the garlic bread scheme had worked), and the boys, whom both he and Anne call the "wee fellas," are in bed. But now it's pouring and Anne announces that the roof is leaking. That gets Graeme blinking and squinting and grinding his jaw.

It's been a long day filled with talk about the past, his plans for the future. This afternoon we walked down to the river behind the house and inspected the site where he will launch the pedal-driven water vehicle he plans to construct for his sons. He aches to make the boys happy. "So I make a point of every day telling the kids I love 'em and they're wanted. I don't remember getting that from my parents."

Anne brews tea. The horizontal rain started this week. Graeme says it will last till spring.

He's writing a book about his struggles, on the advice of his psychologist, who thinks it might help. He is also helping with the movie based on his life, a project that has been in the works since the midnineties, referred to by its producers at different times as "*Rocky* on wheels," "another wonderful Scottish hero story," "*The Full Monty* . . . in lycra," and, since the last suicide attempt, perhaps inspired by commercial considerations as well as matters of fact, "A cross between *Chariots of Fire* and *Shine*."

Obree would like to compete again, to be a champion once more, certainly. A man doesn't triumph twice in the Race of Truth without burning desires and a monstrous ego. But is his longing the manifestation of a conqueror's will or a lethal, seductive siren song? How can he know? How can anyone? One might as well ask what led him to the barn that cold December afternoon. It's so tempting to point the finger at Hein Verbruggen's idiotic intransigence, or Obree's cold, withholding parents, or the corrosive woe that a clumsy, dyslexic boy could never shake, or (as cruel as it is even to contemplate), considering where he fashioned his plastic noose, to blame his horribly misplaced anger toward Anne and her desire to move closer to her horse.

Or maybe it was just a few synapses misfiring, a molecular exchange missed here, another one made there. Maybe it doesn't matter how heroic or tragic your life is, how outsize your dreams and visions, as long as you take your medicine and get enough sleep and eat right and lay off the booze and talk about your feelings. (The corollary to this is, of course, the possibility that Obree's greatest successes might have been mere expressions of bad brain chemistry. Blinding cognitive leaps, flashes of inspiration, remarkable endurance and a high threshold of pain — all common manifestations of the manic phase of bipolar disorder.)

He wants to compete, but he won't. It's too dangerous. He knows he's not supposed to worry. But how can he help it? How could he ever help it?

There's a leaking roof that needs to be fixed. There's a canister of gas that needs to be fetched from ten miles away so he can weld the frames for the two Old Faithful replicas he needs to build for the movie. (The original frame sits in the Scottish Museum, in Edinburgh.) And now the movie producers want the Obrees to drive two hundred miles the day after tomorrow to meet the star so Graeme can teach him how to ride Old Faithful. And since he's going to be the body double in the movie, he needs to get in shape, to shed the lithium flab, especially in his calves, because there will be close-ups. And the newspaper syndication deal needs to be ironed out so he can make some money on his book. And he needs to *write* the book. And he needs to make arrangements for the wee fellas so that he and Anne can go meet the movie people.

He is working his jaw harder than ever, and he is squinting and blinking, and even though Anne just minutes ago served tea and is smiling, hers is a fixed, determined grin. The interview is over. Graeme has too much on his mind to be talking to a reporter just now.

One last question, then: He brought such delight to so many people; was there ever a time he felt it himself? What about that instant in Norway, ten years and a lifetime ago, when he first broke the unbreakable world hour record? Did he take a moment to bask in the ecstasy that descended upon him in the first seconds of that golden year, that magical time of triumph and vindication and affirmation?

I ask him what joy felt like.

"There were no celebrations," he says. "It made me feel

justified, that I'd justified my existence as a person." He is still blinking and squinting.

"As a person," Anne says. She gathers up the tea cups, looks at her watch, then at us, then back at her watch. She is not smiling anymore.

"I'd rather have died on the track than failed," Obree says. "I'd rather have breathed blood than failed."

"And you did," Anne says.

"This was never about sport," says the great hero, the noble champion, before he heads upstairs to his bedroom to rest. "This was never about glory."

2

KINGPIN:

PETE WEBER, BOWLER

I AM NOT A DICK," SAYS THE GREATEST BOWLER IN THE HISTORY OF bowling. He has had a couple of beers, and he's on his third Seven and Seven. When he's not bowling, he golfs. When he's done golfing, he drinks. Sometimes things seem clearer after a few drinks. "When I have a little buzz on, my eyesight gets better" is how he puts it.

This is what the great bowler sees now: cool green hills; loose knots of sweating, fleshy men and lean, tanned women; puddled shadows and the midday sun. He watches through a window from the bar at the Bogey Hills Country Club, near his hometown of St. Louis. The people here smile at him, greet him by name. This matters to the bowler. Once, when he was rich and famous and his enormous gifts were no more remarkable to him than breathing or walking, he didn't care what people thought. Now he's just famous. Now there's talk of the enormous waste the bowler has left behind, of the people he has hurt. He wants another chance. Now he wants to be understood.

"I don't want to be remembered as the guy who destroyed his father's name," the great and tortured bowler says. His eyes are filling. He orders a fourth Seven and Seven.

"I am not a dick," he says. "I am not an asshole. That's all I want. I don't want to be remembered as an asshole."

*   *   *

Pete Weber made a million faster than any other bowler in history. He is one of two men who have made more than $2 million bowling. (He holds the sole distinction of having spent nearly all his gains.) He is neither the best-liked nor the hardest-working bowler ever to play the game. Yet he employs a huge backswing, and he imparts a subtle spin to his bowling ball that results in a vicious hook. The backswing and the hook delight the most casual bowling fan; the spin fascinates and baffles the lanes' cognoscenti.

He is manic and furious, and this is why all but the most emotionally detached bowling fans either adore or despise him. He bowls with an extravagant desperation. He has slammed ball-return devices with his open palm and kicked foul posts and grabbed his genitals, though he can't remember ever doing the latter. He cussed out an old lady during a pro-am tournament. He is one of the most fined, suspended, and disciplined bowlers in the history of the Professional Bowlers Association. But his desperation is fascinating in the way that self-immolating greatness can be. When the PBA wants to draw fans, it knows Weber will bring them. When CBS or ESPN is going to televise a bowling tournament, the producers root for Weber to make it to the finals.

In the spring of 1998, at the Tucson Open, he draws more people than ever. Some want to see redemption; others hunger for rough justice. Some want to see the Pete Weber who bottomed out in 1995, when he earned only $39,795 bowling, winning exactly zero national tournaments. He divorced for a second time that year. He was broke, in debt, still drinking after three stays in drug-and-alcohol-rehabilitation centers (or four stays, depending on who among Pete's friends and family is telling the story).

Others want to see the Pete Weber of 1996, bowling's comeback kid, who, after a third marriage, rediscovered his magical hook and his delicate spin and started winning again.

Going in to the Tucson Open, Pete was the third-leading money earner on the tour for 1998 (more impressive considering that he was thirty-five, old by professional-bowling standards, and that he was suspended during the first three tournaments of the year for complaining about lane conditions), and he held the third-highest average in the PBA.

Will Pete Weber be remembered as the prodigy who squandered his talents or as the courageous maverick who defeated his demons? Bowlers have wondered about this for a few years now. As Pete goes in to the Tucson Open, his family and friends wondered too. So did Pete.

Pete Weber cocks his bowling ball so far back that it sometimes rises above his head, which looks especially dramatic because Pete is five-feet-seven and weighs 127 pounds. Like a lot of pro bowlers, Pete sports a mustache. His nose is thin and long, and his hair is swept back in a pompadour he keeps in place with regular applications of hair spray. He has grayish blue eyes that are soft and almost feminine after he has had a few beers but that go narrow and flat when he is angry or frustrated, which is most all the time when he is bowling. They are narrow and flat now, and he is puffing his cheeks out. He glares at the ground as if it had delivered him some grievous insult. It is late Wednesday morning, the first round of qualifying at the Tucson Open, and Pete Weber has just knocked down nine of ten pins, leaving the nine pin, which sits in the back row, second from the right. In bowling terms, Pete has left a "hard nine." Hard nines make Pete puff his cheeks out and narrow his eyes. They make him hold his arms out and his palms up, or suck air in through his pursed lips, or just scan the bowling crowd with a wide-eyed, wild look his father once described as "something out of the weird movies." Hard nines can also lead to rosin-bag flinging and genital grabbing.

It's not only hard nines. A bowling ball that hooks too much disgusts Pete Weber, as does a ball that hooks too little. Leaving a seven-ten split makes him ready to quit. Spares in general make him think about pushing the rerack button and giving up on the frame and having a few drinks. (He did that once. It was his fourth "ethical misconduct violation" in a year's time, which led to an automatic six-month suspension from the PBA.) Left-handed bowlers get to Pete because he thinks they possess an unfair advantage (their side of the lane is less scuffed and smeared), though he likes some personally. Leaving a ten pin (the rightmost pin in the back row) standing, or "tapping ten," makes him want to throw in the towel. Let's not even talk about gutter balls. The PBA tournament committee nauseates him. "They look out for just themselves. I've said that to them. In fact, I said, 'You guys are a bunch of self-serving motherfuckers.'" Even some strikes make Pete want to puke. Especially lucky strikes when he "goes Brooklyn," which is to say, when the ball hooks too much and hits the head pin from the left (the Brooklyn) side.

Pete goes Brooklyn and hits a strike. He spins around, kicks the ground, stares down the offending patch of wood. "Mother-*fuck*," he mutters.

"Pete has got a little bit of an attitude problem," says Don Fortman, a fan who has driven from Willcox, Arizona, to watch Pete bowl in the Tucson Open. "He gets a lucky break, he doesn't smile. Now a lucky break like that Brooklyn, that puts a smile on most anyone."

But how can Pete smile? How can anyone expect the Greatest and Most Troubled Bowler in the World to bowl for something as simple as fun? Pete hasn't bowled for fun in about twenty years. He says the day he retires from the pro circuit will be his last day in a bowling alley. "He doesn't even like to go in a bowling center now unless he's in a tournament," says his wife, Tracy, who also bowls. "To get him to watch me bowl, I've got to beg."

Pete bowls to pay his child support, his mortgage, and his taxes. He bowls to beat other bowlers. He bowls to show the PBA's self-serving motherfuckers that no one tells him what to do. He bowls because "I've never done anything else." He bowls because that's what he is — a pro bowler — and because if he doesn't bowl well, *that's* what he is.

Pete has three rounds in Tucson to make it to the top twenty-four, then three more rounds to "make the show," to bowl with the top four finishers on television Saturday for one shot at the Tucson Open's sixteen-thousand-dollar first prize.

Just one year ago, the greatest bowler in history, the man who had already earned twenty-one PBA bowling championships, won the Tucson Open at these very lanes. Right after he accepted his trophy, this is what he said about his victory:

"It tells me I'm not a loser."

Many of the bowlers throwing strikes this afternoon are built like Fred Flintstone. This undercuts the PBA's insistence that bowlers are finely tuned athletes. All the bowlers who chain-smoke, like Pete, don't help the PBA party line, either. And not that facial hair has anything to do with athletic performance, but many of the bowlers, like Pete, sport mustaches that call to mind porn stars from the seventies and dentists through the ages. Dentist/porn star mustaches simply do not scream "finely tuned athlete."

The PBA wants to attract larger, younger, richer audiences. Which is understandable because, as the desert sun beats down on Tucson's Golden Pin Lanes (right across the street from Courtesy Towing and Tucson Awning and Screen), and as 108 men with a statistically significant number of extra large guts and dentist/porn star mustaches throw strikes, sluggish little pockets of hunched, white-haired men and women move from lane to lane watching, many of them chain-smoking, some missing teeth, a few with walkers. The air reeks of cigarette smoke and stale beer and disinfectant and sweat.

To counteract this unfortunate impression, the PBA has hired a public-relations company in New York City. Now the PBA is using gold-colored pins and slow-motion cameras on its weekly television show. These efforts to burnish bowling's image make the bowlers happy.

On Wednesday afternoon the PBA's greatest hope and most fearsome nightmare is throwing strikes on lane twenty-four of Tucson's Golden Pin Lanes. Another hard nine. "Mother*fuck*." Pete Weber hisses.

Imagine the Greatest and Most Troubled Bowler in the World as a surly thirteen-year-old. He is scrawny and long-haired, and he pulls his sixteen-pound ball (the heaviest made, just like the pros use) back, back, above his head, flings it down the lane and watches it teeter and hang on the right gutter then hook with murderous intent. Everything about the kid's delivery — the backswing too high, the release too snapped, the hook too hard — is wrong, almost intentionally different from bowling's classic five-and-a-half-step, shoulder-high delivery.

This is much more than merely weird because, in 1975, when the kid is flinging strikes, the most famous practitioner of classic bowling — and not incidentally the most famous bowler in the world — is Pete's father, Dick, or "the Legendary" Dick Weber, as he was and is unfailingly referred to by bowling fans and bowling writers. The Legendary Dick Weber is as renowned for his easy charm, quick smile, and supreme self-control as he is for his bowling prowess. He is sometimes referred to in bowling circles as "bowling's greatest ambassador" and "the Babe Ruth of bowling," a spokesman for and embodiment of the politeness, grace, commitment to hard work, and all-around cheerfulness that the chain-smoking thirteen-year-old with the goofy back-swing doesn't seem to lose a lot of sleep over and that the Professional Bowlers Association so desperately wishes people would associate with the sport. (Actually, PBA officials would be delighted if more people would even think of bowling as a sport.)

It's not that Pete doesn't get along with his dad. No, Pete loves Dick. He especially loves Dick's life. What thirteen-year-old wouldn't? Pete's been on the road with his dad, seen him buy drinks for his bowling buddies, witnessed the fun they have, the parties that never seem to stop.

The thirteen-year-old wants that life for his own. That's why he's flinging that big hook at Dick Weber Lanes. He works on his release, on different angles, on different ways to play different lanes. He throws strikes from each arrow on the lane, six hours a day, seven days a week. Is he good enough to think about hitting the road and buying drinks for the house and hosting the parties that never end? Does he worry about measuring up to his father? He doesn't want to worry about that. He knows what that worry can do. He has watched Richard, his oldest brother, take his sixteen-pound ball and his monogrammed bowling shirt, which unfortunately says DICK WEBER, JR., and follow the Legendary Dick Weber on the tour, a dutiful son with an understated, classic bowling style just like Dad's. "He'll never be as good as his old man," the bowling fans say, until Richard starts worrying, starts wondering, quits. Pete watches John, the next Weber son, as he packs the bowling ball and the WEBER bowling shirt and follows his pop into the family business. John uses the same classic, understated bowling style as his dad, and people talk, and John worries and wonders, and then he quits, too.

Pete was different. "It just made him mad," says Pete's mother, Juanita, whom everyone calls Nete. "It just aggravated him." Pete made a promise to his mother. He told her he'd make people forget about Dick. Told her that one day, when people saw Dick walking down the street, they'd say, "There goes Pete Weber's dad."

A chain-smoking little old lady wants an autograph, so when the second round of qualifying is over on Wednesday afternoon, she makes her move. But it's not Pete she makes her move on.

"Walter Ray," she calls out. "Oh, Walter Ray," she calls out again, and then a third time, until a big, shuffling blond man with a beard looks her way. Only one bowler in history has earned more money bowling than Pete Weber, and it is this man, Walter Ray "Deadeye" Williams Jr.

Williams has a physics degree and a savings account and vague plans to teach high school mathematics someday and six world championships in horseshoes. He throws the ball with graceless efficiency, and he has a little hitch in his delivery that makes bowling aesthetes wince. ("Have you seen him bowl?" one of them asks rhetorically. "It's ugly. It's just brutal.") Williams wins, though, and he possesses a placid demeanor on the lanes that bowling's older female fans particularly adore. But when he signs his name for this fan, he neither smiles nor talks. In fact, Williams, the PBA's adored Abel to Pete's very public Cain, scowls slightly, then turns and gives this little old lady his back, which makes her gasp, then pucker her lips, almost as if one of her grandchildren has thrown some freshly baked Toll House cookies in her face.

She turns to Pete. The older women who frequent bowling alleys are fierce creatures, but she is speaking more softly now. Maybe she has seen Pete react explosively to a few too many hard nines. Whatever the reason, she is positively timid when she approaches Pete.

"Would you mind?" she murmurs, holding out a piece of paper.

"Hey, how ya doin'?" Pete says. "Where are you from?"

She tells him, but warily. Little old ladies — even those who frequent bowling alleys — tend to speak cautiously around men they have watched kick the air while screaming, "Mother*fuck!*"

Pete asks how she's enjoying the tournament. He admits that he's having some problems with the lanes. But, yep, he sure hopes he'll improve as the week goes on.

Emboldened, or maybe shell-shocked, she says, "You know, I used to watch your father all the time."

"Oh, yeah," Pete says, "He was the greatest. He is the greatest. Greatest bowler of all time."

They talk for five minutes.

As she leaves, she reaches for Pete's forearm. It is a gentle, tentative gesture, as if she is trying to convince herself that what just transpired involved flesh and bone and was not some miraculous apparition made up of cigarette smoke and fluorescent lights and beer fumes.

"Thank you," the little old lady says to Pete.

"No," he says, "thank you."

He turned pro at seventeen, a tenth-grade dropout married to a girl he met playing Frisbee in the parking lot of his dad's bowling alley.

The other bowlers on the tour invited the kid to the bar. They knew he liked to drink, so they patted him on the back and bought him drinks.

They bought him drinks because bowlers drink. Even the Legendary Dick Weber had knocked back a few. Actually, more than a few. "Dick got drunk from one coast to the other," Nete says, "and no one ever wrote anything bad about *him.*"

They bought him drinks because pro bowlers are generous. "Back in the day of Dick," says a high-ranking PBA official, "no one made money, because whoever won the tournament hosted the party in the bar that lasted until they packed up and drove to the next tournament."

And they bought him drinks because pro bowlers might be a lot of things, but one thing they are not is stupid. This scrawny little longhair might have good bloodlines, but how many of those vicious hooks could the foul-mouthed little punk roll after he was pumped full of those sweet-smelling, girlie-sounding drinks he liked?

Trouble was, he could roll a lot of 'em. A whole lot. Trouble was, as the pro bowlers found out, not only was Pete an exceedingly nasty drunk (unlike his father, who was a gentle, fun-loving drunk), he was also without question the greatest drunk bowler in the history of bowling.

So Pete would suck back two or four or, on a couple of occasions, eight or ten Long Island iced teas, which was one of his favorite drinks in those days, then he would cock that arm back above his head and let fly, all the while taunting opponents and cussing hard nines and grabbing his nuts and screaming at the world and in general making PBA officials and other pro bowlers regret that Richard Jr. and John had been too sensitive and mild mannered to follow in the big, deep, classic five-and-a-half-step-delivery paw prints of the Legendary Dick Weber.

His first year, Pete was named PBA rookie of the year.

Pete cocks, flings, hooks. He taps ten. "Fuck," he mutters in a tone of voice that is almost pleasant, considering his range of intonations. Then he picks up the spare.

A fan named Jack Iaci nods grimly. "The game is cruel to you," he says with the existential weariness that seems to infect a certain type of bowling fan. "It will rob you. Pete, though, he's the ultimate bowler. He's an artist."

It is Thursday morning, the final round of qualifying. Pete is in twelfth place, and if he bowls well this morning, he'll make it to match play tonight. Some of the other bowlers at the Golden Pin Lanes are flinging the ball as hard as Pete, but they are bigger, stronger, heavier, and younger. They pump iron, jog, take care of themselves. Pete's limbs are skinny, his chest sunken. Some of the other bowlers call him "Bird Legs."

Yet Pete throws the ball so hard, hooks it so dramatically, and imparts such intense forward rotation to it (he's got a "big hand," in bowling parlance) that in the past year he had to switch from a sixteen-pound ball to a fifteen-pound one because the heavier one was driving too powerfully through the pins, not deflecting enough from pin to pin and leaving far too many hard nines. A right-handed bowler with a big hand will inevitably leave hard nines. (Left-handers with big hands leave hard eights.) Pete leaves more hard nines than almost anyone.

"No one throws a ball like Pete," says Brian Berg, a former pro bowler who now works for Storm Bowling Products, Pete's sponsor, and who serves as Pete's friend, equipment manager, and apologist. "Never has. Never will."

"Pete has unlimited talent," says fellow bowler Mike Aulby, the third-winningest bowler of all time, behind Deadeye Williams and Pete. "There's nothing that can stop Pete but himself. And he's done a pretty good job of that."

By the end of the session, Pete is in eighteenth place. He's made it to match play.

Two more days to make it to the show.

In the spring of 1984 — a year in which Pete earned $115,735, turned twenty-two, and used cocaine — Pete checked into a drug-and-alcohol-rehabilitation center in Lonedell, Missouri, after a drunken argument with his then wife, DeeDee. He stayed twenty-eight days. Dick told people his son had a sore wrist.

By 1989 Pete had earned a million dollars faster than any other bowler in history. He was twenty-six, divorced, seeing a woman he had met in a bowling alley (and whom he would later marry), in debt, drinking again, paying child support, and fined and punished more times than he or the PBA officials wanted to think about. (The PBA had never named him its player of the year, and Pete was convinced it was partly because the self-serving motherfuckers flat out didn't like him.)

Even his fans considered Pete a crazed natural, a strike-flinging phenomenon pissing away his greatness. People commented on his tantrums. Bowling writers called him the John McEnroe of bowling. Pete is a lot like McEnroe, but in ways the writers probably didn't intend. Like McEnroe, with his command of spin and pace and angles, Pete is a master of his sport's subtleties, and he "reads" pin falls and lane conditions as well as anyone on the tour. (Also like McEnroe, Pete hates to practice and seldom does.)

The phenomenon was approaching thirty, and genital-grabbing tirades notwithstanding, he was beginning to worry about his reputation. He wanted to be remembered. But he didn't want to be hated.

In 1991 he wrote an article titled "Uncontrolled Emotions Don't Mix with Victory," for *Bowling Digest*. He told the magazine, "I finally got it into my head that liquor and Pete Weber don't mix."

In 1996, after a second divorce and a third marriage, to Tracy Goettel, and a few more attempts at sobriety and a lot more disciplinary actions against him, Pete was bowling a pro-am tournament in Tacoma, Washington, while he drank Seven and Sevens.

The bartender, an older woman, told him he'd had enough.

And that's when the author of "Uncontrolled Emotions Don't Mix with Victory" said, "You can take your fucking bowling center and your fucking tournament and you can shove 'em up your ass."

Turns out she was the mother-in-law of the bowling alley's

owner. The PBA put Pete on five years' probation, which he is still serving.

Pete wishes he had a beer, but the hamburger and fries will have to do because, as Tracy says, "We don't cut loose till the weekend. That's just the way it is." Last night they ate peanut-butter-and-jelly sandwiches in their ninety-nine-dollar-a-night hotel suite, which is more than they usually like to spend. But now it's Thursday afternoon, and Pete has made it to the top twenty-four, and someone else is buying, so for lunch they splurge: Tony Roma's. Tracy goes for the ribs. They're both slightly preoccupied. Tracy knows it costs them between eleven hundred and fourteen hundred dollars a week to bowl on the road, including the four-hundred-dollar tournament entry fee, and that if Pete doesn't bowl well in the next three sessions in Tucson, they'll lose money on this trip. Pete's first wife is suing for more child support, even though, Tracy says, "I went though the checks he wrote last year, and I found another eleven thousand dollars that he spent on the kids, including paying for their braces." She knows Pete's a soft touch, always lending money to his friends and even to some people Tracy doesn't think are his friends. She knows how Pete is about paying bills and that he loves to gamble: he once won twenty-five thousand dollars in a single night and he can lose just as big. She knows that he spends most of his afternoons in St. Louis back at the Bogey Hills Country Club, which she doesn't like, but what can she do other than make him promise to call her to pick him up so at least he won't be driving drunk? She knows golfers bet sixteen hundred dollars in one afternoon at Bogey Hills. She knows that not too many years ago the PBA had to send Pete's tournament checks straight to his mother. "We bailed him out two different times," Nete says. "Had to do that. He owed the IRS forty-three thousand dollars one year, and we helped him. We also had to pay his American Express bills."

Tracy knows that, and that's why she shops for peanut butter and jelly and Wonder Bread. That's why she buys Pete's hair spray for $2.48 a bottle at Walgreens. That's why she keeps the books and keeps him out of bars and off the golf course during tournaments. "I worry about him drinking when he's golfing, and besides, these guys might say they're his friends, but they're bowling against him, too, and I wouldn't trust one of them. I mean, who would you like to knock off the tour?"

Pete grabs a french fry, describes his typical day on the road. "I bowl, then I eat lunch, then I go back to my room and don't think about bowling. Then I bowl again."

"Yeah, babe, you're bowling great," Tracy says. Pete works over his burger. Tracy dispatches a baby back.

Tracy knows all about Wayne Webb, the PBA's twelfth-all-time-earnings leader, who is better known to bowlers and bowling fans as "the King of Karaoke." That's because Webb, a forty-one-year-old with a diamond stud in his left ear and a blond dentist/porn star mustache, has for three years been lugging his karaoke equipment in a U-Haul trailer from tournament to tournament, setting it up in bowling-center bars, where he serves as master of ceremonies three nights a week. He gets $250 a night.

Pete finishing his career manning a microphone in a bowling-alley bar? Tracy doesn't think so. Not if she's around. And she plans to be around. Tracy knows how much she loves Pete. But what she doesn't know is what will happen if Pete doesn't keep winning, if Pete doesn't start saving.

"That's a scary thought," she says. "No, I don't know."

"THE KING OF KARAOKE!" the PBA guys shouts into a microphone, and Wayne Webb trots onto lane thirty-two and squints into the spotlight. It's a Friday night, the final eight games of match play, and the PBA is doing its best to ratchet up the tension. The fluorescent lights are turned off, rock-and-roll music is pumped up, and the PBA guy is shouting player introductions with all the manic energy he can muster. A new group of bowling fans has shown up for the final night of match play. They are younger, mostly men, and they wear sleeveless shirts and baseball caps. Some have tattoos.

When a bowler is introduced, the young men yell. "One of only three players ever to convert the seven-ten split on national TV!" the PBA guy screams, and Jess Stayrook waves, and the young men yell "Yarghhh!"

"The comedian of the tour!" the PBA guy hollers, and Randy Pedersen waves, and the young men yell "Yarghhh!"

Most of the players sit in groups with friends, and they laugh and cheer and make fun of whomever happens to be the bowler in the spotlight. Pete sits alone, smoking. He knows what's at stake. So do the bowling-ball companies, which pay incentives to those fortunate four who make the show.

Pete is in ninth place, 109 pins from the show. He yawns. "Because I'm not bowling," he says.

Friday night, with four games left, Pete still has a chance for the show.

He strikes.

"Atta babe," Tracy says softly, because she is his wife and she loves him. Also she wants a new outfit. "That's the deal. If he makes the show, I get a new outfit to wear on it." He strikes again.

"Yeah, Pete," Brian Berg says, because Pete is his friend and his favorite bowler and because if Pete makes the show, Brian gets an incentive check from Storm.

He strikes yet again.

"Yarghhh!" yell the young guys in the sleeveless shirts, because they know that when Pete's on TV, if he's hitting strikes, he'll sometimes imitate Diamond Dallas Page, his favorite professional wrestler, and he'll make the Diamond Dallas Page hand sign (a diamond in front of his crotch) for the crowd, and he'll also do the Schwarzenegger pump-you-up flex thing every once in a while. And though the young bowling fans haven't yet learned to articulate their existential weariness, they yell "Yarghhh" because Pete embodies the disaffected, free-floating rage they admire, and they don't like the self-serving PBA motherfuckers any more than their hero does.

Pete strikes again, pumps his fist.

"Atta babe," Tracy says.

"Yeah, Pete," Brian says.

"Yarghhh!" the guys in sleeveless shirts yell.

But bowling is a cruel sport, and it will rob you.

Four games to prove he's not a loser and Pete goes Brooklyn, leaves four pins. Then he hooks too early with his spare ball, leaving a pin. An open frame. For a pro bowler, a disaster worse than a gutter ball.

Brian Berg stares at Pete, then at the remaining pin. "His attitude stinks right now," Berg says. "That spare he chopped? He didn't even try."

Pete won't make the show, and he knows it. That last game Pete bowls in Tucson is a meaningless 222. After one strike, for the first time on the lanes all week, he smiles.

He's had four beers and two Seven and Sevens, and his eyesight is good. Friday night in the Golden Pin Lanes bar, less than an hour after match play concludes, and this is what Pete sees: Tracy, sitting across from him, working on her second screwdriver; the King of Karaoke twirling dials and gesticulating; bowlers at the bar, drinking and waiting for their checks; and in front of the room eight young women in halter tops and shorts, singing a giggling, wiggling version of "Harper Valley P.T.A."

"Here's some girls looking to meet a bowler tonight," Tracy says, with a hard smile at the singers.

The PBA tour director enters the bar waving a wad of checks for the twenty finishers who didn't make the show. Tracy snatches Pete's twenty-one-hundred-dollar check for his tenth-place finish. "We got gambling money for next week in Reno," he shouts.

When the teenyboppers sit down, Brian Berg takes the mike and eases into "Mack the Knife." A pro bowler turned bowling-ball-company representative who can wring beauty from a song is a rare thing, and with each phrasing and pause, another patron of the bar seems to realize his precious luck, until the room is quiet and attentive as Brian nails the big ending of the song. And then bowlers holler, and bowling groupies scream, and Pete and Tracy drink up, and Mackie's back in town, and here at the Golden Pin Lanes bar no one is suing anyone else for child support, and no one's mother-in-law is cutting anyone off, and seldom is seen a hard nine. The King of Karaoke invites another singer to the mike, and Pete and Tracy order another round. Just one more. Well, maybe two, and then, Pete says, "We'll probably go to the hotel bar. We'll probably close the bar, actually."

The greatest bowler who ever lived has another ten years to earn some money, put some away, leave whatever bowling legacy he's going to leave, and get on with the rest of his life. Even though Pete will be inducted into the PBA Hall of Fame this month, even though he has a huge hand, even though Pete is the greatest drunk bowler in history, he is still going to be looking at more seven-ten splits and open frames in the next decade. "And ten years is pushing it," Dick Weber says. "Being forty-five, trying to keep up with these twenty-year-olds, especially now — that's tough."

Sometimes Dick blames himself. He remembers times he

let little Petey watch him drink with his pals and wonders if it all looked like too much fun. So he and Nete try not to drink in front of their youngest son. It saddens Dick when people think unkindly of Pete, "that he's a violent person, because he's not. I would say, yes, they're right, when he drinks. But when he's Pete, he's the most kind, the most generous person going. I mean, we didn't believe in the tough love. I guess we're just not that kind of people. So I don't regret not doing the tough-love thing. I still couldn't do it."

Nete wishes Pete would quit drinking. "But what Pete does he does and he will admit it. And what he says, you can bank on it being the truth. And he doesn't sneak around and do things. And I happen to know a lot of the bowlers out there who do the same things Pete does and nobody notices it. In fact, I wrote a letter to the PBA once telling what some of their 'nice guys' did."

("Have a player tell Juanita to get fucked, like Pete told that guy's mother-in-law," says a PBA official, who wisely requested anonymity, "and then see what happens.")

"What do I want people to know about Pete?" Dick Weber asks. "That he's loved by his family. He's just so loved by his family. We just love him to death."

Pete Weber is sitting in the bar of the Bogey Hills Country Club. He has had two beers and four Seven and Sevens, and has just ordered a glass of merlot. He has expressed a wish that people not judge him too harshly. He has said he would like to be remembered as a "nice guy." He has fought back tears. In an hour or so, he will call Tracy, who will have to drive out to pick him up. But now he is studying the glass of merlot in front of him, telling the story of his life, remembering how it began, wondering what might have been.

"If it wasn't for bowling," he says, "I would have ended up dead."

3

"IT'S GONNA SUCK TO BE YOU": THE MEN AND WOMEN OF THE HARDROCK 100, ULTRA-MARATHONERS

THE FIRST TIME HE TRIED IT, THE VOMITING STARTED AFTER sixty-seven miles, and it didn't stop until six hours later. The last time, his quadriceps cramped at mile seventy-five, so he hobbled the last quarter of the course. But Kirk Apt is a resilient, optimistic, obsessive — some might say weird — man who describes experiences like being trapped on an exposed peak during a lightning storm as "interesting," and that is why he's here, in Silverton, Colorado, cheerfully tucking in to a plate of pancakes, eggs, and bacon at 4:00 A.M., discoursing on the nature of fun while he prepares to take on, yet again, the most punishing hundred-mile footrace in the world.

It's called the Hardrock Hundred Mile Endurance Run, even though it's actually 101.7 miles long, and it is known to the small and strange band of people who have attempted it as the Hardrock 100. Or, simply, the Hardrock. In 1992, the first year of the race, just eighteen of forty-two entrants finished. Today nearly half of the 118 men and women who set off into the mountains will quit or be told to stop. Based on medical opinion, history, and statistical probabilities, death for one or two of them is not out of the question.

Apt could not look more pleased. "Enjoy yourself," he says to a fellow racer, a man staring fearfully at a strip of bacon. "Have fun," he blithely exhorts another, a pale woman clutching a cup of coffee, clenching and unclenching her jaw. Apt says "have fun" frequently enough to sound creepy. Even among other Hardrockers — many of them sinewy scientists from New Mexico's Los Alamos National Laboratory who tend to describe themselves with staggering inaccuracy as "mellow" — the thirty-nine-year-old massage therapist from Crested Butte, Colorado, is known as Mr. Mellow.

It's race day, the first Friday after the Fourth of July (the 2001 Hardrock will start on July 13), and Mr. Mellow is working over his pancakes at a worn wooden picnic table inside a café hunkered at the northern end of the only paved road in town. Silverton, population 440, is encircled by peaks, nestled at 9,305 feet in a lush mountain valley in the southern San Juans, at least an hour away, via the most avalanche-prone highway in North America, from fresh vegetables, a movie theater, or a working cell phone. If you didn't know about the fifteen feet of snow that falls here every winter, or the unemployment rate that's four times the state average, or the knots of bitter, beery ex-miners who gather at The Miner's Tavern toward the southern end of the paved road most every night to slurrily curse the environmentalists they blame for shutting down the mines and trying to ban snowmobiles downtown, you might think that Silverton was quaint.

Outside, the sky is a riot of stars, the air clean and cold and so thin it makes you gasp. Inside the café, it's warm and cozy, a perfect place for Mellow to break bread with Terrified.

"The most important thing about the race," Apt says, "is to remember to make sure to enjoy yourself." Yes, there can be crippling cramps and hair-raising lightning bolts — big smile — but there are also remote, deserted vistas, long and lonely treks up mountains and across ridgelines, precious hours spent alone among old-growth forest and fresh wildflowers.

It sounds cleansing. If you didn't know about the dozens of

unusually fit people who every midsummer collapse into near-catatonic, weeping blobs of flesh, their faces and hands and feet swollen to grotesque balloons because entire clusters of the racers' capillaries are breaking down and leaking (more on that later), you might think the Hardrock was fun.

Apt unfolds his six-foot-one, 168-pound frame from the cafe's picnic bench. Broad-shouldered, long-legged, clear-eyed, and, above all, mellow, he strides out of the emptying restaurant. He won the Leadville Trail 100 in 1995, and, though he's completed six Hardrocks, he's never finished first. Maybe this will be the year. Maybe not.

Big, big smile.

"How lucky are we?" he says.

Five minutes before six o'clock, the sun still not up, the competitors are turning in small circles on the gravel road outside Silverton Public School, taking in the surrounding peaks, scanning the distance for answers to questions most people never even consider. "Will I be hospitalized before sunset?" for example. They will spend the next day and at least one sleepless night in the deepest backcountry, almost constantly above ten thousand feet, climbing, sliding, wading, hiking, staggering, limping, and occasionally running. (Unlike other hundred-mile racers, the fastest and most fit of the Hardrockers will jog no more than 60 percent of the course.) They will face five mountain passes of at least thirteen thousand feet and one fourteen-thousand-foot peak. Those who complete the loop will climb and descend sixty-six thousand feet (more than would be involved in climbing and descending Mount Everest from sea level, as the race organizers like to point out). A large number of racers will vomit at least once. One or two might turn white and pass out. The slower runners will almost certainly hallucinate.

One of the most horrifying Hardrock visions is often all too real. It occurs when a race official informs a racer that he or she is moving too slowly to finish within the prescribed forty-eight hours. Getting "timed out," whether at mile seventy-five or at the finish line itself, is a bitter experience. Just ask Todd Burgess, a thirty-two-year-old newspaper-page designer from Colorado Springs. Five-foot-ten and 175 pounds, Burgess is cheerfully cognizant of his limitations and aspires only to finish and enjoy himself along the way. So last year he snapped pictures, meandered in the wildflowers, gamboled through the old growth. But, toward the end of the race, he saw that, unless he hurried, he wasn't going to make it. He sprinted. He stumbled. He panicked. And when he crossed the line at forty-eight hours, three minutes, and thirty-five seconds — which means that, officially, he didn't finish at all — another racer told him, "It's gonna suck to be you for the next year."

It was a cruel thing to say but, as it turns out, somewhat prophetic. For Burgess the last year has been one filled with doubts, fears, and horrific training sessions — twelve-hour runs and fifty-mile practice races and Sunday-morning sleep-deprivation workouts. While it has sucked to be him, it would suck more to be timed out again this year.

It's been said that recovering alcoholics and bulimics and drug addicts are disproportionately represented among Hardrockers, which is tough to confirm, but it makes sense if you consider that addictive tendencies and compulsive behavior would come in handy with the training regimen. It's also been said that full-time Silvertonians tend toward the same kind of ornery optimism and obsessive, clannish, and sometimes perversely mellow brand of masochism exhibited by many of the racers. That's equally difficult to nail down, but, having spent the better part of two winters here, I can vouch for the general soundness of the theory. It's no surprise that Silvertonians and Hardrockers tend to get along.

A few dozen townspeople have awakened early this morning to see the racers off, partly because three Silvertonians are entered, including one of the Hardrock's most popular hard-luck cases, fifty-two-year-old Carolyn Erdman, who has tried and failed three times to finish. Also at the starting line is the only Silvertonian ever to complete a Hardrock, Chris Nute. Nute, thirty-three, will be pacing Erdman in the second half of the race. He is not entered this year largely because of his wife, Jodi, thirty, who is with him for the start and whom no one has ever accused of being mellow, especially when it comes to the Hardrock.

The year Chris Nute ran the Hardrock "was the only time I ever thought we might get a divorce," Jodi says. "I couldn't understand wanting to do that. The training time sucked. And it made me feel out of shape. It totally gave me a fat complex. I had a [terrifying] vision of the future: that I was going to be married to an ultra-runner."

Dawn. Race director Dale Garland yells, "Go!" and about fifty Hardrock volunteers and spouses and Silvertonians watch as Apt, Burgess, Erdman, and their fellow racers jog and walk down a gravel road, turn southeast, and then head into the mountains — and toward the cold and dark and pain.

Some hundred-mile races are more famous. Many are more popular. Most have more corporate sponsors. None approach the Hardrock's brutality.

"This is a dangerous course!" warns the Hardrock manual, a fantastic compendium of arcane statistics, numbingly detailed course descriptions, grave warnings, and chilling understatement. When it comes to the temptation to scale peaks during storms, for instance, the manual advises, "You can hunker down in a valley for two to four hours and still finish; but if you get fried by lightning your running career may end on the spot."

Though a forty-four-year-old runner with a history of high blood pressure, Joel Zucker, died of a brain aneurysm on his way to the airport after completing the race in 1998, no one has perished during a Hardrock. But, according to the manual, "It is our general opinion that the first fatality . . . will be either from hypothermia or lightning!" (A Hardrock-manual exclamation point is rare as a Sasquatch sighting; one suspects typographical error, grim subject matter notwithstanding.)

"There's a reasonable chance somebody could die," says Tyler Curiel, forty-five, a Dallas-based doctor specializing in infectious disease and oncology who's run eleven hundred-milers and "fifty or sixty" ultras (any race longer than 26.2 miles). "I've fallen into ice-cold water, almost been swept away by a waterfall, walked six hours alone at high elevations in boulder fields," he says of his Hardrock experiences. "Had I sprained an ankle then, I might have been dead. I almost walked off a two-thousand-foot cliff in the middle of the night once. Two more steps, and I would have been dead for sure. And I'm fairly competent. So, yeah, there's a reasonable chance."

By late afternoon, after ten hours of climbing and sliding and "EXPOSURE" (the manual lists dehydration, fatigue, and vomiting as "minor problems," so racers tend to take capital letters seriously), the fleetest and most fit of participants are a good five hours from being halfway finished. At this juncture — the fifth of thirteen aid stations, Grouse Gulch, mile 42.4 — one would expect the appropriate emotion to be grim determination. So it comes as something of a shock to onlookers when a slender young man named Jonathan Worswick skips through a light rain, down a narrow, switchback trail, and across a stream into Grouse Gulch at 4:27 P.M. He is smiling. The thirty-eight-year-old runner from England is on pace for a course record.

The Hardrock old hands are unimpressed. These are retired runners, longtime observers of ultra running, in demeanor and worldview much like the leathery old men who hang around ballparks in Florida and Arizona sneering at the fuzzy-cheeked phenoms of spring and their March batting averages. The old hands have seen young studs like Worswick before. Seen them tear up the first half of the course only to be seized later by fatigue, cramps, nausea, and a despair so profound they can't even name it. Besides, the promising dawn has turned into a chilly, wet afternoon. And this is Grouse Gulch. Dangerous things happen at Grouse Gulch.

It doesn't look dangerous: a wooden yurt twelve feet in diameter, a canvas elk-hunters' shelter with three cots and a propane heater, and a telephone-booth-size communications tent where a radio operator hunches over his sputtering equipment, all hugging the west bank of the fast-flowing Animas River.

But if you've just trekked more than forty miles, climbed 14,000 feet and descended 10,000, confronted Up-Chuck Ridge ("ACROPHOBIA"), which is nearly three times as steep as the steepest part of the Pikes Peak Marathon, tackled the 14,048-foot Handies Peak ("Snow fields, altitude sickness, fantastic views"), where through a freezing rain you looked out upon the world and pondered the sleepless night (or nights) and the long hours that lie ahead, and now you are staggering down rocky switchbacks through pellets of freezing rain . . . well, then Grouse Gulch is danger itself. And nothing is more menacing than its banana pudding.

If there is some Higher Power watching over Hardrockers, urging them on, then surely there is a corresponding demon tempting them to stop. What the fiend wants is for them to taste the pudding. Not the oatmeal, or soup, or mashed potatoes, or individually prepared breakfast burritos (meat or vegetarian) — though all are tempting. No, it's the pudding, whose scent floats along the riverbanks and up the mountain slopes as easily as the Sirens' lethal song wafted over the wine-dark sea.

The pudding itself is creamy, smooth, not quite white, not quite brown. (The recipe is absurdly prosaic: one large package of Jell-O instant vanilla pudding mixed with four cups whole milk and three fresh bananas; makes eight servings.) But for the weeping runner who has been slogging up and down talus slopes and through marshes for fifteen hours or so, the pudding . . . for that person, the pudding whispers to them.

"Stop," it whispers. "Rest." The rush of the river blends with the hushed static from the radio equipment, but the pudding won't shut up. "Don't go on," it whispers. "Have some more pudding."

Worswick wolfs a vegetarian burrito — he won't even look at the pudding — and leaves ten minutes after he arrives. Fourteen minutes later, Kirk Apt strides across the bridge, looks around the aid station, sits down, changes his socks, and frets. Things are taking too long; he's wasting precious minutes. By the time he is ready to go, Mr. Mellow is thoroughly agitated. When he leaves Grouse Gulch, he starts too fast, realizes he's too "amped up," and has to breathe deeply in order to regain the calm he regards as essential.

Apt spends less than ten minutes at Grouse Gulch.

Todd Burgess had planned to be here by 6:00 P.M., but at 10:00 he is still struggling down the mountain, thighs burning, tentative, taking baby steps, fearful of falling.

He enters Grouse Gulch at 10:12 and leaves at 10:28.

Carolyn staggers in at 10:30, loses sight in her left eye, then leaves at 10:36, two minutes ahead of her planned forty-three-hour pace.

Others — swifter, more accomplished, less tortured — are not so strong. Scott Jurek, twenty-seven, who two weeks ago won the Western States hundred-miler, hits Grouse Gulch at 6:05 P.M. and takes a rest. He will not go on. Eric Clifton, who has won thirteen hundred-milers since 1989, walks into the aid station two minutes later and also stops for good.

Soaked and cold and exhausted, other racers hear the rushing river and the steady drizzle and the devilish gibberings of the

Pudding Master, and they feel the propane heat, and then they cast their weary eyes on the cots, soft as dreams.

Twenty-three Hardrockers quit at Grouse Gulch.

Vomiting, cramping, collapsing, whimpering hopelessly before the devil's pudding, and/or surrendering to that despair so profound that it's difficult to name are all variations, in Hardrock parlance, of "bonking." Typically, when a runner bonks, he or she also quits the race, as Apt did when he couldn't stop puking in 1992. Sometimes a runner bonks and keeps going, and even finishes, as Apt did when his quadriceps cramped and he trudged the last twenty-five miles of the course in eleven hours in 1999. To continue after bonking earns a runner enormous respect among fellow racers, most of whom have bonked at some point in their running careers. These people appreciate speed, but they revere grit.

When male Hardrockers bonk, they tend to quit. This is accepted wisdom among the racers, as is the fact that women bonkers, in general, do their best to finish. A racer can bonk without timing out, and he can time out without bonking. All things being equal, it's better to have bonked before being timed out than the other way around. Nonbonking runners who are timed out — especially late in a Hardrock — suffer the fate of Todd Burgess (it sucks to be them).

The Ouray aid station, at mile fifty-eight and an elevation of 7,680 feet, would provide an excellent place to quit. Though there is no pudding of any sort here, nor heated tents with cots, next to the aid station is a parking lot, and next to that, a highway. Silverton is less than an hour's drive away in a heated car.

But there will be no quitting here for Jonathan Worswick,

who arrives at 7:42 P.M., still leading, and leaves at 7:56. Not for Kirk Apt, who arrives at 8:20 and leaves at 8:27 — "psyched," he says, "but in a relaxed, calm way."

Neither will there be any quitting for Todd Burgess, who trundles toward the aid station the next morning at 5:14. His pacer, Fred Creamer, urges Burgess to run the last mile or so to the aid station, but Burgess wants to conserve his energy until he eats something. He's sure that a meal will give him the boost he needs for the second half of the course. In Ouray he takes a bite of warm roast turkey, a long pull of Gatorade, and vomits.

Creamer asks Burgess if this has ever happened to him during a race, and, when Burgess says no, Creamer considers ending their journey. But Burgess says he feels great. He does feel great. Creamer feels grave concern. They continue.

Like Burgess, Erdman approaches Ouray in the predawn darkness, moving fast enough to finish in less than forty-eight hours, but just barely. No one — not the aid-station volunteers and not pacer Chris Nute — entertains the slightest suspicion that she might quit in Ouray. Not that they wouldn't welcome such an event.

Erdman entered the race for the first time in 1997, when she was forty-eight, eight years after she quit smoking and one year after she and her husband left their cattle farm in Wisconsin and moved to Silverton. Nute paced her that year, and she made it eighty-five miles before race organizers told her that she was moving too slowly and that she was done.

In 1998 she entered again. Four weeks before the event she ran a fifty-mile warm-up race in Orem, Utah. Three miles into it she fell and scraped her left knee. There was blood and a little pain, but she thought it was no big deal. By the time she finished, she could see her patella; she was shocked at how white it was. The doctor in the emergency room told her she was lucky he didn't have to amputate the limb. She spent a week in the hospital with intravenous antibiotics. Surgeons operated on her twice.

In 1999 she was timed out at mile ninety-two.

Erdman has long gray hair that she wears in a braid, the lean body of someone half her age, and brown eyes that sparkle with an intensity peculiar to religious leaders and Hardrockers. She runs ten miles a day, more in the midst of Hardrock training, through rain, snow, and blistering sun. Her dedication has unified Silvertonians — like many residents of small mountain towns, notoriously resistant to unification unless it involves railing against silent black helicopters and the craven, jackbooted federal thugs who claim the choppers don't exist. But they're worried about her. Will she endure too much just to finish? What if she doesn't finish?

Nute knows that Erdman would sooner end up on an operating table than quit, and that's one reason he's agreed to pace her. They're friends. He wants her to finish, but he also wants her to live.

After thirteen minutes at the station, they walk along the Uncompaghre River out of Ouray and onto a dirt road, which they climb steadily through thick forest. The air is moist with dew and sweet with pine; birds are starting to sing. Though Erdman is falling farther behind her forty-three-hour pace and hasn't slept for a full twenty-four hours and won't for another twenty-four, the approaching dawn invigorates her — for about two hours. Then she wants to take a nap.

Not a good idea, Nute tells her.

Leafy undergrowth and lush, grassy ground beckon. Just a few minutes lying in that pillowy green would be so nourishing, so healing. It would make her go so much faster.

Really not such a smart thing to do, Nute says.

She pleads. She whines. She begs.

Pacers are valuable precisely because they warn their

charges not to surrender to their worst temptations — like gobbling fistfuls of ibuprofen and taking ill-advised naps. But Nute is also Erdman's friend, not to mention a fellow Silvertonian. OK, he says, one nap. They settle on seven minutes.

She nearly cries with happiness. She spreads her jacket, makes a pillow of her pack, and lies down in a perfect leafy spot. But it's not perfect enough. She picks everything up, moves to another leafy spot, and lies down again. Nute watches, looks at his watch; eight minutes have passed. She doesn't like the position of the pillow, so she adjusts it. Then she adjusts her jacket. Then her body. Three adjustments later, she sighs. It is a pitiable little sound.

"Go!" she chirps to Nute, who is sitting down, staring at her. "Start timing."

This is when Nute starts to worry.

Back in Silverton, Jodi Harper Nute is worried, too. She has watched over the past week as Chris has helped with various Hardrock tasks, handing out literature, signing in runners, helping pace Carolyn. Jodi watched him chat with other runners. She watched him study the course map. She watched him huddle with the old hands, doubtless revering grit.

And what she feared has come to pass. Just last night Chris told Jodi he wants to race again. (The couple has since moved to Durango, where less snow makes it easier to train.) "Goddamnit," Jodi says. "I can't believe this." Pause. "Yes, I can. I was wondering why I've been so pissy the past few days. Now I know why. God*damn*it."

While Jodi worries, Hardrockers trudge 10.4 miles and 5,420 feet up to Virginius Pass (elevation 13,100 feet), then 5.3 miles and 4,350 feet down to the aid station at Telluride. They have traveled 73.7 miles and have another 28 to go. Soon they'll have to tackle Oscar's Pass, 6.5 miles away and 4,400 feet higher. "Basically," says Jonathan Thompson, editor of the *Silverton Mountain Journal*, the local biweekly, "straight up a friggin' mountain."

After Oscar's ("Acrophobia, exposure, cornice") surviving runners will face Grant Swamp Pass, the most difficult climb of the course, a murderously steep scramble over boulders and loose scree ("rock and dirt that will slide back down the hill with each step you take"). It would be daunting on a day hike.

Erdman has been awake, racing, for thirty-one hours. It's now one in the afternoon, and, after she wolfs a slice of pepperoni pizza, she and Nute leave Telluride, climbing straight into the zone where Hardrockers too proud, too foolish, or too dense to quit often get themselves in danger. In 1998, as two-time Hardrock champion Dave Horton was ascending Grant Swamp Pass, a melon-size rock dislodged by a runner above fell and struck his right hand. "A little later," Horton, fifty-one, wrote in his account of that race, "I noticed that my glove was soaked through with blood." After finishing (of course) he realized that it was a compound fracture.

Many runners ignore puffy faces, hands that have ballooned like boxing gloves, feet like clown shoes, telling themselves it's merely a lack of sodium or some low-level kidney failure. Probably not fatal. They'll try to ignore the moist rattling they hear with every breath. Chances are the swelling and rattling are the result of damage to the body's capillaries. High-altitude races tend to starve capillaries of oxygen, which makes them leak fluid, which pools in the racers' hands and feet. "The danger," says Curiel, the doctor from Dallas, "is that one of the largest capillary networks is in your lungs, and when those capillaries start leaking, you have difficulty breathing. Pulmonary edema. In a really bad case, your lungs can fill up with water and you'll drown."

Digestive problems barely merit consideration. Jonathan Worswick left Ouray still in the lead but vomiting every few miles and suffering stomach cramps and diarrhea. Mr. Mellow stalked him during the climb, enjoying the view, confident in his uphill power, even more confident that Worswick had expended too much energy too early. Just before passing Worswick and crossing Virginius Pass, Apt said later, "a mental shift occurred for me. I knew I was in this race and really had a good shot at winning."

Worswick overtook him on the downhill to Telluride, but Apt was having fun. Just after beginning the brutal assault on Oscar's, Apt told his pacer he wanted to "get after it." Minutes later they blew by Worswick, who was too sick to fight anymore. He bonked. But he continued.

Burgess hasn't puked since Ouray, and, though by midafternoon he's suffering fatigue, muscle soreness, chills, and a slight loss of motor coordination, he's still in the race.

Erdman? She regains her sight near Telluride. But three miles later she begins to gasp.

She turns to Nute. "I'm not going to make it," she says.

Nute knows she might well be speaking the truth. He's been monitoring his watch, worrying as Erdman has slowed to a forty-minute-mile stagger. He's been despairing that she'll never make it out of the next aid station, Chapman, at 83.1 miles, before the cutoff time. But Erdman is the one who inspired Nute to run his first and — depending on Jodi — possibly only Hardrock. Plenty of people have told Erdman to stop. Nute's not going to be one of them.

"Let's sit down for a minute," Nute says. "Let's just process this. Let's do the math."

But what calculus of the spirit can take in to account years of training, hours alone, broken bones, and the taunting of the devil's pudding? Has an equation yet been written so elegant that it can encompass impossible dreams?

They sit, and they sit some more. They peer upward, above

the tree line, where the skies are black with monstrous storm clouds. Lighting crashes.

Erdman does the math. Instead of a number comes a word. "All I can think," she says, "is why?"

She doesn't bonk, and she isn't timed out. But after seventy-seven miles, Erdman drops out of her third and — she says — final Hardrock.

Ten miles from the finish, Todd Burgess forgets how to walk a straight line. Counting, he decides, will solve the problem. If he can put eight steps together, one ahead of another, without wavering, and name the number of each step, he won't swerve into the wilderness and be lost forever. He is sure of this. He counts aloud for an hour.

When he steps onto the abandoned rail bed that will take him the last two miles to Silverton, Burgess can see the gentle, aspen-covered hill ahead. Once he climbs that, he'll be able to look down to the town. He'll be able to see the finish line below. He knows he's going to make it. Only one thing can stop him.

He knows it's a silly fear, most likely the result of exhaustion and chills. If he knew about leaking capillaries, he might ascribe his anxiety to that. But Burgess's attempts at rationality won't banish a dreadful notion, born of sleep deprivation, or cellular rioting, or the desperate, fearsome need to finish under forty-eight hours.

This is what he thinks: "This would be a terrible time for a nuclear bomb to fall."

Burgess isn't the only one losing his mind. Gigantic June bugs wriggle from the soil and onto the damp and wobbly legs of Hardrockers unlucky enough to find themselves on the course after dusk on the second day of the race. Ghostly condominiums waver on top of mountain passes. Severed elk heads bob in the arms of grinning aid-station volunteers.

It's probably not capillary leakage. The visions seem to visit the slower runners, the ones who have been awake the longest.

"We know that people who have been sleep deprived have been noted to have visual, auditory, as well as tactile hallucinations," says Dr. Clete Kushida, director of the Stanford University Center for Human Sleep Research. "They can also suffer irritability, as well as changes in memory, focus, and concentration. And psychomotor deficits."

That's one way of putting it.

After forty hours, phantom Texans in ten-gallon hats walk beside the sleepiest Hardrockers at thirteen thousand feet, drinking beer and laughing. Grass turns to snow, rocks morph into Chevy Suburbans, plants transmute into Gummy Bears and bows. Before he died, Joel Zucker saw Indians.

Burgess finishes at forty-seven hours, forty-one minutes, and three seconds, the fifty-eighth of sixty finishers (none of them Silvertonians). Then he sits on the ground.

Race Director Dale Garland walks to Burgess and asks if he would mind turning off the digital clock when it hits forty-eight hours. "I think this is good therapy," Garland says.

Burgess sits next to the clock and stares at it. At forty-eight hours he pushes a button, but the clock keeps going. Burgess keeps sitting, staring at the running numbers.

Jonathan Worswick finishes sixth, at thirty hours, forty-six minutes, sixteen seconds.

Kirk Apt wins in twenty-nine hours and thirty-five minutes — beating the course record by more than thirty-five minutes. His legs tremble, and he weeps. Some onlookers get teary, too, even a few of the old hands. They don't like to talk about it, but they know that some of the fastest finishers are the most patently competitive, the loudest, the least liked, and the most likely to quit when outright victory seems impossible. Then there's Apt, who bonked and walked the last twenty-five miles of the course last year, enjoying the scenic vistas and the lonely ridgelines. Cramped. Limping. Having fun.

Local newspaper reporters gather round the champion. It's almost noon, clear and sunny. Apt tells one notetaker that he consulted a nutritionist before this year's Hardrock and that his "homemade goos" (various combinations of blended hard-boiled egg, potato, tofu, avocado, rice, yogurt, salt, honey, and chicken liver) helped him stay the course. He tells another, "I'm really not that competitive, but I saw I had the opportunity to win, so I thought, why not?" He mentions that he ran about sixty of the one hundred miles — "the flats and downhills, and I ran a few uphills, too."

The reporter from Durango has one last question.

"What interesting things happened in the race?" she asks.

Interesting things? Mr. Mellow grins.

"The flowers were just amazing."

4

LOST AND FOUND:
GERRY LINDGREN, RUNNER

S PEED WON'T BRING VICTORY. THE BOY KNOWS THIS. SPEED CAN'T *possibly save him. All he can hope for is to avoid shame. The boy will do anything to avoid shame. But he knows only one thing. He needs more speed.*

It is late afternoon on a midsummer day, July 25, 1964, at the Los Angeles Coliseum, long before anyone suspected the boy's secrets. He has run nearly four miles. He has two to go. It is 93 degrees on the track. The two men in front of him are world-class, race-hardened. He is eighteen years old, five-feet-six, 118 pounds, barely a month out of high school. To sprint now is madness. It is self-immolation. On the curve, where they won't see him, he sprints. He sprints to the outside. He sprints past one, then, fifteen yards later, the other. Of course it is folly. Later he knows he'll fail. But he has no choice.

He sprints around the curve and straight into California's setting sun. It's no use. They won't break. He hears their footsteps. Kritch-kritch. Kritch-kritch.

He beat Steve Prefontaine. He beat gold medalist Billy Mills. He lapped Jim Ryun in a two-mile race of the nation's greatest schoolboy runners. Most astonishing, in a sport where genetics, nutrition, technology, and training techniques conspire to make records ephemeral, Gerry Lindgren, in 1964, broke the high school two-mile record by nearly a minute. The same year, he ran five thousand meters faster than any American schoolboy ever had — or has.

"There was no frame of reference for what he was doing," says Bob Payne, who as a young reporter for the *Spokesman-Review* in Spokane, Washington, covered Lindgren when the runner was a high school senior. "There'd never been anything like it before. And it's safe to say there never will be again."

To study contemporary track records is to pore over knots of present-day phenomena and twenty-first-century dates. But look closely at the high school record books and rub your eyes. It must be a misprint, yet there it is, "1964," next to Lindgren's name in category after category. Second-fastest two-mile and three thousand meters ever. Sixth-fastest mile ever. Eighth-fastest fifteen hundred meters ever.

In the world of track, ignominy and immortality are separated by hundredths of seconds. Half a second looms — an impregnable barrier. High school records routinely fall within months, even weeks. It took fifteen years before a high schooler could break Lindgren's two-mile record. It took twenty-two years before a boy could shave five-tenths of a second off Lindgren's three-thousand-meter time. The number that can't possibly be real, the record that defies all running logic: 13:44. In more than forty years, no schoolboy has ever run five thousand meters faster than Lindgren.

He was neither graceful nor classic nor, much as it defies belief, blazingly swift. At the height of his powers, he couldn't step onto a track and run 440 yards in less than fifty-three seconds. Among elite runners, that's pathetic. But he could run a fifty-five-second 440 when others couldn't — at the end of a punishing six miles. What he was, was indomitable. He took on Olympians. He took on the Soviets at the height of the Cold War. He took on the ruling bodies of the sport. He helped ignite the first American running boom.

And then something went terribly wrong. Or maybe it was wrong from the beginning.

His wife awoke on January 15, 1980, and found a note on the kitchen table. Sell the business, it said. Get a divorce. He would be back in touch with her and their three children when he could.

They never heard from him again.

We meet in a hotel lobby under a three-story, 280,000-gallon aquarium filled with manta rays and black-tipped reef sharks, the room thick with the odors of suntan lotion, garlic, and salt water. Across the street lap the waves of Waikiki Beach, where Lindgren sold water-filled insoles called Happy Feet from a pushcart after washing ashore here more than twenty years ago.

Writer and former Olympic marathoner Kenny Moore tracked his old friend and running partner here in 1987. In *Sports Illustrated* Moore told of a champion who never believed in himself, a husband and father crushed by the demands of family life, a track legend living under an assumed name.

I had called from the mainland a month earlier to try to find out what had caused such wreckage — and to see if Lindgren had discovered the peace that had always eluded him or whether he was more lost than ever.

"Aloha," the voice on the other end said cheerfully, musically.

"Gerry Lindgren?" I asked.

"Never heard of me!"

I called again a few weeks later and got his recording. "If you want to leave a message for Gerry or Gale . . ." Gale Young was the name he had adopted when he had disappeared. He was still using it?

He is fleshier than the scrawny schoolboy who sprinted away from modern track's demigods, but still slight at 138 pounds.

He wears unfashionably large wire-rim glasses that frame his soft blue eyes. In the center of the blue iris is a shocking golden ring, which you can see when he gazes directly at you, which he doesn't do often. His teeth are graying. He wears a tank top, running shorts, and flip-flops, and his upper arms are soft and undefined. (He doesn't believe in weight lifting, and never has.) They jiggle when he gesticulates, which he does when he tells stories. His right big toe is blackened and blistered, no doubt from the fifty miles he runs every week. His hair, brown but graying, is carefully combed and looks as if it might be held in place with hairspray. He is an unremarkable-looking middle-aged man. Only one thing about his appearance sets him apart. His thighs are knotted, industrial-looking. He leans back in the couch beneath the placid sharks, and his feet dangle, not quite to the floor.

We talk about his origins as a runner, the self-doubt that drove him and continued to plague him through his record-setting career. "I was stupid and wimpy, and no one liked me," he says, "and I thought sports might help. I never did believe in myself. I hated myself from the time I was little."

He says his schoolmates hated him, too, that the coaches at his junior high school hated him and drove him from their teams, that, when he ran through the streets of Spokane as a youngster, the local police arrested him seventeen times, once firing a bullet that creased his hair. He says that the Army kidnapped him and held him in an abandoned men's room without food or medical attention before releasing him with a bleeding ulcer, and that when he defied the National Collegiate Athletic Association (NCAA) to run in an Amateur Athletic Union (AAU)-sanctioned race, a "famous football coach from an eastern university" told Lindgren he knew where he lived and that if he ran, the coach would burn his house with gasoline. He uses the words "stupid" and "wimpy" to describe himself so many times I lose track.

He recounts all this in perfectly reasonable tones, in a high-pitched, slightly excitable voice that his former friends and competitors still remark upon, and he frequently says "Yah?" in a rising inflection at the end of sentences, a vocal marker from his heritage and birthplace in the Pacific Northwest.

I broach the subject of his family. He tells me he was never married and has no children.

He was always a joker. He told a reporter at the 1964 Tokyo Olympics that right-footed runners had an advantage at long distances. Another time he said the intense heat of a summer race hadn't bothered him because he had (uncharacteristically) stayed behind in the shade of the front-runners.

"I must remind you," Bob Payne, now retired, e-mailed Lindgren last year after the runner requested comments on a memoir he wrote and was trying to get published, "that your humor sometimes has whizzed right over the heads of your listeners — and that in some of those cases, their reaction was not laughter but anger and irritation."

But he is not joking. He insists. The other kids did hate him. The coach did threaten him with fire. He was arrested seventeen times. A bullet did crease his hair. No ex-wife. No children. Fiction. "Not true."

He was Eleanor Lindgren's third boy, her most difficult birth. Eleven days before the end of the winter of 1946, the baby was in the wrong position. The doctors had to turn him. When Gerry entered the world, he did so with a broken arm, struggling to breathe. His mother didn't see him for two weeks. Nurses told her he'd been almost black from oxygen deprivation.

"I knew then he was special," Eleanor told Kenny Moore in 1987.

His father, Myrl, apparently didn't agree. Gerry was tiny and weak, but Myrl picked on him just like he did his two older brothers. Eleanor wouldn't stand for that. She defended her baby. That made things worse. On good days Myrl came home from his job as a mechanic at Spokane's Kaiser smelting plant, sat in his rocking chair, read his paper, and smoked his pipe. Little Gerry would watch wisps of smoke float through the house, catching the last light of day as it flooded in through the picture window.

Most days were not good days. Most days Myrl stopped off at the tavern before he came home. He was a big drinker. When he drank, he hit. Once, Gerry says, Myrl hit his wife so hard that her dentures broke in three places and flew across the room. Another time, when Lindgren was just three and sitting at the dinner table — on two dictionaries that had been placed there for him — he sang a song. "Open all the windows," he sang. "Open all the doors." His father hit him in the face. There would be no singing at the table. The child fell out of his chair, then returned and sang again. His father hit him again, knocking him to the floor. Again the toddler got up. Again he sang. Frustrated, his father stalked out, back to the tavern.

Myrl continued drinking and continued hitting, "many, many other times," Gerry says. The family avoided him when they could. Usually they couldn't. Gerry got the worst of it. The more his father hit him, the more he hated himself. "I always had in my head," he says, "that my father wouldn't have to be like that if it wasn't for me — if I was a better kid."

In eighth grade he tried football and failed. He tried basketball and failed. He tried baseball and failed. He ended up on the track team, where he was the slowest runner on the B squad. Nobody got cut from the track team.

Freshman year at John R. Rogers High School, in the cross-country pack, his teammates bumped him, and they elbowed him in the face. He hated getting hit. The only way out was in front, so he became a rabbit, darting to the lead, where he was free from blows. He stayed in front until his body failed him.

First one runner passed, then another, then the entire team. The next day, barely able to walk, he planned to quit the team. The coach, a man named Tracy Walters, urged him to stay. Locally famous for his character-building speeches (he was also the school's guidance counselor) and his winning records, Walters told the boy that his tiny stature and squeaky voice were gifts. If he could lead his teammates even for short stretches, Lindgren recalls the coach telling him, it would inspire the bigger, stronger runners to do better.

Every day he would dart to the front. Not for himself but to help them. Every day the pack would pass him: first tall, rangy, and aptly named senior Len Long, then senior Arvid Anderson, then everyone else. But each day the little freshman would stay in front longer and longer. Then one afternoon, as the team ran a weekly time trial through the streets of Spokane to the southern edge of the high school, he found himself in front with half a mile to go. This had never happened before. He kept churning, three steps for every one of Long's. The boy weighed only 108 pounds then. His legs burned. He kept churning. Was he running from the drunk who beat him, who broke his mother's teeth? Or was he sprinting toward his hero, the man standing twenty yards away clutching a stopwatch? Was he doing both? He still hated himself, but now he could chase victory and tell himself it wasn't for personal gain. No one would beat him for his efforts. He was still wimpy; he was still stupid; he was still unworthy of honor, incapable of saving himself. But he wasn't doing this to save himself. He was doing it to inspire others.

Long and Anderson didn't have a chance.

The scrawny, squeaky-voiced kid's very first victory. God, it felt good.

As a sophomore he would run six miles upon waking, do his team workout after school, then wake up at 2:00 A.M. and run another ten miles. In the summer he would run ten miles to Peone Creek to go fishing and swimming, or fifteen miles to the radio station. He would run forty-four miles to Mt. Spokane. By the fall of Gerry's junior year, Myrl had left the house for good and Gerry was running twenty-five to thirty-five miles a day.

For fun? For victory? To push his teammates? "You are constantly being judged," he wrote in his unpublished memoir, a remarkable compendium of race strategy, stream of consciousness, preposterous adventures, inspirational pieties, and a studious avoidance of anything credible beyond his life as an abused child and a championship runner. It's told in the first person, from the point of view of Lindgren's shadow. There is no mention of a wife or children. "Every workout is a test," he wrote. "For you to become the vessel that serves all mankind, you will be tested constantly. Your courage and dedication has to be proven through pain and agony."

What happens when you bring together a boy who hates himself and a coach who believes in him? What happens when the only way a boy knows to express love is through self-annihilation?

This is what Lindgren did his senior year of high school: he set national high school records in the fifteen hundred meters, mile, three thousand meters, two miles, and three miles. The two-mile mark was 9:27 before Lindgren lapped a field of all-star schoolboys (including Ryun) on his way to a 9-flat record. Two weeks later, he ran 8:46. Three weeks after that, he ran 8:40.

At California's Compton relays, on a dusty track in Modesto during a night meet, organizers set up light bars above the track every fifty-five yards so spectators could see better. Bursting from blackness into light, then disappearing into darkness, then bursting forth again, over and over, Lindgren ran five thousand meters faster than any American schoolboy ever had. "I was thinking," he wrote, "if running killed me, it'd be better for everyone anyway. I think that helped."

*   *   *

Since the USA-USSR dual track meets had begun in 1958, no American had ever won the ten thousand meters. Lindgren's fastest time was a full minute slower than world-class pace. Still, the coach of the American team, Sam Bell, then the coach at Oregon State, asked Lindgren to run. It was 1964, the summer he graduated from high school. "He was a midget," says Bell, now seventy-six, who went on to coach at Indiana University from 1970 to 1998 and is a member of the United States Track Coaches Hall of Fame. "But he had a huge heart."

Bell told the boy that the world thought of Lindgren and his ilk as "lazy Americans." Yes, the coach knew the Soviets would defeat the boy; chances are they might even lap him. But wouldn't it mean something if the boy could put up a brave fight? Wouldn't it be inspirational if the boy could stay with the mighty Soviets for at least a little while? Could Gerry stay with them for a few laps?

Did Bell have any idea how ravenously Lindgren devoured his plea? For others he would run. This is what Lindgren heard, and this is what he would do. Not for himself. Never for himself. For his country.

Lindgren turned to Tracy Walters. Back in Spokane, Walters had enrolled in a masters program in education. He took time off from studying to train his protégé. Every day for six weeks, they met at the high school track where their connection had been forged.

Walters might have been a beloved counselor, but he was also a painstaking tactician. He had studied accounts of the Soviet races, their times, the speeds at which they raced certain segments of the distance. He had discovered something. At the fifteenth of twenty-four laps — right at four miles — they would suddenly surge. They would shift from sixty-nine-second laps — a very fast pace to hold in a ten-thousand-meter race — to a sixty-three-second pace. After a lap at sixty-three seconds, they would return to sixty-nine seconds. Other runners, unaccustomed to such bizarre midrace speed, would let the Soviets go during the sprint lap, knowing they would have to slow down. What other runners didn't realize is that the Soviets had hardened themselves to never go slower than sixty-nine seconds — race pace. After one surge, no runner could ever catch them.

"They were Pavlovian trained," Walters says. "That was the way they broke people down."

There was only one way to beat the Soviets.

First, he made Lindgren put together consistent seventy-second laps. That wasn't a problem. They boy had always been good at holding pace. Then, after hours and hours of grueling intervals, he added a sixty-second sprint after a seventy-second lap. Lindgren could do that, too. Other runners could do it as well. To sprint in the middle of a long distance isn't as difficult as many might think. What is difficult — what is near impossible — is to continue the race after the sprint, to return to anything other than a flailing, gasping lurch. But that's what the Soviets did. That's what Walters asked Lindgren to do. Run a seventy-second lap, sprint a sixty-second lap, then return to pace without flagging. Lindgren did it. Do it again, Walters said. Lindgren did it. He got to the point where he could do it twice in a row.

Afterward Walters made Lindgren run up hills and through sand. "It was gut-busting," says the retired coach, now seventy-three, an orchardist near Spokane. "I've never had anybody I trained who could handle that."

At the end of a workout one day, just weeks before the teenager would face the Soviets, teacher and pupil lay on the infield grass at the Rogers High School track. They talked about how they met and what the boy might do in the future. They talked about a lot of things. "Life and one thing and another," Walters remembers. "And Gerry says, 'You know, Coach, what would be really cool? After they do a fast lap, and I stay with them, what if I do one of my own?'"

A lap at pace followed by a sprint lap was difficult. Pace followed by sprint followed by pace was very, very difficult. Pace a lap, sprint a lap, sprint another lap?

The coach remembers what he said. "I said, 'Gerry, you're blowing my mind.'"

When the boy takes the lead, the spectators scream. It has been only eight months since the presidential assassination and convulsive national grief. More than fifty thousand people have come to the coliseum for the ten-thousand-meter race, Robert Kennedy among them, and they continue to scream as Lindgren sprints. But he hears something through the screams, right behind him. Is there a more terrifying noise in a race? Kritch-kritch.

He finishes his sprint lap, still ahead. Now he will blow their minds. He sprints another lap. But the footsteps stay with him. So he does something he hadn't planned. He begins a third sprint lap. It is insane, inspired. To run as Lindgren is running is to court injury, to insure ugly, total defeat.

Still they scream. A supernova is a tragic thing, but it is awesome. In the stands, Robert Kennedy weeps. Four laps to go and the boy has nothing left. He can't go on, but he does. He tries to sprint a fourth lap, a fifth, a sixth. The footsteps have faded. Where are they? When will the Soviets pass? The boy looks at Sam Bell, standing on the infield, then puts his hands together, a foot apart, then jerks his thumb over his shoulder. How far back? The coach yells something, but it makes no sense. The boy continues sprinting.

Here come the footsteps again, faster, more insistent. Irrefutable evidence of his weakness, his failure. Kritch-kritch. Kritch-kritch.

In the fall of 1964, Lindgren enrolled at Washington State University. The next year he ignored threats from the NCAA and faced Billy Mills in an AAU-sanctioned six-mile race, setting a world record with Mills in a photo finish and breaking the NCAA's stranglehold on the sport in the process.

During his college career, he set eleven track and cross-country records (breaking Jesse Owens's national mark of eight) and handed Steve Prefontaine his only college defeat (in 1969, at the Pacific-8 cross-country championships. Lindgren was a senior, Prefontaine a freshman). There were failures, too. A sprained ankle cost him a medal in the ten thousand meters at the 1964 Olympics in Tokyo. An inflamed Achilles tendon kept him out of the Mexico City Olympics in 1968. In 1972, after spending a disastrous forty-seven days in the army before being discharged with his bleeding ulcer, he tried again. Training for Munich, he pushed himself to fifty miles a day. Two weeks before the trials, a car hit him, injuring his knee and ending that Olympic bid.

The next year he joined the International Track Federation, the short-lived professional track tour. He also did a stint with Glenn Turner, the Florida supersalesman who operated a pyramid scheme of cosmetics franchises; Lindgren served as an international motivational instructor until the enterprise was shut down. By 1974 he'd married his college sweetheart, Betty Caley, and they had two boys and lived in Oxnard, California, where Gerry managed a Straw Hat Pizza restaurant.

On weekends he'd disappear, sometimes to race, sometimes to do who-knows-what. "He was leading a double life, living like he was single," says Betty Caley Lindgren. "He was flirting around, acting like he was a college kid."

In 1976 Lindgren was charged with fathering another woman's child the previous year and ordered by the state to pay seventy-five dollars a month in child support. He left home without telling Betty where he was going. Months later she tracked him to San Francisco. "As soon as he saw me, he packed up his stuff and we moved back to Tacoma," she says. They opened two athletic-shoe stores, one in Tacoma and one in Bellevue — both called Gerry Lindgren's Stinky Foot. They also had a little girl. Life was settling down. Or was it?

He still disappeared on weekends. And when she drove him to work at one of the shoe stores, he'd ask her to drop him off at the edge of the parking lot, like he didn't want to be seen with her. Betty says he didn't tell any of the store employees he had children. "He was a good liar then," she says of their life in the 1970s. "I used to believe him because I wanted to."

When she found his note that morning in January 1980, typed, with no signature, she crumpled it and threw it in the fireplace. Gerry Lindgren had run again.

The boy is fifty-eight now. For six days in a row, an hour a day, we meet to discuss running and life and one thing and another. He comes straight from his job as a manager of a string of parking garages. We meet under the giant aquarium, or next to a banyan tree in the shadow of Diamond Head, or on a high school track.

I ask about the "Gale Young" pseudonym. He says it's not really a pseudonym, that the original Happy Feet businessman was named Gale Young, and that after Young left Hawaii he'd kept the name because it made business sense. When Kenny Moore found Lindgren in 1987, Lindgren told him that he created the Gale Young alias in Los Angeles. "I didn't choose the name," Lindgren said. "It just worked out that way." He later told a reporter from the Associated Press that it was all an innocent mix-up — that a friend had been unable to run after entering a race and that Lindgren had run under his name and people had become confused.

He says he's married to a woman in Hawaii named Yoshiko. One day he tells me he's been married "almost twenty years"; another day, "I think I met her on a beach in Waikiki ten years ago." None of the runners I talk to in Hawaii, a few of whom Lindgren describes as friends, knows he's married. But a photographer who visited his rented bungalow in Hawaii Kai says a woman lives there with him. According to the county records office in Honolulu, the renters are Gale E. Young and Yoshiko Young.

He says he left Tacoma because, after he complained about the United States' decision to boycott the 1980 Olympics, "I suddenly started having trouble with the government. They came in and closed my stores to look in to my taxes. Immigration came in and closed my stores because they were checking for illegal aliens."

He says he never knew Betty Caley or the woman from Oxnard who claims to have borne his child. He speaks calmly, reasonably. But he says crazy things. I tell him that if I quote him, people might think he is mentally ill. He thanks me for the warning. "You've tapped my heart," he says, "and I appreciate that."

Then he says more crazy things.

"In 1937," he says, "in a little town in Ohio, there was a man who stayed off the ground and flew under his own power for thirty-seven seconds. After 1937, for two years, there were people trying to fly — there were five instances of people staying off the ground for up to seventeen seconds of free flight. Then, in 1939, the Ecumenical Counsel of Churches came out denouncing human flight as against the will of God, and it stopped."

Another time he tells me that cancer is caused by chemical-secreting parasites, and that many doctors know this but refuse to cure people because there's not as much money in it.

One day Lindgren says the woman and children who claim to be his family don't exist. Later he says he knows who they are but never knew them and was not married to the woman. Another day he says, "I had a relationship with this woman. I loved this woman. Or I liked this woman. She had cute little kids. They used to come in my kitchen and bang my pans."

Steven Lindgren flew to Hawaii three years ago. Gerry's eldest son wrote down thirteen questions on a scrap of paper. "I didn't expect him to turn into a dad," Steven says. "I just wanted to look him in the eye — I just wanted to see why he left."

When Gerry disappeared, the shoe business went under. Over the years Betty has worked as a dry cleaner, a census taker, a summer-camp administrator. For the last fifteen years, she's taught school in Tacoma.

When he was home, Steven remembers, his father took him and his little brother and sister for walks in the gully that ran behind their backyard. He made them pancakes. If you're a small child when a parent leaves, memories are few, and you hoard them. Steven was ten when his father left. He's thirty-three now, a hoarder. "He was always eating protein pills," his son says. "I remember getting into his protein pills and eating them when he wasn't looking."

During their meeting in Hawaii, Steven remembers, his dad said the reason he had left the family was because "my mom ran him off. That he was just kind of tired of it all . . ." Steven told his father he'd like to keep in touch. Gerry has neither called nor written since.

Steven says he always knew his father was coming back from his long, mysterious absences. So when he left for the last time, "I assumed he was coming back again, and I'd ask and ask when he would be home. After a while, I just quit asking."

Consider the boy, a country's sacrificial offering. Jug-eared, with an overbite, he is not a handsome youth, but, with his blotchy skin and

*baggy shorts and desperate, logic-defying dash — much too fast, way too
early — he is beautiful as only the doomed can be.*

*Think of him then, in his frantic, foolish dash, almost a half cen-
tury ago, before he disappeared, before the false identity and the grieving
wife and the confused children and the countless lies, before he forced
track fans to reconsider their notions of heroism and courage. The Soviets are pounding down the track behind him and he is doing the only
thing that might spare him shame, the only thing that might set him free.
He is doing the only thing that ever brought him any peace. It won't save
him, but he knows nothing else. He is running.*

*It's no use. Behind him, proof of who he is, of who he will never be.
Kritch-kritch.*

Is it the isolation? The simplicity? The way pain and glory are
so inextricably bound? How else to explain why running —
compared with sports like football and basketball and baseball —
produces such a disproportionate number of religious leaders,
motivational speakers, and, depending on your perspective,
charismatic maniacs or divinely inspired champions? Eric Liddell, the Scottish sprinter portrayed in *Chariots of Fire*, ran with
his chest out and head lifted toward the sky. He told a reporter
who asked him how he knew where the finish line was, "The
Lord guides me." Billy Mills, the 1964 ten-thousand-meter
Olympic gold medalist and national spokesperson for Running
Strong, an organization dedicated to helping Native American
youth, wrote on his Web site, "Your life is a gift from the Creator.
Your gift back to the Creator is what you do with your life." Jim
Ryun, the first schoolboy four-minute-miler, has leveraged his
success into a Kansas congressional seat and preaches the gospel
of the born again. "Running with Jesus," he has written, "will
give you the peace and joy you long for." Even the gloriously
profane Steve Prefontaine has gained in his early death deitylike

status among the more romantic and stoned of long-distance runners.

The most spiritual runner of them all might be a middle-aged parking-garage manager. A squeaky-voiced, possibly delusional jogger. A compulsive fabulist whose life is more fantastic than any of the lies he can't seem to stop telling.

He's neither rich nor famous. He doesn't have fourth-row season tickets to the Sacramento Kings, as Mills does. He doesn't have a press secretary, as Ryun does. He has neither a movie (Liddell and Mills each had one, Prefontaine two), nor a book nor the fame accorded lesser, less disturbing former champions. The state of Washington finalized his divorce from Betty in 1999. His parents died more than a decade ago; he hasn't spoken with his brothers in years.

What he has are the Coconut Road Runners, a collection of recreational joggers he trains, for free, five days a week. And the Niketown gang, the scores of Honolulu runners he joins for a four-and-a-half-mile jog that takes off from the Waikiki store every Wednesday afternoon. And Gerry's Joggers, a loose and informal collection of Hawaii's premier athletes, along with their coaches and parents, who solicit his wisdom (also free), who pass his cell-phone number and e-mail address among themselves as primitive tribes might have passed a potent and secret talisman.

What he has are the sixteen pairs of worn and scuffed size-eight Nikes that he lugs around in the trunk of his 1980 Mercedes 300 diesel, next to a cooler filled with 23.5-ounce cans of AriZona Green Tea with Ginseng. (Ten more pairs of running shoes sit at home.) What he has are the empty jars of homemade apple butter and huckleberry jam that Tracy Walters sends him at Christmas and a tiny backyard where, every night after he runs, he dangles his naked feet in a koi pond and listens to the plaintive birdsong from the trees above. What he has is his unpublished manuscript and his forty-year-old record and his spooky conspiracy theories and his odd, infuriating, unshakable faith.

He so wants to share it. Three years ago he got a call from Tia Ferguson, a freshman at a local high school. She had just lost by three-tenths of a second in the fifteen hundred meters at the state meet, to a senior. The girls became friends, and, before the senior left for college, she bequeathed to the freshman a precious secret — Lindgren's phone number. That summer and much of the next year, Ferguson and Lindgren ran together, e-mailed each other, talked on the phone.

"I gave her a magic pillow," he says. "Told her when she felt tired, just to lean back into that magic pillow."

As is often the case, I don't know if he's speaking metaphorically or literally, if he believes what he's saying, if he wants me to believe it. He laughs, shakes his head. I catch a split-second glimpse of the gold in his irises. "You don't have to be realistic when you run," he says. "It's a magic world."

A gasping, middle-aged man struggles to keep up with his teenage daughter. Just behind him is a slightly pudgy woman in baggy shorts and T-shirt. Ten yards back three rangy young men glide. It is late afternoon in Honolulu, the same time of day Lindgren challenged the Soviets. Shadows lengthen across the McKinley High School track. Lindgren jogs behind the pudgy woman, ahead of the gliders. The greatest high school distance runner who ever lived doesn't move from the middle of the pack.

He has put the Coconuts through warm-ups, sprints, cooldowns, intervals. Now they jog. Sometimes he asks them about their lives. Sometimes he exhorts them to run more, to add distance. Sometimes he tells them stories.

"He'll tell us about the Russians or about Billy Mills," says Rolf Kvalvik, a twenty-six-year-old environmental consultant.

"If we were running into a really strong headwind," says Buffy Whiteman, who runs with Lindgren with the Niketown group on Wednesdays, "he'd say, 'Think of it as your ancestor trying to push you back, trying to hold you and challenge you.'"

"It's fact-based," says Michael Tunick, a twenty-eight-year-old who spent a year in Hawaii before enrolling at the University of Michigan law school this fall, "like a parable."

The first time Lindgren met Tia Ferguson, he asked why she ran. "Gee," she said, "I dunno. I'm just a sophomore." For months they ran, and they talked about running and life. He instructed her in the subtleties of pace, in strategy and keeping her knees up, but those are not the things that were most important.

"If you don't know why you run," he told her, "you're not going to last." She had never heard of Billy Mills or Jim Ryun. She had no idea of Lindgren's records, his defiance of the NCAA, his place in running history. She just knew he was funny and fun to run with, an inspirational teacher, "one of the most grounded, present people that I know."

"You have to have a reason to run," he told her. "Run with your heart."

Her sophomore year, after her sessions with Lindgren, Ferguson won state titles in the fifteen hundred and three thousand meters. She was all-American at three thousand meters last year. This fall, she'll attend Duke, where she'll run track and cross-country.

The magic pillow? "That's something I use to this day — the philosophy of leaning back. Even today when I'm nervous about something my mom will go, 'Now, Tia, remember about Gerry's magic pillow.'"

And what does Lindgren do when he's nervous about something? Is he ever nervous? Always? The last time we meet, I ask if he's happy.

"I think that ever since my dad departed, I have had a happy life," he says. "I don't worry about things. I don't let things get me down . . . I can take it. Any problems, I know I can solve any kind of a problem that comes up."

On the McKinley High School infield, girls playing soccer giggle and shriek. Outside the fence around the track, past the banyan and palm trees, Honolulu rush hour thrums. The air smells of grass and paradise and something sad and sweet. The shadows grow longer and longer; pink pudgy clouds scrape the impossibly green mountains in the distance. The seven runners move around the track in a knot. Lindgren, the ferocious front runner, doesn't budge from the middle. He's chasing no one, and no one's chasing him.

When they first saw him, track fans laughed at him, then they were mystified by him, then they loved him, because he ran the way we all like to imagine ourselves running — absent self-consciousness, elementally, as animals run — for survival and for sheer joy and for both. They screamed for him.

But they've never screamed as they are screaming now in Los Angeles. They started screaming as Lindgren shot by one Soviet on the curve, then by the other. They screamed as he bolted into the setting sun. The more he sprints, the more they scream.

The boy has sprinted — or flailed, or lurched — for the past seven laps. Somehow he has endured. Now the bell sounds, and the boy is shocked. He won't be lapped. Now the sound of screaming is nearly deafening. Still it doesn't drown out the noise behind him. He can't go faster, but he must. The sound behind him: remorseless, world-class, conclusive. Kritch-kritch.

You won't see his likes again, so, once more, look at the boy. Look closely. Regard the would-be hero, the utter failure. Forty years ago, another world, more than half his lifetime, and Gerry Lindgren is running for his life. What choice does he have? The terrifying sound is getting louder. Closer, closer. He needs more speed. No use. It was never any use. Kritch-kritch. Kritch-kritch.

Only when he breaks the tape, only when the screams turn to cries of national pride and triumph, only when he knows he has won does he dare turn to look behind him. There is no one there. The closest Soviet is 150 yards back.

The boy has been running from the sound of his own footsteps. Now, one last time, regard the boy. Look at him in his moment of triumph and revelation. Is he ecstatic? Is he relieved? No?

What's wrong?

5

THE UNBEARABLE LIGHTNESS OF BEING
SCOTT WILLIAMSON:
SCOTT WILLIAMSON, HIKER

YOUR FATHER AND THE MAN KNOWN AS "MR. BEER" FIND THE deaf girl at a store in town and they learn that she's been chasing you for seven hundred miles. When they bring her to your campsite, you don't know it, but that's the moment your grief finally starts to lift. That's when you find what you need, what you have always needed. It's a year ago, May 14, and maybe that's where your story begins.

But starting there leaves out too much. It leaves out the crazy man with the gun and the miracle of the corned-beef hash and that sad day on the river when the magic ducks honor the dead boy. It doesn't even mention Hobo Joe and Walking Carrot and the Wall and the Abominable Slow Man and Real Fat. And what about the nightmares? What about the years of failure? What about the autumn of loss, the seasons of mourning?

To understand those things, it's better to begin with the day searchers find a bear feeding on your best friend's body. Or the afternoon you lose the deaf woman. Too grim? It's your story, and it's filled with the strangest and most unexpected gifts, so maybe it's best to begin on the rock in the snowfield where you find her again. But that's too happy. It's misleading. What about in a spot you know all too well, where you have spent way too much time: under sodden skies and sneering peaks during an early winter blizzard, as you sink to your thighs and know that you are — once again — doomed to defeat?

You've always struggled with beginnings and endings. How can anyone expect you to say when you started, when you finished? Might as well ask when you decided to start living.

Still, an epic journey — and if your journey is anything, it's definitely epic — must begin somewhere. The first step, the first time out of Mexico? That's accurate but inadequate. The victorious stroll last November into the crowd of photographers and friends? Touching but incomplete. No, better to begin in the midst of setback, struggling. Better to start with what you know. Better to start with isolation and pain.

It is exactly ten minutes until five in the afternoon — you remember that because the man in the hooded sweatshirt asks you what time it is and you tell him, right before he shoots you in the face. It is 4:50 in the afternoon on January 20, 1996, and you aren't scheduled to work that day, but when the convenience-store owner calls and asks you to come in you say yes because you can always use extra cash. You work hard when you work — tree felling, logging, construction — so you can take off for months at a time, and such an approach to labor and to life has made for many sublime sunrises and peaceful sunsets and occasional moments of Zen oneness with nature and . . . a job in a convenience store. You are reading an article in the *New Yorker* when the man in the hooded sweatshirt comes in and asks what time it is and you look at your watch and tell him, and then you notice he seems nervous, his eyes are darting, he is rocking back and forth, and then he lifts something and points it at you and you feel heat and searing pain on your cheek.

The bullet enters the left side of your face, clips your jaw, rips through flesh, and stops. You run to the back of the store and the door is locked so you hit it with your shoulder. It is a steel door with a deadbolt but you tear it from the wall. The man in the hooded sweatshirt follows and fires six more rounds and you keep running. You keep running and running until you see a man and a woman and their young child lifting groceries out of their car and you tell them you've been shot.

They take you inside and you call 911 and you worry because even with a towel you're dripping blood on their floor.

The doctors give you morphine and they check for nerve damage. They tell you that the salivary gland on the left side of your mouth might never function again. They tell you it's too risky to remove the bullet, which is lodged near your spine, and that another quarter of an inch and you would have been paralyzed. You leave the hospital and you have nightmares and get spooked when you see men in hooded sweatshirts, and you resolve to change your life.

Some men might bend their will toward jobs with desks and health insurance and 401(k)s, away from double shifts at convenience stores. Not you. You decide that life is short, that the future is uncertain. You decide that time is precious. You have already hiked from Mexico to Canada once, a huge summer trek on the Pacific Crest Trail (PCT). It was wonderful, but now that you've been shot in the face and reevaluated your life, you want more than wonderful. You decide you will hike from Mexico to Canada again, but this time, rather than celebrating at the border, you will turn around and hike back to Mexico. You will need to travel lighter this time and pack smarter and move very, very fast to beat the winter storms before they make the southbound journey impossible. You will need to hike more than twenty-five miles a day, every day, for almost seven months. No one has ever accomplished such a feat before. No one has even tried it.

Maybe the moment you make the decision is the best place to start.

*   *   *

But even that's not right. No, if you want the best beginning to your story — the real beginning, the *right* beginning — you need to start with the kid. The first time you see him, he is crouching next to a spring at the bottom of a canyon, feral, like a wild child. It's May 3, 1993, and you have been hiking for a week, on your way to Canada on the PCT, one way, just like any other young man longing to escape life and find himself. The kid is seventeen years old, skinny and overpacked, and he's in trouble. That's the first thing you notice. His pack must weigh ninety pounds — it's bigger than he is. He carries a gleaming stove and a fat down sleeping bag. Shiny pots and kettles hang from his pack. Countless straps and bungee cords. He has the newest and heaviest of everything. A kid who must have read some books, who has no idea that the secret to happiness out here is packing light and moving fast. He reminds you of yourself when you first made the trip the year before. You made it to Oregon, and you suffered, and you learned, so this time you've come stripped down. This time you carry only twenty pounds.

You're not very nice to him. You don't need extra baggage of any kind on your hike. That's something else you've learned. But he's delighted to be outdoors, delighted to meet you, delighted to learn from you. He's even delighted to learn how little you think of his style. He tags along, and every day he digs a hole and buries a piece of equipment, or a piece of clothing. He wants to do it like you.

You have never met such a person before. Wake at 4:00 A.M. for a predawn march? No problem. Log forty-five miles in one day? Can do. Climb every mountain, ford a gazillion streams? Now, *that's* living! You have no idea about the sadness he carries, the sadness he will bequeath to you.

It's funny — you're only twenty-one and already you have chosen a life of long-distance hikes and labor high up in trees and meticulous, solitary planning, and you spend more time alone on the Pacific Crest Trail than probably any person on earth, but every so often a person crashes into your life and, even if you're careful, even if you're not very welcoming at first, even if you're not very nice, your plans get all screwed up.

When he leaves the trail to return to his mother's house, you're surprised. Not that he's leaving — even burying so many things, the kid was still carrying too much. You're surprised that you miss him.

Then, one day in early July, at the post office in Sierra City, you see his name in a register: Kenny Gould. He's come back and he is trying to catch you. He doesn't realize he's already ahead of you. Every few days you see his name in another log. The kid is humping forty miles a day. You cover distances like that every once in a while, but the kid is doing it day after day. No one can keep up that pace.

You didn't make this trip to babysit anyone, to save anyone from himself. You didn't start in Mexico in order to make friends. But something happens. It's funny how a man's plans can change in spite of himself. You start logging monster distances, too. It takes you two weeks to catch him. When you find him at Crater Lake, in Oregon, he is carrying next to nothing. He has taken scissors and a knife to his pack, slicing off all the hanging straps. When the kid does something, he's all in. That summer, you're all in, too. You hike together through the rest of Oregon and all of Washington to Canada. Over campfires and at sunrise and in meadows you talk about the misapplication of technology in the world, how it is serving powerful interests rather than people. He's just a kid and you're barely an adult. You talk about how society is going down the tubes, how neither of you will be sucked into the machine. You talk about the tricky business of living in a troubled world without becoming part of the trouble. He is impulsive, carefree — sometimes to a fault. You help him settle down, think things through. And you are meticulous, painstaking — sometimes to a fault. Hiking with Kenny, you quit planning so much and start living more. Kenny talks about how nothing is impossible. You can't help it. You believe him.

The next summer, while Kenny climbs in Yosemite, you hike the Continental Divide Trail from Canada to Mexico. The summer after that — Kenny's still climbing, and you hear he's going through some tough times with his family — you travel the Appalachian Trail, but you tack on the Florida Trail first, then walk 450 miles of road between the two. You want to make it from Florida to Maine. Now you have achieved the Triple Crown of long-distance hiking, which is as rare as it sounds. What's next?

The kid has an idea. You run into him that fall at a meeting of long-distance hikers. His folks have split up and he's spent a little time in a psych ward, where the doctors told him he's got a mental illness, and he's ashamed about that, but you tell him it's no big deal, they're just words, like "flu" or "virus," that he doesn't have anything to feel bad about. He appreciates that; it makes him feel better. Do you want to hear his idea? You do.

What if next year, Kenny asks, you try something *really* ambitious? What if next year, you hike the PCT again? But this time, instead of stopping in Canada, what if you turn around and hoof it back to Mexico? And what if he tags along? You promise to think about it. And then the man in the hood walks into the convenience store and you decide life is short and a man can spend too much time thinking and you decide that you and Kenny will embark on a great adventure.

You lug your sewing machine up from Richmond to Kenny's mom's house in the Sierra foothills, in Auburn, California. One night she looks in and sees you and Kenny, both long-haired and bearded and plotting, each one of you hunched over a sewing machine. You are sewing your own sleeping quilts, and she shakes her head at her woolly son and his woolly friend and thinks, "Gee, this is never going to work." But she's smiling and laughing, and, though you might not know about it, she knows the sadness her son carries and you seem like such a nice boy and Kenny seems so at peace when he's with you — she worries often about him but never when he's with you.

She takes you boys — to her, you are boys — to dinner at Auburn's Mongolian Barbecue for all-you-can-eat dinners, and the Chinese proprietor smiles when he sees the three of you coming, and you might not know it, but Kenny's mom knows: he hates the sight of you three because you and Kenny sit at the table for hours, plotting adventures and talking about the trail and spinning dreams, but mostly piling bowl after bowl after bowl full of rice and broccoli and spinach and bamboo shoots, mashing the food down, and eating and mashing it down some more and eating some more, and it's a wonder you don't drive that restaurant out of business. Kenny's mom loves her son and she's beginning to love you, but — she can't help it — she feels sorry for that little Chinese man.

A young man can imagine great adventures in the foothills, in the winter, over sewing machines and bowls of rice and vegetables. And you do. You both do. But the adventure is greater than even you can imagine. It's funny. For all your great plans, the greatest times happen when the plans fall apart. It happens after a snowstorm — there are so many snowstorms in the life you have chosen — and you and Kenny are short on food, so you bushwhack forty-three miles through the mountains to the nearest town and you know it's going to take at least three days to even make it back to the trail. You buy onions and garlic and lemons and a roll of tinfoil and a six-pound bag of rice and some fishing gear. Not what most people think of as fishing gear. No, you buy two spools and a couple of hooks and a few lures.

And now you are standing in the middle of a river in a hidden canyon, holding a stick. Standing upstream, holding another stick, is your hiking partner, who has somehow become your best friend. The stream carves through a canyon, which slices through a section of California's High Sierra that is very difficult to find, even on a map. You have tied the hook to one end of the spool and flung it into the river. It is a foolish, absurd way to fish, but in hidden valleys, life is foolish and absurd and bountiful and the word "failure" doesn't mean much. Kenny catches a fish. Then you. Golden trout. You have been a vegan for five years. But Kenny has taught you, so, just like him, you look into the golden trout's eyes and you bash its head on a rock and you feel its life slipping from its body, and you have always thought of meat as something people buy in grocery stores, but you will never think this way again. Years later you will say that this is the moment you learned that death not only is part of life but that death can sustain life. For three days and nights you and Kenny toss lines into clear water and make your way upstream and east, along the river and up a snowy path toward the Pacific Crest Trail, and for breakfast and lunch and dinner you feast on golden trout over crackling fires, and the days and nights are cold but you are warm and well-fed and alone and together in a place that is difficult to find, even on a map. He tells you wild, hilarious stories about the people he met in the psych ward, which always make you laugh. And he calls you "Duckface" because you carry a rubber duck that you found in the street in a mountain town and sometimes you start quacking, which always makes Kenny laugh.

You make the turn in Canada and head south and make it all the way to Reds Meadow, near Mammoth, where it starts snowing on October 18 and doesn't stop until a week and five feet later. It is your first and most glorious failure.

You try again the next year, alone, because Kenny has taken up white-water rafting, and he's busy with that. You struggle through so much snow on the way north that you stop at the Canadian border. The next year, you read the weather reports and you know it's impossible, so you start in Canada and take a leisurely stroll south with your girlfriend, a poet and student named Rebecca. You try to make it both ways in 1999 and 2000, but each time blizzards stop you before you're even out of Southern California. The rest of your life? Off the trail? There are the tree-felling jobs, and a winter spent logging in Maine with Rebecca, but with all the trips and hiking a relationship is tough, and you split up. Your mother has been sick with lung cancer for a few years. She's a chain-smoker, and that makes you angry, and things have never been easy between you two, with her always telling you to get a regular job, buy a house, settle down. And besides, she carries her own sadness. People scare her, and open spaces and new things, so she avoids all that. When you were a kid and friends came over, she would hide in a room. Those friends remember fleeting glimpses of her, in a hat and dark sunglasses, peering from behind a door. "Agoraphobic," doctors said, but to you, it's just a word. She's your mother. The last summer of her life, you don't hike. She dies in October 2001 and you don't hike the next year either.

That summer, on July 6, you meet a pretty girl with sun-streaked hair outside a restaurant called Chop Stix, near Santa Cruz, where you're doing some tree work. A month later you and the pretty girl, a climber and acupuncture student named Michelle Turley, move in together. Women have always been attracted to you, and you to them. And in January you're on a day hike together and you tell her that, come spring, you think you're going to try yo-yoing the PCT again, and she says that's nice, what exactly does that mean? Well, it means you might be gone for seven months. She's not happy, but she's a climber and a good sport, she believes in you, so she works on your résumé and on letters trying to drum up publicity and sponsors, and she helps organize a slide show and rents a hall in Santa Cruz and gets some local musicians, and she helps you raise $250. Then she drives you to the border, and when you call her after your first day and tell her your knee hurts, she puts together a package of moxa and ginger — Michelle practices Chinese medicine, too — and sends it to you.

Your knee gets better, but the weather worsens. You have never seen so much snow so early in the season. Every day it dumps more, and at Cedar Grove, on June 7, 2003, you hike for fifteen hours and make it exactly fifteen miles. That's when you quit. It's your fifth try, your fifth failure. You don't know if you'll ever try again.

Kenny? The kid who gave your story the best beginning, the right beginning? While you're trying to yo-yo the PCT, Kenny is making himself into one of the premier extreme kayakers in North America. While you're financing your hikes by climbing giant redwoods and little fruit trees in Santa Cruz, Kenny is scaling communications towers for pay near Auburn, hanging vinyl on tall buildings. One day in the spring of 1999 you visit him at his mom's, and while you're on a day hike together he tells you he's been having a tough time, that he has to take pills every day just to feel normal. You hadn't known, but you aren't shocked. Kenny had never been what you would call normal. You find out later that different doctors called Kenny's difficulties different things. Bipolar disorder. Schizo-affective disorder. Brief reactive psychosis related to stress. It doesn't matter to you. They're just words. Kenny is your partner, your best friend. Somewhere along the way, Kenny has become your brother.

In the early winter of 2002 you climb North Palisade, a fourteen-thousand-footer. It's so cold your equipment is freezing, and you have to take your gloves off to brush the ice away and eventually your fingers freeze up and you have to turn back, just three hundred vertical feet short of the summit. You don't know it, but Kenny returns a few weeks later and completes the climb.

You talk to him again that spring. You and Michelle have driven up north and you're going to hike to a waterfall that Kenny took you to once, down a remote canyon of the American River. You call him from a pay phone near the river. Does Kenny remember the waterfall? Can he give you some tips on how to get there?

Does he? Can he? There's a slot canyon, and you can rappel down it, and the bottom is hidden but unbelievably beautiful, another world! It's incredible! It's amazing! Kenny is so enthusiastic, shouting so loud, you have to hold the phone away from your ear, smiling. You remember that. It's funny the things you remember. Michelle, standing next to you, can hear him, too. She has never met Kenny, but she has heard you talk about him, has seen your scrapbooks filled with pictures and writings from him. You don't know it, but she worries about you a lot. This is the first time she hears his voice, and she loves how it makes you smile.

You hear from him one more time — in early September. He calls and leaves a message: "Hey, it's me, call me back," but you're busy. Would things have turned out differently if you had called him?

You don't know it, but things are bad. The sadness isn't coming and going anymore. It's staying. Kenny checks himself into the hospital, but that doesn't work. He takes medication, but that doesn't work. Now he's doing free solo climbs, hazarding riskier and more dangerous falls. He talks to people about kayaking off Yosemite Falls with a parachute. He talks about sky diving in a kayak, "to see how it handles."

Kenny's mom tries to help, but she doesn't know what to do. She wishes Kenny had a kindred spirit in his family — someone who could understand him. But his dad and his older brother are doctors, nose-to-the-grindstone kind of men, and Kenny has never related to that life. He has a younger sister, but what can a younger sister do? What can a mother do? Kenny's mom thinks of you. She worries about Kenny all the time, but she never worries about him when he's with you. She tells Kenny — OK, maybe she nags him a little — why doesn't he call you? Why doesn't he pick up the phone so the two of you can plan another one of your epic hikes together? But he doesn't call.

He makes eight trips to the hospital, and the doctors do their best, adjust his meds, but each trip is worse than the last. When he leaves the eighth time, he's so desperate, so crestfallen, his mom tells him she doesn't want him to ever have to go back, and he says he doesn't want to go back either.

You pick up the phone on the first of October 2002. No one has heard from Kenny in four days and Kenny's mom is scared; she asks if you know where he is. She calls back on the fifth. Searchers have found his truck parked near the top of a rocky bluff. They had combed the area for days with no luck, and then one of the searchers had looked down and seen a bear at the bottom of the cliff. It was feeding on Kenny's body.

When Kenny's mom is going through her son's things, she finds a note. It's addressed to you. It's a good-bye note. He didn't want to go back to the hospital. He hated his pills. He didn't see any other way out.

You give the eulogy on the banks of the American River, where Kenny loved to hike and fish and raft. You tell the four hundred mourners that you have lost your best friend. Three other speakers say the same thing. Weird how such a young man, carrying so much sadness, could have so many best friends.

After Kenny's friends speak, the preacher rises, walks to the front of the crowd. He begins to talk and at that instant a flock of ducks flies overhead, quacking, and they land behind him, on the river. He raises his voice and they quack louder. The preacher keeps trying, but the ducks quack so loud no one can hear what he's saying. You and Michelle look at each other. "It's him," she says.

It is a terrible winter, a season of grief, and Michelle is worried sick about you; she hopes spring will bring healing, but it doesn't. The next winter is terrible, too. You write to Kenny's mom. "How do you go on when you lose your best friend?" You talk to her once a week and she tells you she has lost a son and you have lost a mother, but now you have each other. You can't sleep. Mornings, you're bone-tired. The times you manage to drift off, you wake screaming. You wake Michelle. And some nights Michelle wakes on her own and finds you staring at pictures of Kenny, holding the scrapbooks with records of your hikes together. You avoid other people, spend more and more time alone. She doesn't know what to do. Ever since she met you, she has worried about you. But she never worried when you were with Kenny. She tells you to get outside, to hike, to climb. Michelle knows the climbing community in Santa Cruz, they're her friends, so she calls them. She calls people she knows, asks them if they'll climb with you, then tells you — OK, maybe she nags a little — that they're waiting for your call, but you don't call. Sometimes, desperate, she prays. Not to God. She prays to Kenny.

You and Michelle break up in February — it just got too intense — and you don't have any work lined up, or anything else tying you down, so you try again. You leave Mexico April 22, 2004. You're not sure you're going to yo-yo. You're not sure of anything.

On the trail, you grieve for Kenny, but you don't worry about him anymore. You don't have to. And you don't have to worry about how sick your mother is, or what she wants you to do with your life, or the sadness she carries behind her dark sunglasses, in her dark little room. You don't have to worry about your next job, or packing, or whether you are going to attempt the hike again. All you have to worry about are water and food and shelter, and it's liberating. Maybe no man is an island, but, god, the seas can be choppy, they can drown a man if he's not careful, and there is something to be said for hiking alone in the Sierra in early spring, with no girlfriend, no job, no family, no skinny kid carrying unbearable sadness in his stripped-down, strapless pack. You have your beans and corn chips and tarp and sleeping quilt. You think you have everything you need. You're so wrong.

When your dad and the man known as Mr. Beer take you to her, the first thing you notice about the deaf girl is how weathered she looks, how worn-down. She scribbles notes. She says she has been trying to catch you since she left Mexico two weeks ago, four days after you. You work that out in your head. She has been covering more than thirty miles a day. She says she has covered all of Southern California without a trail map. She says she is trying to break the women's speed record from Mexico to Canada.

As you scribble back and forth, literally comparing notes, you look at her again. She has just walked through a section of the American West where water sources are sometimes thirty miles apart, where the best way to locate them is with a map, and the second best way by sound. She has just hiked through a region infested with rattlesnakes (she has seen ten). And here she is, to your eyes malnourished, still without a map, cheerfully outlining her plans to race to Canada.

Later, when you remember meeting Patti, and you talk to strangers about things like inner peace and karma and living in harmony with the universe, you will apologize, use words like "cheesy" and "New Agey." But here, late at night next to the Current River, you can't ignore what you see. What you feel. It's spooky. It shakes you a little. You have met only one other person in your life who approached absurd difficulties and daunting challenges with such unreasonable joy, such blithe good humor. Climb every mountain? Ford a gazillion streams? Now *that's* living. You never thought you would run into anyone else like him. Can a man be sad and bursting with joy all at once?

The next morning, your father drives away — he'd come all the way down from Richmond just to see you for a night — and the man known as Mr. Beer, whom you met on the trail and camped with for one night, takes off. Then it's just you and the deaf girl, Patti Haskins. She has a master's degree in biochemistry, and she works at a day-care center in Yosemite Valley. She's fast, but you're faster, and you move ahead. You wait an hour for her in a meadow, and then an hour and a half. Then you leave a note. Gotta go.

A man travels fastest when he travels alone. You camp alone that night and hike the next day and it surprises you, but you're worried. And maybe you miss her a little. And at the end of that next day, skirting a snowfield, you hear a strange sound. There she is, yelling on a rock, like she knew you would find her — or she would find you. She had lost the trail, had simply continued north, mapless. It's funny how people can shake up your plans. This was going to be a solo trip. The rest of the summer, all the way to Canada, you hike together.

You learn to sign. You tell her that the Top Ramen and Cup-a-Soup she has been eating is wearing her down, that she should start eating organically, like you. She tells you that for someone who talks so much about organic food, you eat an awful lot of SNICKERS bars whenever you're near a store, and, by the way, you should start slathering on sunscreen, like she does. She sticks with Top Ramen. You stick with SNICKERS and bare skin.

You watch out for each other. When Patti gets sick and has to go to the bathroom twenty times one day, you worry. When you bite down on a chip and a molar on your right side breaks, you spit it out. Now the nagging about the SNICKERS gets intense. She spends a lot of time peering into your mouth, at the half tooth, worrying about decay and infection.

But those are minor things. They're bonding things. Life in the mountains with Patti is OK. It's more than OK. One evening, she walks to a stream to fetch water and she disappears around a bend, and then you hear her scream. It's a weird thought, you have no idea why it comes to you, but you're certain she has found a body. You have never heard such screams. You sprint down the creek, around the bend, panting. And there she is, screaming and singing. Patti is a beautiful woman, all dark hair and smooth limbs and sharp angles, and she is trilling with joy. She's holding a bullfrog as big as a cantaloupe, laughing and singing. Only one other person in your life ever found such wild, outsized delight in nature.

On sunny days you plunge into frigid alpine rivers, then scramble out and lay down in sun-soaked beds of wildflowers. On rainy nights you huddle together underneath your tarp. And the more OK things get with Patti, the more you worry. Not about her nutrition or her intestinal health. You are now just weeks from Canada, and you suspect that this time you have a shot at making it all the way back. You also know how people can creep into your life and shake up your plans. You know that a man travels fastest when he travels alone. You remember the last person you loved like you love Patti. He was just a boy, and then he was a man, and it's different, of course, Patti is beautiful and soft, all smooth limbs and sharp angles. But it's the same, too. You never thought you would meet someone like him again and now you have and it scares you. You know what loss feels like. You know what loss can do to a man. You walk into Canada on August 8, 105 days after you left Mexico, 101 days after Patti started. She misses her record by a week, and, since she has no money left, she catches a bus back to Yosemite. Hiking south, alone again, you cover forty-three miles your first day. The second day, you walk forty miles. The third day, thirty-eight miles.

Late summer in the Cascades is a glorious time. Long days and lush flowers and torrents of water and plenty of time to think. You think about Patti and your mother and your damaged salivary gland and the man who shot you, the man in the hood, and how you'd like to teach kids about the wilderness, about how tree felling is a young man's occupation and how you're thirty-two and you won't be able to do it for much longer and maybe you ought to really consider college. You think about beef and spinach and coffee, you think hard about those things. You think of the long days and nights talking with Kenny about how difficult it was to be true to yourself when you were surrounded by wage slaves and soulless corporations and creeping technology, and how you told Kenny that a man couldn't spend his entire life on the PCT, the important thing was to find balance in your life, and Kenny did his best and his best wasn't enough. You wonder how the man known as Mr. Beer is doing back at home in Sapporo, Japan (which is why he's known as Mr. Beer). You think about all the hikers you have met over the years — Hobo Joe, the homeless Vietnam vet who every few years scrapes enough money together to hit the trail, and does fine until he hits a town with a liquor store, then ends up in the county jail for a few nights; and Maineiac, who lives in Maine; and Walking Carrot, who loves carrots; and Real Fat, who is really fat; and the Abominable Slow Man, who is astoundingly pokey; and the Leprechaun, who stands six-feet-eight.

The kid? He comes to you at the oddest times. In southern Oregon you run out of water and hike fifteen miles to a stream near Mt. McGloughlin to refill your bottle, but the stream is dry and it's fifteen miles until the next one and you're thirsty and in trouble and then, there, right on the trail, is a water bottle, sixteen ounces just sitting there, and you know it's cheesy, you know it's New Agey, but you can't help it, you think about death, and life, the cosmic wheel and all that, and how even when someone leaves you, maybe he's not gone at all. You feel Kenny's presence then; you know he's with you.

You think about Michelle, who really is sweet, and supportive, and beautiful, and all-around great, and you wonder if the two of you might ever get together again. And you think of Rebecca, in Maine, and the poem she wrote called "The Mandible Bullet," about the convenience-store shooting. Rebecca was sweet, too, and you loved that poem, you wish you still had a copy of it. And you think about other former girlfriends, and how women are great but relationships are complicated, especially when you have a goal, and maybe you're better off not exactly in one right now. And of course you think some more of Patti, whose trail name is Silent Running, which even by trail-name standards is weird, because she's deaf, not mute.

Michelle meets you at the trail in Echo Lake, near Tahoe. She drives ninety minutes from her home in Truckee, where she moved shortly after the two of you broke up. You are still good friends and, before you met Patti, you had been writing or talking with Michelle almost every day — in Southern California in the mountains there is excellent reception and you have a cell phone — and she has been writing you on the trail, telling you how much fun it would be to see you and hang out, and you have agreed. She meets you at 7:00 P.M. and it's great to see her. It's really great. You hang out at the store next to the lake harbor, and you look at trail books together and tell her about the trip, and it's comfortable. You tell her you had a hiking partner most of the way north, and she says, oh, and you tell her a little about Patti, and she says, OK, and then you show her a picture of Patti and she says *oh*, OK. But Michelle is sweet, and she looks great, and as the air gets chillier and shadows lengthen over the lake you tell her how wonderful it is to see her and maybe the two of you could hang out that night, you can hit the trail the next morning, and at that instant, like in a movie or something, here comes a 4 X 4 with a camper shell squealing around the bend and out jumps this beautiful brunette making funny sounds and she jumps on you — that's how Michelle sees it, the brunette friggin' *jumps* on you, and she doesn't even look at Michelle, it's as if Michelle doesn't even exist. And even though Michelle is sweet it pisses her off a little bit, and of course it's Patti; Michelle recognizes her from the picture you showed her. Patti has driven three hours from Yosemite to surprise you, and after a few minutes you tell Michelle, well, you guess you'll be hanging out with Patti tonight, and Michelle says, OK, no problem, she understands, it's not like you two are together or anything and, besides, you and Patti were only hiking partners, no big deal, and she drives the ninety minutes back to Truckee, and you don't know it, but the entire ride, for an hour and a half straight, behind the wheel driving west on Highway 89, Michelle sobs.

Women are tricky. Relationships are tricky. The trail is simple. You wake at 5:30 and by 6:00 you're hiking. You hike till 9:00 and you stop for a fifteen-minute meal and then you hike till the early afternoon, eat another quick meal, and then you hike a few more hours. You stop just to chop some garlic and to mix your dried beans with water, and you hike another few hours, and then you have dinner, a leisurely thirty or forty minutes, and then you hike until it's dark. Every day you hike at least thirty-five miles, and most days you don't see a soul. From Crater Lake to near Tahoe — one thousand miles — you don't see anyone on the trail. You're alone. Days and days alone.

Why? Because you can't survive off the trail? Because things like steady work and marriage and a house fill you with fear?

Because the only place you feel safe is here, strolling through fields of golden yarrow and red maids and prickly poppies and yellow-and-white monkey flowers, sleeping under wheeling constellations? That's what Michelle thinks. To her, God is everywhere, but she's pretty sure you feel Him — or Her, or It, or the Great Whatever — only on the trail. Or do you do it because you love deeply and grieve deeply and sometimes you don't know the difference, and you're trying to come to terms with your friend's death? That's what Kenny's mom thinks. She didn't start to feel better about Kenny until she visited the rivers he rafted and the trails he hiked — all the spots he'd been happiest. She's sure you're on a journey of acceptance and healing.

And you? What do you think?

"Kenny's death played a part," you say politely but firmly. "So I suppose you could say I did it for him. But as I've told a lot of people, the only reason to do something like this is for yourself."

You can tell the temperature within two degrees just by the viscosity of the mucus in your nose, and you can predict snow by how the air feels on your skin. But you have never been very good at explaining yourself, at dissecting your feelings, at sharing your inner life.

Still, even a man as self-contained as you, even a man who has been shot in the face and whose mother has died and whose best friend has killed himself — even a man who has responded to injury and loss and death by walking away from others and into the woods — even a man like you must feel joy and relief and a tremendous sense of accomplishment as he closes in on the goal that has eluded him for nearly a decade.

How do you feel? "Very neutral," you say, with profound and oddly moving blockheadedness.

You reach the Mexican border on Saturday, November 13, 2004, and there to greet you are your father, who has driven twelve hours from Richmond, and Patti, who has driven eight hours from Yosemite, and Kenny's mom, who has driven twelve hours from Auburn. There is a photo crew, too, and dozens of long-distance hikers who know about you. You tell Patti you can't believe it's over. You tell her that finishing makes you sad. Kenny's mom hugs you and tells you that Kenny would be proud. And that's a sweet ending to your story, but it's not the best one. It's not the right one.

It leaves out what's next. It leaves out Patti asking you to spend more time in Yosemite, and Michelle asking you to visit Truckee more often, and you feeling guilty and annoyed that you can't do either — that you don't want to do either. It leaves out the way the daily e-mail with Patti becomes weekly, then bi-weekly, then merely occasional.

It leaves out where you are now, living in a 1984 Toyota 4 X 4 in the Santa Cruz mountains, taking the occasional tree-felling job. It omits the fact that until recently, fifteen rolls of slides from your trip sat in your father's freezer because you couldn't afford to have them developed. He did it for you as a Christmas gift. It leaves out how you can't afford to rent a room somewhere. How you can't afford to fix your tooth.

You'll figure it out. Or you won't. You turn thirty-three in May. You have many trips in front of you. Or you don't. The money will come. Or it won't. The answers will present themselves, or not. You have to be patient. You have to avoid gazing too far into the future. These are the lessons that any would-be yo-yo hiker must learn. You have learned them. You have to savor each day, to love the journey. A step at a time, a mile at a time. An hour at a time.

So let's pick a good hour to end your tale. There are so many to choose from. What about the afternoon in San Diego, where you and Patti drove after Mexico, where you swam in the ocean and floated on your back and marveled at how everything flows from the mountains and ends up in the sea, and you were no different; where you visited the tacky T-shirt shops next to the beach and drank cup after cup of coffee and ate plate after plate of spinach salad? No? What about rush hour in the East Bay, stuck in traffic, doing your best to apply the lessons of the trail — the lessons of patience and acceptance and grace and being a part of the troubled society you and Kenny talked about — to life? No? What about midday in Barney's Burgers, on the Berkeley border, where you tuck in to a one-pound monster patty and a half order of curly fries and a blackberry milkshake and spin tales about Hobo Joe and Real Fat and the Wall and the folly of long-distance hikers who leave the trail and reenter society with rage and bitterness and hatred for things like traffic jams and jobs, not realizing that those things are as much a part of life as soaring hawks and fragrant sunrises?

No? You have always had difficulty with beginnings and endings. You have been through enough grief. So why don't we pick a moment in the middle? The right ending. Let's choose a moment of peace.

It has been raining for a week. It's late July and you and Kenny have been on the trail since March 2, through blizzards and windstorms and hidden canyons filled with golden trout. And now, in Washington's Glacier Peak Wilderness, headed north, at mile 2,450, high on a ridge, your food supplies are practically gone and you're not only cold and wet, you're hungry. A chilly, damp twilight and you throw off your packs and set up your tarp and try to build a fire to dry out and get warm, but most of the wood is wet. Kenny scrabbles in the dirt at the base of a tree, looking for dry kindling. It's a western hemlock. Isn't it funny the things a man remembers?

Kenny shouts. "I found a beer!" It's a Miller Icehouse. You remember that, too. Then he shouts some more. He has dug up six cans of food. Chili and corn and corned-beef hash and okra. But only one beer. You and Kenny convene for a crucial Pacific Crest Trail yo-yo summit conference. Together you decide that half a beer simply will not do, that one of you should drink the entire thing. You flip a nickel and Kenny wins. Has a single beer ever filled anyone with such utter, outsize delight?

It's the spring of 1996 and the left side of your face is missing a functioning salivary gland. You don't have a steady job or health insurance. You don't know if you'll make it back to Mexico this year, or even if you'll make it to the Canadian border. You have no idea about the difficulties and pain that lurk in the decade ahead, about what loss will do to you. It doesn't matter, though. You are blessed, rich beyond anyone's wildest dreams. You have the mountain peaks and the stars and a warm fire and corn and chili and okra and corned-beef hash and your tarp and your very good friend drinking a beer, your brother who you have tried to teach about balance and who has taught you so much about joy. You have never been good at beginnings and endings, but that's OK, because beginnings and endings don't really matter here. Maybe there is no beginning, no ending. Maybe — yeah, it's cheesy, it's kind of New Agey — life and death are part of the same cycle, and sometimes one death can sustain another life, the cosmic wheel and all that. So maybe the story ends in 1996. Maybe it begins there, too. Maybe all that counts is the journey, and you have that. Maybe there is only now, and you have now. You have this moment, underneath the branches of the western hemlock tree, with your hiking partner, who has become your best friend, who has become your brother. You have everything you need. You have everything you will ever need.

6

FALLING STAR:
MARSHALL ROGERS, BASKETBALL PLAYER

O
N GOOD DAYS, MARSHALL ROGERS CAN ALMOST REMEMBER WHAT
*it feels like to be rich and famous. Flipping through the scrap-
books he never allows to leave his room, he is struggling to
make this a good day.*

*"I scored fifty-eight here," he says and stabs a finger at a yellowed
clipping, then at me. "Here," he says and flips the page, "this is where I
had scored my thousandth point. There. That's Lamar. I used them up.
I had eighteen the first year we played them. The next year I had forty-
four." He flips to another curled piece of paper. "I had fifty-eight points
here. This is important. Look at this."*

*It is late July, the kind of hazy, sweaty day when even little children
in this North St. Louis neighborhood stay off the streets and cling to
patches of shade on their front porches. We are sitting in Rogers's bedroom, on the top floor of his mother's house. A fan blows hot, stale air
around the cramped room, over the chessboard that sits on a footlocker
between two beds, ruffling the pictures of naked women that plaster the
walls. In a corner, nearly hidden, is a shiny, bronzed basketball engraved on its base. It says, "Marshal [sic] Rogers, The National Scoring Champ, NCAA Division I 36.8." Rogers received it in 1976, the
year he scored more points than anyone else in major college basketball.
He picks it up, rubs the top of it, mutters something to someone who is
not there.*

Then he shouts. "Hey, you've heard of Willie Smith [former basketball player at Mizzou]? They retired his number, right? Willie Smith never scored fifty-eight points. They're crazy. Don't you think so? See what I'm saying?"

People remember Marshall Rogers. He was one of the inner city's success stories. A role model. By the time he graduated from Sumner High School in 1971, he wasn't just a high school all-American basketball player. He was also the school's scholar-athlete. And when he left the University of Texas-Pan American on a spring day in 1976, he held, as well as a slew of scoring records, a bachelor's degree in history.

Did mothers tell their little boys about Marshall? Did they say it was OK to run outside and play, as long as they remembered to study — like Marshall? The children surely paid attention, because Marshall was living their dream. People paid him to play basketball. He was on television. For a few glorious months in the winter of 1977, he worked for the Golden State Warriors, and on days he wanted to tool around the San Francisco Bay area, he hopped into a green Cordoba, or a lavender Mark V. Sometimes he tooled around in a yellow van with "Warriors" emblazoned on the side. He made forty-five thousand dollars per year. That was a long time ago.

This past June, a downtown drugstore manager spotted Rogers stuffing something into his gym bag. When the manager searched it, he found a bottle of Mennen Skin Bracer, a stick of Adidas deodorant, a pair of white sunglasses, and three Baby Ruth candy bars. Total value: thirteen dollars.

Rogers has lived with his mother for at least three years. He hasn't worked steadily this decade.

Hometown heroes often fall, but rarely from such dizzying heights, and seldom to such public lows ("Ex-Sumner, Pro

Player Held in Melee," read the headline in the *St. Louis Post-Dispatch*). Marshall Rogers seemed to have it all, and when he lost it, those who knew him groped for explanations.

"Living in the past," said a man who played against Rogers in high school. "Like a lot of inner-city kids," said one of his college coaches, "who can never give up that dream of playing big-time basketball."

Impatience, said his mother. "He always wanted to jump fast. You can't jump fast if you're new."

Pride, said one of his two ex-wives. "He probably feels that things should be better because they were better. . . . He will have to go back down, in a sense, to get back up."

Rogers is proud, of course, and impatient. Those qualities, as much as his enormous physical gifts, helped him claw his way to success. And, yes, he clings to the past, and to the dream he should have long ago abandoned. But those are small problems. What's wrong with Marshall Rogers is more serious. And more frightening.

"I was drafted number thirty-four in the second round, but I would have been in the first round, playing with the New York Knicks. But some important people didn't want me in New York."

We are sitting in Pope's Cafeteria in Central City Shopping Center. Rogers is halfway through his lunch — a pork steak, a plate of roast beef, a large salad soaked in Thousand Island and Italian dressing, a roll with six pats of butter, green beans, a large pickle, two cartons of milk, a piece of apple pie, and a bottle of Budweiser. Before he digs in, he shakes salt over everything but the drinks and the pie for five seconds, then pepper for three seconds, until there is gritty layer of black and white covering his food. "Hey," he yells when a waitress walks by, "where's the ketchup?" She promises to bring some. "And bring some Tabasco and A.1. sauce, too."

Between huge bites, Rogers talks about basketball, and college, and women.

After he left the pros and before he returned for good to St. Louis, Rogers went back to Pan American in Texas to take some graduate courses. He dropped out because "every time I went to take a test, they were using a machine to clear my mind."

"A machine?"

"Yeah."

"Who?"

"I can't tell you. You know what this place is called?"

"Pope's?"

"Yeah, exactly."

He attacks his pork steak, and we eat in silence. Then he tells me how he and his team almost defeated the University of Nevada, Las Vegas basketball team twelve years ago. "We were hooping 'em to death," he says, until "they were using some kind of animation machine to help them score in the second half."

"An animation machine?"

"They have these rays that grab the ball in midair."

"Who does?"

"I can't tell you."

Roast beef and green beans then, and more silence.

I ask how many children he has.

"I don't really know."

"Five?"

"No, about twelve. I have some white ones, too. When I was at Kansas, I had some white girlfriends, and they had my kids. They wanted some money for the kids, and cars and stuff, and they asked the regime, and they got the cars and money and places to live."

"You mean the athletic department got that stuff for them? Coaches? Alumni?"

"No, the regime. Pope John Paul, Queen Elizabeth, King Arthur, and Hercules."

*   *   *

Marshall Roger was the sixth of seven children. A bright little boy, he paid attention and worked hard. Before long, he was riding the bus to Sportsman's Park with all the other straight-A students to watch the baseball Cardinals. He decided he wanted to be a teacher when he grew up. That, or a professional baseball player. His heroes were Ken Boyer, Mike Shannon, and Bob Gibson.

In third grade he discovered basketball. He was the best player in his class, "but the dudes used to beat on us." For a while, anyway, Marshall stuck with marbles and hopscotch. But his mother bought him a shiny new basketball that year, and, when he wore it out, she bought him another. By the time he graduated from Sumner in 1971, Marshall's mother had bought her baby boy ten new basketballs. Every year, a new ball.

In the summer he went to the baseball games with the other straight-A students. In the spring he set sprint and long-jump records for the Sumner track team. And always there was basketball.

He played for the state championship team when he was a sophomore; when he was a senior, he averaged 26.7 points per game and led his team to a 22–4–1 record (a near riot forced the tie with Vashon). When practice was over and the rest of the team had showered and gone home, Rogers stayed in the gym. Coach John Algee stayed, too, and when Rogers dribbled and shot, Algee slapped his star's wrist. Or he smacked his star's elbow.

"I wanted him to get his rhythm down," Algee says, "to help him learn to shoot with people hitting him."

He learned — on the court and in class.

"My favorite course was probably history," Rogers says. "Math was good, too. Cutting class was the best, though. Just to talk about what happened yesterday, or last night."

John Algee: "I can't say enough about him as a high school

athlete. He was one of the greatest basketball players that ever played for me. . . . He was a very good student, carried himself well.

"But he was more or less a loner — stayed by himself. I don't think he had any best friends."

"My mother stole one of my tank tops." He has finished everything but the pie. He will take that home. He is sipping his beer and smoking a cigarette. "Someone probably called her — the pope or the queen, and told her, "Steal Marshall's tank top so he won't look so good.'"

Rogers left St. Louis and moved to Lawrence, Kansas, where he had accepted an athletic scholarship at the University of Kansas. He led his undefeated freshman team in scoring and assists and enjoyed the social opportunities available to a healthy young athlete in a college town. His freshman coach, Bob Frederick (now athletic director at KU), says he "really enjoyed" Marshall but remembers that "he did have a little bit of a temper. He'd flare up pretty quickly."

He had plenty of chances to flare up the next year. The KU Jayhawks employed a slow-down offense, which could not have been less suited to the insect-quick Rogers. His scoring average fell to 7.6. The team went 8–18. "I was unhappy," Rogers remembers. "We were winning quite a few games in the first half, then losing. There were some inner-squad squabbles. The teammates got upset."

During his sophomore winter of discontent, Rogers happened to pick up a magazine on one of the Jayhawks road trips. He spotted a story about a coach named Abe Lemons, legendary in basketball circles for his explosive offenses.

"Dear Coach Lemons," Rogers wrote. "My name is Marshall Rogers. I'm 6-foot 2-inches and 180 pounds. I averaged

24.3 points and 6.0 assists respectively for the Kansas fresh-men team last year. My main strengths are speed and quick-ness . . ."

Fourteen years later, Lemons still has the letter.

"I just thought he was the nicest kid," the coach says. Lemons was especially impressed that Rogers didn't badmouth his Kansas coach. "And he wrote a real nice letter."

After his sophomore season, Rogers left KU and transferred to Pan American, where Lemons was coaching. When he showed up at the campus in Edinburg, Texas, and laid eyes on his new coach, the "nice kid" demanded money. "He asked if I was going to give him plane fare for his trips back to St. Louis," Lemon remembers. "I said no. He asked if that was the way it was for everybody on the team. I said yes. He said, 'Well, I can live with that.'"

While Rogers was waiting to become eligible to play for Lemons, he joined a city league in Edinburg. "They kicked him off," Lemons says, "and they told me he would never be able to play for me because he shot too much."

They didn't know Lemons. Famous for his cowboy boots and his drawling one-liners, the coach never met a jump shot he didn't like. And if some of Marshall's shots were, shall we say, in-ventive, well, Lemons took to splash and dazzle the way other coaches take to crew cuts and blazers.

For two years the city kid and the country coach created a defensive specialist's worst nightmare. Their supporting cast could have been dreamed up by Ring Lardner. At one guard was Jesus Guerra, a short (five-foot-ten), skinny kid who grew up on the Mexican border. He penetrated and passed. Teammates called him "Chewey." Fans called him "Little Jesus." In the pivot was Pete "Pizza" Severa, a six-foot-five, 250-pound man-child who worked during the day at — where else? — Pizza Hut then threw opponents around at night. "He was what we jokingly called our center," says Lemons, who now coaches at Oklahoma City University.

The Pan American Broncs often scored more than a hundred points in a single game. And the biggest scorer and main attraction of the hardwood circus was Rogers.

"He was the best pure shooter I've ever seen," says Jim McKone, Pan American's sports information director for the past eighteen years. Likeable? Rogers is one of two Bronc athletes McKone ever had to his house for dinner. Tough? McKone remembers a game — it was January 29, 1976 — against Houston Baptist University. Rogers drove the lane in the opening minutes, and when he stretched toward the basket, Houston Baptist's seven-foot center caught the nation's leading scorer in the jaw with an elbow. "He was out on the floor," McKone remembers, "absolutely cold." A minute passed. Rogers didn't move. Two minutes. Nothing. Three minutes. Rogers got up, walked to the free-throw line, and sank two shots. He ended up with forty-five points. Final score: Pan American, eighty-one, Houston Baptist, seventy-nine.

Rogers averaged 26.7 points in his junior year. The team went 22–2. In his record-setting senior season, he hit 36.8 per game. The team was 20–5.

"He was amazing," said Guerra, now head basketball coach at Roma (Texas) High School, in the border town where he grew up. "Coach Lemons kept stats every day, and Marshall would shoot forty out of fifty, twenty-five out of thirty. He was the most dedicated player I've ever been associated with."

"He was one of the best," Lemons says. "He had the size, the ability. There wasn't anything he couldn't do in a game. . . . He was what you'd call an all-American boy. He made his grades, worked hard, got along with everybody. He was a coach's dream."

*   *   *

Rogers: "We were playing the University of Hawaii. The queen called me on the phone and said we had to beat them by fifteen points. I scored forty-seven points, but we had to play them the next night again, and I was too tired. So one of my brothers, who looks just like me, from Africa, he played."

Rogers was selected in the second round of the National Basketball Association's annual draft, and in the fall of 1976 he signed a forty-five-thousand-dollar contract with the Golden State Warriors. He played in twenty-six games that year and averaged 3.8 points. "I was hooping 'em to death," Rogers says. "I should have been playing more."

The next fall he attended veteran's camp, where he continued to ride the bench. In October 1977 the Warriors played the Los Angeles Lakers in an exhibition game in Reno, Nevada.

"I should have been starting," Rogers says. "I got kind of upset. . . . You get real upset and feel like hurting somebody. It's best just to get away so you don't get into trouble."

He left the team.

We are driving to Shoney's in North County. Rogers is in the passenger's seat, stroking an invisible baby he holds in front of him. He is talking out of the right side of his mouth, addressing something outside the car.

When we sit down, he calls to a waitress. "I'll have an apple pie à la mode while I order," he says. She brings it, and he asks for spaghetti with extra meat, and a turkey club sandwich, and the salad bar. He gives it all the salt-and-pepper treatment and asks for ketchup and A.1.

"On May 30, 1976," he says, "I went to the Olympic camp in Raleigh, North Carolina. There were two practices a day for three hours each time. It was grueling. It made you tired. And mean and mad. I did real well before the animation machine got in my way.

"Wait," he says after we finish and I start to stand. "I have to do

something." He stands in the aisle, turns and crosses his arms under his chin, elbows outstretched. "That was the pope," he tells me later, "telling me to do that."

After leaving the Warriors, Rogers stayed in the Bay Area. He played in pickup games, in tournaments. He was a substitute teacher in Hayward, California. And he was unhappy.

In September 1978 he tried out with the San Antonio Spurs. "I was doing good enough to be in the top seven. I didn't see anyone else hitting as many jump shots as me. [But] people in the underground were saying, 'Marshall likes himself too much 'cause he scores too much.' That's why I didn't play. But I'm thinking about trying out again."

"The last I heard from him," says Coach Lemons, "seems like he was down in San Antone. He called and said he needed one hundred dollars, so I telegrammed it to him."

Rogers is standing at the free-throw line in the gym at Vic Tanny on Dorsett and I-270. His right arm is cocked in a U, and a scowl splits his face. He hits thirty-four free throws without missing and without smiling. Then he hits thirty-one without missing, then seventeen. The only sounds are the clanking of the weight machines nearby. That and the occasional bounce of the basketball on the floor, and the swish of the net. And Marshall's muttering. He is talking to the voices.

KU's Bob Frederick heard from Rogers last winter. "He wanted to know if I could put in a word for him with" Topeka's semipro basketball team. "He told me how he and his friend were hooping everybody at the Forest Park Community College."

Frederick clears his throat. It pained him to hear from Rogers. It pains him to talk about him.

"I don't want this to sound wrong," Frederick says and clears his throat again. "It was like he was just a year out of college instead of eleven years."

Roma's favorite son, Guerra, doesn't know what to say when he learns of his old teammate's troubles. First come the adjectives: "hardworking," "gifted," "dedicated." Then the memories of specific games, particular feats of athletic heroism. There is a realization that "it was very rare when we got together" socially, and a few halfhearted attempts to understand why some people succeed and others fail. Finally, there is simply a request.

"Do you have Marshall's phone number?" Little Jesus asks. "I need to call him."

We are driving to O'Fallon Park with a photographer to shoot some baskets and some pictures. Rogers is expansive — laughing, smoking, jiving. He is telling us how he played one-on-one with a local teenager a few days earlier. "He was woofing on me. I smoked him. I'm gonna steal his mother from him now. She knows me from high school. She knows me from when I was a superstar."

It is Thursday afternoon, August 27. Today, Rogers turns thirty-four years old.

Narrating his own life story, Rogers will gladly rattle off dates and statistics. December 2, 1974: the Broncs steal the ball three times in the final thirty seconds to erase a five-point deficit and beat Arkansas State in Jonesboro. January 3, 1976: the Broncs lose to the University of Nevada, Las Vegas, and Rogers feels the "animation machine." May 16, 1976: Rogers graduates from Pan American. September 1978: he tries out with the Spurs but is cut.

And "that's it," Rogers says. "Right there. You don't need to write about any of that other stuff."

*   *   *

Kurt Gull used to work as a security guard for St. Louis Centre. He was on duty Wednesday, June 24.

"We got a call from Walgreens. They said they had a shoplifter in custody. I was the first person on the scene. When I got there, Marshall and the manager were arguing and pushing and shoving.... [The manager] explained that he had seen him take some items, and that he and the assistant manager had talked Marshall in to going into the back room, and they checked the gym bag and found the items. What they were pushing and shoving over was that [Rogers] didn't like the idea of them getting into his gym bag.

"I said, 'OK, I'm placing you under arrest.'

"He said, 'OK, what's going to happen now?'

"I said, 'I'll have to handcuff you until the police arrive, and you'll probably get a summons, and you probably won't have to go anywhere.'

"He said, 'OK,' and I put one handcuff on his left hand and he went crazy. He jumped back, slammed me against the wall. He swung, he pushed, he shoved."

By then, two more security guards and a police officer arrived.

"I'm five-feet-nine, two hundred twenty-five pounds, fifty inches across the chest, and he was tossing us around like we were rag dolls."

In September Rogers was convicted of assault. He was placed on probation.

After the Spurs cut him, Rogers returned to St. Louis. Except for a brief attempt to take graduate courses at Pan American in the fall of 1979 (where the machine "cleared his mind"), Rogers has never ventured out again. One of college basketball's greatest scorers hasn't done much the past ten years.

He taught at McKinley High School and O'Fallon Technical Center in 1978 and 1979. He left McKinley because "the principal was upset . . . because the students were acting crazy, and one girl especially, and I started to curse her out." He has been married twice and has at least two children. His second wife, who asked that her name not be used, says, "He probably feels that things should be better because they were better." His mother says he "does funny things with his hands." She wishes he would see a doctor.

Rogers spends much of his time sleeping and eating. He wakes up early every day — sometimes at 5:30 or 6:00 A.M. — and makes breakfast. A typical meal is two eggs, two hot dogs, two pancakes, milk, and Kool-Aid. After that, "Sometimes I go back to sleep. Sometimes I cut the grass. Sometimes I just sit on the porch. Sometimes, but not all the time. Sometimes it's fun. Sometimes it's boring."

He usually skips lunch, and, after a typical afternoon of "just relaxing," his mother cooks dinner. After that, he usually hangs around the house until he decides to go up to his room and go to sleep, which could be any time between 7:00 P.M. and 2:00 A.M.

"Sometimes I get mad at the voices," he says, "and I can't go to sleep. And I say, 'Leave me alone.'"

We are sitting in a courtyard on Laclede's Landing. Rogers is here with mixed feelings. He doesn't want anything written about his recent troubles with the law, and he would rather talk about how many points he scored against Lamar than his difficulties finding a job. On the other hand, without a car he doesn't get a chance to leave the house much. And I'm buying lunch.

I ask who his friends are.

"No one."

"No one?"

"Sometimes, I'll be with friends, but not very often. Nowadays, I'll be by myself at home."

"You ever get lonely?"

"Sometimes. Sometimes. But not all the time."

"What do you see yourself doing in five or ten years?"

"Some type of work. . . . With a job, I could get around and do more things I want. I could go to a discotheque and buy some drinks that I like — that's why I need to get some work. You know, I haven't been having a real good time lately."

"What plans do you have for looking for work?"

"I don't know. I haven't thought about it."

"You have any regrets about what happened at Walgreens?"

"It's over with."

"Do the voices bother you?"

"I'll be trying to lay down, and it really upsets me when I'm trying to lay down and go to sleep and I don't feel like standing up and they tell me to stand up."

"You told me you talked to a doctor about this once."

"That was someone else. That really wasn't me.

"Sometimes they say things to me that don't pertain to what I want to do. They tell me to do something while I'm playing and I don't feel like doing it, and I just say, 'Shut the fuck up.' Sometimes it gives me a headache."

"Do you ever think now about seeing a doctor?"

"I don't need a doctor. I just need to go to sleep and not talk to them anymore."

7

UP FROM THE GUTTER:
RUDY KASIMAKIS, BOWLER

*S*O WE PULL UP IN THE PARKING LOT OF THE BOWLING CENTER; IT WAS *after midnight. I knew who he was. . . . I knew that sometimes in matches like this, you either lose a lot of money or, if you win, you're lucky to get out of there. We look around the parking lot. . . . I'm thinking, 'We're gonna get mugged.' I'm thinking, 'This is ugly,'"*
— professional bowler David Ozio, remembering bowling an action game against Rudy Kasimakis

Most men don't leave bowling alleys at sunrise, but he has left many then. He has staggered out of bowling alleys into cold dawns. He has opened bowling alley doors and blinked at fragrant mornings and hot, sticky mornings and cool, autumnal mornings, exhausted but fulfilled, his pockets bulging with so much cash he would rather not discuss it. He has walked out with nothing, "no gas in your car, no toll to get home sometimes, you're not eating for three days." This has been his job. He has driven five hours to bowl six hours. He has drilled holes in thousands of bowling balls, until he made himself expert in the ways they were balanced and weighted. He has x-rayed bowling balls. (In self-consciously ironic moments, he refers to himself as "a recovering ballaholic.") He has bought advertisements in small newspapers and challenged top professional bowlers — "professional" in a legitimate, corporate-endorsement type of way, from a clean, well-lighted world he once tried and failed to enter — to meet him late at night in smoky, loud places filled with hard, unsmiling men, and many of the professionals have come. Hours later, oftentimes, he has swaggered into the sunrise with gas money to burn. He has taken money from many other less-famous bowlers, too. He has made a good living at that, a much better living, it is safe to say, than many of the bowlers who labor in the clean, well-lighted world he once tried and failed to enter.

He has bet on frames, high odd scores, high even scores. He has bet on a single ball. (He has not bet on "towel games," where bowlers fling their balls from towels, or "concourse games," where bowlers fling their balls from the scorer's table, though he has beat players who have). He has bowled where lowest score won (but only if you hit at least one pin per ball). He has bowled "telephone matches," where two bowlers meet in a town and open a phone book and one player closes his eyes and stabs at the page listing the bowling centers, and, wherever his finger lands, that's where they bowl. He has bowled badly on purpose, to persuade other bowlers to play and to bet against him. "To keep the fish interested. I was always cleaning the bottom of the tank. It was dirty and I had to clean it." He has bowled "four game freezeouts," where the first bowler to win four games in a row won everything. In the world of action bowling, which is where Rudy Kasimakis has ruled for the past fifteen years or so, "everything" can represent a large sum of money, oftentimes bet by hard, unsmiling men. Think of a good year's salary. That sum, large but intentionally vague at Rudy's request, might be what's at stake in a single action game.

Action bowler's most successful practitioner is pulling himself from the game now. He is once again trying to leave the four game freezeouts and bleary sunrises behind, so that he can enter the clean, well-lighted world with the television lights and corporate endorsements. He is attempting success on the Professional

Bowlers Association (PBA) tour — at thirty-four years old going legit. But like Joseph Kennedy and George Steinbrenner and Don King and Mark Wahlberg and other skilled men who have tried to leave one disreputable world in order to enter a different, better-lighted, and more complicated one, his trip is fraught with complications. And in the case of action bowling's greatest action bowler, a question: Why?

Most bowling fans know him as Rudy Revs, because, when he cocks his bowling ball back, his right hand points straight up and he torques his wrist and then releases the ball with more power than almost any other bowler alive. Among bowlers, Rudy is said to possess a "high revolution" ball. Thus Revs. He weighs 240 pounds and stands five-feet-eight and he has forearms like thighs and a neck like a waist and dark eyes that glower and burn in a head like a boulder. He is loud and swaggering in victory, and moody when he loses. He is obsessed with winning. His survival depends on winning. Professional and top amateur bowlers speak of "throwing" a bowling ball. In Rudy's case, the expression is accurate. When Rudy strikes, pins jump and scatter with cartoonish alacrity. When he doesn't strike, he leaves more pins than a professional bowler should or can afford to. He is known as an "all-or-nothing" bowler. His wife, Nancy, knows what a spectacle he creates in a bowling alley. She likes it. "Someone comes into an alley," she says, "and they look at all the bowlers, and then they see him. People are saying, 'Who is that? Who is that?' And I turn around and say, 'That's Rudy Revs!'" He has a heavy New York accent and a reputation for betting big money in games that he has helped fix. He looks and sometimes acts like low-rent muscle, and he is making a life change for the loftiest kind of ideal.

*   *   *

"He gets right in your face and says, 'I'm the best, you can't beat me, I'm the best, there's no way you can beat me.' He'd just demoralize a guy, the guy would just be shaking.

"I bowled him twice, beat him twice. The last time I beat him, two straight games, and he was in my face at the end of the second game, still screaming, 'You can't beat me, you can't beat me!'"

— former professional bowler Brian Berg

There are two commandments that action bowlers live by. The first, especially for an action bowler who wants to keep his belly and his gas tank full, is you play the percentages. "You don't play a straight guy in a straight guy's house if you're a hook bowler," says David Ozio, the thirteenth-winningest professional bowler in history, a man who has bowled his share of action games (and still does).

The second imperative is you play anywhere. "The code of any good action player," says PBA commissioner Mark Gerberich, a man who has a strange and twisted relationship to action bowling and action bowlers like Rudy, "is 'anytime, anywhere, any amount of money.' That's what action bowling is — you and me, you get done working, I get done working, we're gonna lock the doors and we're gonna bowl."

To thrive as an action bowler — and Rudy has thrived better than any other action bowler — means devising a way of synthesizing two ostensibly conflicting dictates, two absolute imperatives that appear to be mutually exclusive but are in fact subtly interconnected. In some ways, it's like being a pious murderer.

So action bowlers try to make sure the lanes they are bowling on are oiled to their liking, and not to their opponents. Oil patterns influence how a ball hooks, where it hooks, even *if* it hooks. Some action bowlers arrive at a lane early and tinker with the pin-setting machine, which can favor balls thrown from certain angles — angles that happen to be the ones those bowlers who tinker are best at.

One action bowler, a man who throws the ball even harder than Rudy — "His ball could basically knock down tree trunks," Rudy says — used to travel to action games with four cases of Brunswick 3-8 Red Crowns in the trunk of his car. "That's three pounds eight ounces." At the time the Red Crowns were four ounces heavier — and more difficult to knock down — than normal pins.

In the world of action bowling, where Rudy has long been the chief aquarium cleaner, strange and exotic creatures scurry and skitter in the murky light. There are "gutter players," men with sweeping hooks who spend their entire careers bowling on the board right next to the gutter because they've made sure the rest of the lane is heavily oiled. A gutter player's ball avoids the oil before hooking at the last minute into the head pin. A gutter player's opponent usually bowls down the middle of the lane, only to watch helplessly as his ball slides and slip out of control. There are "dump artists," excellent bowlers who make most of their money placing secret bets against themselves — on other, lesser bowlers — then losing on purpose.

One dump artist became so notorious that one night, with one ball left to bowl, a ball that would decide the outcome of the game, many of the hard, unsmiling men who had — perhaps foolishly — bet on the dump artist thought he might throw the game and so threatened him with grievous bodily harm if he didn't make his spare. But other hard men, who were counting on his dumping the game, threatened him with grievous bodily harm if he *did* make his spare. So the dump artist faked a heart attack. "Clutched his chest, yelled, fell over, the whole bit," says Rudy with a laugh that is at least a little admiring. "Made an ambulance come to get him outta there."

Dump artists and gutter players are unpopular creatures, shunned by other denizens of the action aquarium. But their cunning and skill are recognized, sometimes even honored. Such is the case with the man who in the early seventies discovered that if he soaked his bowling ball overnight in a chemical resin that he had found in a hardware store, the ball would become soft and it would grip the wood of a bowling lane with amazing traction and hook powerfully into the head pin. The year he made his discovery, the bowler, a career journeyman, made more money than any of his colleagues and was named PBA player of the year. He is described at the International Bowling Museum and Hall of Fame in St. Louis as "an innovator in the game."

Rudy is not above gimmicks and trickery. When he bowls at his favorite action spot, Deer Park Lanes, in Deer Park, Long Island, he makes sure the match takes place on lanes eleven and twelve. "Lane eleven is the easiest lane in America to throw a strike on," he says. "Lane twelve hooks early and stops in the back; you have to circle the lane, make sure you get the ball to come around the corner and kick the ten." It takes a while for Rudy's opponents to figure that out.

Bowlers who have opposed Rudy at Deer Park Lanes refer to the venue as "the Cage," in part because it always seemed to be crowded with hard, unsmiling friends of Rudy. Rudy would yell at other bowlers there and slap his hands in front of them after he had bowled a strike. He'd say, "Now that's a *real* strike." He would belittle his opponent, insult his game, and then he would watch his opponent. Rudy knows that, when a man is bowling with his own money, he is often scared, and Rudy senses others' fear and he feeds off it.

"I'm kind of like a dog that way," he says. "When I can sense him shaking, it's kind of like a high."

"He was an animal," says Norm, the eleventh winningest professional bowler in history. "The hardest thing about bowling Rudy was not being intimidated. He took sixteen pounds and made it look like a piece of popcorn."

"I bowled him at the Cage," says David Ozio. "That was suicidal on my part. Everyone feared Rudy in the Cage."

*   *   *

He tried the pro tour twelve years ago, but he didn't make it. There are no fish on the pro tour, and there's more oil than on regular lanes, and the oil patterns are equally tough on everyone. And where Rudy's all-or-nothing ball scares opponents in dark, dim alleys, it doesn't scare anyone on the PBA tour. Too many times, the all-or-nothing ball was nothing. The most successful PBA bowlers aren't the men who make the pins jump and whose balls can knock over tree trunks. The men who make the money on the PBA tour are consistent, mostly quiet men with consistent, mostly quiet bowling styles. The man even Rudy says is the greatest clutch bowler in the game — the man "I'd bet my last dollar on to throw one single ball" — is Norm Duke, who is five-feet-five, 123 pounds, unfailingly polite to bowling fans, and who says "thank you" and dips his head when people applaud. "The Duke," as he is known, is not flashy, but he's consistent. The richest bowler in history is a man named Walter Ray "Deadeye" Williams Jr. Williams doesn't throw a particularly powerful strike ball, and if his style is notable for anything, it's for a certain clumsiness. But he's accurate, and he's consistent.

To succeed on the tour this time, Rudy knows he'll have to adjust more, go for broke less. He also knows that even with his three sponsors — Hammer Bowling and Turbo 2-N-1 Grips, and Ultimate Polish — giving him weekly checks plus incentives if and when he wins, competing on the PBA tour means spending about thirteen hundred dollars a week on travel and expenses. Rudy stands to make much less money as a pro than he has made as an amateur (though rule changes in bowling's amateur ranks have made it more difficult for Rudy to clean the bottom of the tank with such consistent success). In fact, he stands to lose money, anathema to an action bowler.

"Everybody's ego exists to the next level," says David Ozio, by way of explaining Rudy's otherwise inexplicable return to the

PBA. "If you don't do it, you'll always wonder how you would have stacked up against the best of the best."

Rudy is having lunch with PBA commissioner Mark Gerberich at an Applebee's restaurant in a mall on the outskirts of Scranton, Pennsylvania, which is like the most notorious and trash-talking street basketball hustler you have never heard of sitting down to break bread with National Basketball Association (NBA) commissioner David Stern, though they probably wouldn't end up at Applebee's, or in a mall outside Scranton. Gerberich is at the table because he knows what an action bowler with Rudy's dark charisma and big hook and boulder head with glowing eyes can do by way of drawing fans to the sport, and he knows what Rudy's penchant for mano-a-mano, in-your-face confrontation can do for television drama, and because he also knows that some people already think badly of bowlers — think they're less skilled than other professional athletes, somehow ruder, louder, meaner, *seedier* — and Gerberich worries that too much of Rudy's dark charisma and boulder head and mano-a-mano confrontation might reinforce that notion. So Gerberich, who has bowled action himself and who loves the color and drama of action, who loves the *action* of action, wants people to know about Rudy. But the commissioner also knows about the bad image that some people have of bowling and he doesn't want them to know *too* much about Rudy.

Rudy is here because Gerberich asked him to be here.

"There are some pro players who couldn't win an action game if their life depended on it . . ." Rudy says.

"What Rudy means," Gerberich says, "is that while pro bowlers are the best in the world, when it comes down to a single match, with everything on the line —"

"Bowling action," Rudy says, "means you're putting up your own money, on one game, everything riding on it, and it means you're facing some serious consequences depending on how you bowl."

"What Rudy means —"

"What I mean is, to bowl action, you gotta have ice water in your veins and a set of big keisters. I remember one match, it was Royal Lanes, in West Hempstead, I got beat up so bad, I left that place in a body bag and —"

"He doesn't mean he literally left in a body bag," Gerberich says.

"Yeah," Rudy says. "Not literally. But he beat me up bad. I was talking to myself that night."

Gerberich thinks Rudy could be just what the PBA needs. He hopes he'll bring some of the drama and flair of the action game to the PBA. But Gerberich worries that too much drama and flair might scare some people, might jeopardize the already fragile alliance the PBA has built with its corporate sponsors. Gerberich would like to make professional bowling more colorful without alarming the middle-class audience it is trying to broaden.

"You wanna do that?" Rudy asks. "Here's how you do that. When Walter Ray wins the next TV tournament, I walk up to him after, while the cameras are still rolling, and I say, 'Hey, Walter Ray, you might have won the tournament, but I don't think you're so hot.' Then I say, 'How about me and you just go to an alley down the street and we just rough it up, just me and you?' Then we do it, and the cameras follow us. Now that would be something."

Gerberich tells Rudy to hold off on that idea for a while.

8

TOUGH:
DANELLE BALLENGEE, RUNNER

HE WAS A BAD DOG. THAT WAS AN AWFUL THING FOR THE runner to think as she lay dying. He had curled next to her that first night in the hidden canyon, after the accident. He had put his snout on her belly and licked her face as she stared up at more shooting stars than she had ever dreamed. And that first morning — could it have been just the day before? — when it was so cold she had to crack the ice on top of the miraculous puddle, he had played with a stick, run in little circles, and barked with what she thought was happiness, and he was such a good dog then. He made her think that maybe things weren't so bad. She saw an eagle glide overhead that morning. It was beautiful. It was a beautiful morning. She was in a beautiful spot. Red rock and sandy soil and a juniper tree and the soft sighing of the high-desert wind, and to lope through it would have been a wonder for a runner whose body wasn't broken and bleeding inside.

All she had was the puddle and her dog. And then she didn't have the dog, because when she was screaming, when it took her two hours to reach behind her head to fill a water bottle from the puddle, the dog ran away. She couldn't stop screaming. She screamed because she hurt, and because she needed help and because she was afraid that help might not come in time. The dog came back, but he wouldn't lie down next to her that second night. It was just last night, but it seemed so long ago. There were no shooting stars the second night. The second night she saw things in the sky that made no sense, and heard a strange voice from the dark, and it made no sense, either.

Today, the third day, the dog was gone. Then he was back. Then he was gone again. Maybe she was hallucinating. Even though she was well known for enduring things others could not, for persevering through heat and cold and all manner of punishing climate and topography — even though she was one of the most accomplished endurance runners in the world, she still had her limits. On the third day, in the hidden canyon, her body broken, bleeding inside, she discovered them.

And then the dog was back, and now he was coming closer, and now he was lapping at the puddle, her only water source, and she couldn't help it, she yelled at him. It was the only water she could reach. Couldn't he find another puddle? Bad dog!

No one knew where she was. It would be dark again, and cold. No one could hear her scream. No one was coming. Today, her third day on the rock by the puddle, she allowed herself to see the truth.

She had won the Pikes Peak Marathon four times. She had raced up Colorado's fifty-four fourteen-thousand-foot peaks in less than fifteen days, faster than any female in history. She had competed in 441 endurance events since 1995 and finished in the top three in 390 of them. Three times she had been part of the team that won the Primal Quest Expedition Adventure Race, a four hundred–mile trek over land and water, mountain and desert. She had earned six U.S. Athlete of the Year titles in four different endurance sports. She had kept going when others had told her she had to stop. Now she couldn't move.

It was midafternoon on a Friday. She had degrees in biology and kinesiology, and, as much as she had invested personally and professionally in the awesome power of the human spirit, she also possessed grim knowledge regarding the limits of flesh and bone. It was ten days before Christmas. That's when Danelle

Ballengee, just thirty-five years old, prepared to die. That's when the runner who never gave up, gave up. It really was a beautiful spot. She felt peace. And then she heard another sound. And it didn't make sense, either.

Two days earlier, on Wednesday, December 13, she had left her house on Cliffview Drive in Moab, Utah, at 10:00 A.M. She had to communicate with sponsors, to write articles, to answer questions from teammates and, because she also worked as a trainer, clients. There were landlord duties, too. She owned three rental properties in Colorado, and she rented out space in her Moab house, and one of her tenant's friends had stolen some money, so she had to go to the bank to file a fraud report. Only then could she begin the highlight of her morning: her run.

With her dog, Taz, a three-year-old reddish brown mutt with a long jaw and a broad chest, she climbed in her white Ford Ranger truck. She stopped at a Burger King for a chicken sandwich and french fries and a large coffee because she had forgotten to eat breakfast. The dog got a bite because the dog always got a bite. She had spoiled him since the day she got him from the pound, when he was just a few weeks old.

It was a good day for a run, cloudy but not too cold. She listened to "Beautiful Day," by U2. She thought about the guy she had met a few months earlier at a race in Leadville, Colorado, and smiled because she thought there was potential. When she got to the parking area at the Amasa Back trailhead, five miles out of town, she kept driving, continued a quarter mile north on the road to a turnoff near a cliff. She did it because she wanted to shave a quarter mile off her run. The endurance runner was feeling lazy.

She put on a pair of cheap orange sunglasses, grabbed her MP3 player and a large plastic bottle filled with water and a raspberry-flavored energy gel. She wore running pants, a fleece hat, silk long underwear, a polypropylene shirt, and a thin fleece jacket. The temperature was in the forties, but she wanted to be prepared. She invested as much in preparation as she did in the power of positive thinking. Just before she locked her wallet and cell phone in the car, she spotted a fanny pack in the back seat. She had forgotten it was there. She grabbed it, stuck her water bottle in, and took off.

She would run an eight-mile loop. She would start on the Amasa Back Trail, popular among bikers and hikers, especially in spring and fall. But she would veer off of that after just a few miles, just before the top of a mesa, where she would follow a seldom-used jeep trail into a hidden canyon, then she would scramble up the rocks of that canyon, toward Hurrah Pass, onto another seldom-used jeep trail, through another canyon, up some more rocks, and she would eventually land back on another jeep trail that would take her back to her truck.

She had done this route five times already, knew she wouldn't see anyone else on her run. That suited her. Taz ran alongside her, panting happily. An hour in, she had covered five miles. She had drunk half her water. She was scrambling up the rocks in the first hidden canyon, Taz just behind her. It really was a beautiful day.

If you stopped to think about the things that could kill you, you could drive yourself crazy. Another second in an intersection. Another inch on a highway. One misstep on some ice-covered slickrock. Or maybe it was just slippery lichen.

One second she was one of the best endurance runners in the world, out for a late autumn loop in the high desert, breathing in the soft, juniper-scented air, barely paying attention to the low, grayish clouds scudding by. One second she was a world champion out for a light workout.

And then the second was gone. Now she was sliding like a kid down a giant waterslide. That's what she thought at the time, that it felt like a waterslide. Past lichen, past rocks, past sand.

She slid on her butt, hit "a little bump," then "another little bump." Then she came to "a little ledge."

People hear "Primal Quest" and they see adrenaline junkies. People read about Danelle Ballengee and they think "risk seeker." But in her kayak she steered clear of white water. On skis she descended carefully, avoided steep out-of-bounds areas. She had no interest in bungee jumping. Other adventure racers yipped with glee at sections that demanded hanging from ropes. That was the point in the race when Ballengee frowned and gritted her teeth.

She kept picking up speed. According to a newspaper account published a week after the accident, she flew off a cliff and plummeted the equivalent of two stories, landing on her feet. The reality was messier and more plain. She ended up halfway down the hill, prone. She caught her breath. She had survived eight sun-baked days in the Morocco Eco-Challenge. A leech had attached itself to her eye in another race, given her a corneal ulcer, blinded her for three days. That was punishing. This was just a nasty tumble. But she was smart and careful. She had her two degrees from the University of Colorado. She would be methodical. She put her right hand on her right leg, her left hand on her left leg. *Whew.* That was the word she thought. *Whew.* She wasn't paralyzed. This was her next thought: "Man, it's gonna be a long walk out of here." A moment later she realized she couldn't stand up.

She would crawl to the bottom of the canyon. She would drag herself downhill, thirty feet over rocks and boulders and through scrub, then, once she was on sand, she would crawl the three miles to the Amasa Back Trail and someone would see her. It was noon when she started.

Her left leg wouldn't move. She scooted forward on her right knee, balanced, then reached back with both hands and pulled her left leg forward. She knew things were broken. She knew she was in trouble. When she reached the bottom of the canyon, she looked in her fanny pack to see if there might be something to help. There was an old pack of raspberry energy gel, and a shower cap, and two ibuprofen. She ate the medicine, kept crawling. She crawled through sand and brush and some snow, and, by the time she arrived at a flat rock and a sinkhole filled with water, the air was getting cold and shadows in the canyon were lengthening. It was 5:00 P.M. She had crawled a quarter of a mile and it had taken five hours.

She laid down on her back, drank the remaining half of her water, put her hands between her legs because they were so cold. She decided she would refill the water bottle from the sink-hole — she didn't care about Giardia. But it hurt too much to turn over. So she reached backward over her right shoulder and filled the water bottle without looking. She thought about how cold she was, and how it would be dark soon, and how she was next to a water source. She decided she would spend the night next to the sinkhole.

She did crunches with her head and neck to keep warm. Her knees were bent and she tapped her feet on the rock. She rubbed her hands together. She reached for the shower cap in the fanny pack, but she couldn't find it. Taz curled up next to her. He put his chin on her stomach and looked at her. The temperature dipped into the twenties. She lay on her back, freezing, exhausted, and looked at the moonless sky. She saw the Milky Way and shooting stars. She had never in her life seen so many shooting stars.

She wondered what the guy in Leadville was doing. She wondered if someone would see that her truck was missing from her house. Then she realized how dumb that was. She loved working with others in the endurance challenges, but she hadn't told anyone where she was going. And what she was most fa-mous for was enduring. Why would anyone worry about her?

It was so cold. She didn't want to die. She couldn't die. There were friends and family she wasn't ready to leave. There was the guy from Leadville, and that had so much potential. She continued her crunches, her heel tapping, her finger curling.

At first light she saw Taz playing with a stick. That cheered her. She ate one of her energy gels. She tried to refill her water bottle, but the water in the sinkhole had frozen. She reached over her shoulder and broke through it with the cap of the bottle.

She decided she would crawl out of the canyon. She tried to roll over, to get on her hands and knees, and she screamed. She felt pain radiating down her legs, up her back. Taz licked her face and she lay back down on her back to gather her strength. And she screamed for help in case anyone could hear her, and when she looked up Taz had gone.

Then it was 3:00 and he was back. She wasn't sure how so much time had passed, but it had. It would be dark again soon, and the cold would come. She screamed for help even though she knew no one was coming. That's when she saw the shower cap — it was a just a couple of feet away. It was too far. She raised her head, lowered her voice. She looked at Taz.

"I'm hurt," she said. He looked at her and tilted his head, first to the left, then to the right. She knew it was ridiculous, but it looked like he understood.

"Taz," she said, "you know, maybe you could go and get some help for me."

He tilted his head again, didn't move. She told herself not to be stupid, that he was a dog. Just a dog. And then Taz ran away again, down the hidden canyon.

Now it was 4:00. She had to get the shower cap. She would need it for the night, to keep what meager body heat she still had. Two feet. It took an hour to get it. And now the sun had left the hidden little canyon and it was getting colder again, and she felt a swelling in her midsection, a lump the size of a water bottle, and she knew it was blood, that she was broken inside and bleeding. Then Taz was back, which was comforting, but it meant that he wasn't magic, he didn't understand English, he was a good dog, but he was just a dog. No one would be coming down the hidden canyon to rescue her.

She started the crunches again, the feet tapping, the hand rubbing. Taz refused to curl up next to her. Was it an animal's instinctive recoiling from imminent death? Did he want softer ground? It made no sense to her. Every so often, though, he would place a paw on her chest, lick her face. "Good dog," she would say.

It got colder and colder, and darker. She gazed up, looking for shooting stars, for the Milky Way, for evidence that the world hadn't ended. That she hadn't ended. But there were no stars. She saw only stripes. Long, white stripes slicing through the black night sky. She knew her body was shutting down, her brain malfunctioning. She was seeing things. She cried. She cried for her family and her friends and the nascent romance with the guy from Leadville that would never go anywhere. She is not religious, and she did not pray. What she did was plead.

"Please," she begged. "Please, somebody, notice that I'm gone."

Dorothy Rossignol is seventy-six years old, a "nosy neighbor" by her own account. Others in Moab call her a "piece of work," a "little old lady," and "the busybody of the neighborhood." She is childless, a widow since 1990. She loves mining, and if there is a town in the American West that ever produced a significant amount of any valuable mineral, whether gold, silver, or lead, she can name the town along with its mineral. Chances are she lived there with her husband, who mined it. "My husband would rather mine than eat," she says. They first came through Moab in 1957, a young bride and her husband, a miner looking for work during the uranium boom. They returned in 1969 and settled there for good. Moab was something in the boom years. "Parties you wouldn't believe," she says, ". . . dancing girls from Spain."

Life is slower now, nights quieter, days longer. She volunteers at the Dan O'Laurie Museum of Moab, eats lunch four days a week at the Moab senior center ("I'd eat there five days, but they're closed on Thursdays"), tends to the five peachcot (peach trees with apricot fruit grafted on) trees in her front yard, which have been growing for sixty years and whose fruit she still enjoys. She likes to talk about the boom years and the cultivation of her peachcot trees and all the movies that used to be filmed in Moab, "especially the ones with John Wayne."

Rossignol liked the young woman who moved next door five years ago, which is saying a lot. "I don't rush over to meet new neighbors right away, because you don't know what kind of people they are."

But the young woman seemed nice, and quiet, and she bought a puppy who jumped over the little metal fence separating the yards so often and scratched at the widow's door so relentlessly that she finally gave up and bought a bag of dog biscuits. Every day Taz would come over, and every day Rossignol would give the mutt two biscuits. He'd eat one there and take the other one home. Ballengee was gone a lot — "training for one of those adventure things" — so Rossignol fetched her mail, made sure her pipes didn't freeze in the winter when she was traveling.

They would do yard work together and chat "about everything in general and nothing in particular." As nice as Ballengee was, she wasn't so great on following leash laws. "So when I see the police or the dog catcher," Rossignol says, "I tie him up."

Taz didn't come to visit on Wednesday, December 13, and that night Rossignol looked through her window and saw that Ballengee's truck wasn't there. She also saw that Ballengee had left her drapes open, her lights on. She saw Ballengee's computer, also open. She knew that Ballengee was a free spirit, that when she wasn't training or visiting her parents in Evergreen, Colorado, she sometimes left to visit friends. She knew that

Ballengee sometimes didn't tell anyone where she was going. The widow didn't exactly approve of all that gallivanting. On the other hand, she had to admit, she admired it. They weren't all that different, the endurance runner and the miner's widow. Self-sufficient women in a man's world. Rossignol might have been a nosy neighbor, but she wasn't a scaredy cat. She would feel foolish calling the police if her young neighbor was out just having fun. She went to bed.

On Thursday afternoon Rossignol looked again and saw the open drapes, the blazing lights, the computer. That's when she called Gary and Peggy Ballengee in Evergreen, Colorado. She told Danelle's parents she was worried.

She was so tired. And cold. What was the point of tapping her feet? No one was coming down the hidden canyon. She stopped tapping. Then she heard a voice, commanding her. She knew she was alone. She knew there was no one telling her anything. She didn't believe in God. She knew there couldn't be a voice. But there was. And it wouldn't shut up. Keep tapping, the voice said. She kept tapping.

Police suspected the friend of the tenant — the guy who had stolen the checks — but they quickly cleared him. Word had spread through town, along with rumors, and someone from the bicycle shop called someone else who called the guy from Leadville. I promise, he told Ballengee's parents over the phone, I did not take your daughter to Mexico. I don't know where she is.

Police spent three hours inside Ballengee's house that Thursday. When they arrived Rossignol was waiting. She told them her neighbor was in trouble, that they should be looking for her truck and her dog. She told them she would show them where things were inside the house, where to find the clues that showed the runner was gone. When they refused her entry, she stood on the sidewalk outside. She stood on the sidewalk for three hours.

One of the police officers was a woman. She listened to the nosy neighbor's requests and suggestions and urgent entreaties. Then the officer gave her a card. It was dark now. If Rossignol heard anything, the cop said, feel free to call. Then the cops left.

The voice had stopped. The stripes were gone. It was light and she was alive. But the water in the puddle was frozen again and Taz was gone. She broke through, filled her bottle. She ate her last raspberry energy gel. No one was coming. She estimated she couldn't make it more than a few feet an hour and wondered if was worse to die trying or to die next to her little puddle. She started crawling.

She dragged herself off the rock, and her pants came off because she couldn't lift her pelvis off the ground. She found herself in a shallow depression. She was stuck. She saw the stupidity of her decision and crawled back onto the rock. A round trip of four feet. It took two hours. Now she was hyperventilating. Now the ball of clotted blood and swollen flesh was moving around inside her. And now it was 1:30 P.M. She would never leave this hidden canyon. Why had she wasted hours and precious energy to go four feet? Why hadn't she told someone where she was going? Why hadn't she told more people she loved them? And where the hell was Taz? What was wrong with that dog?

Craig Shumway grew up in Moab, dug in its soil for uranium during the last years of the boom. He loves the high desert, the wide open spaces. He has been in law enforcement for seventeen years, a Moab detective for four. On Friday morning, December 15, he was sitting in his office at the police department on

East Center Street when Sergeant Mike Wiler walked in and sat down.

Wiler told Shumway there had been a missing-person report the previous night. He said it looked like someone had left a house unsecured and was going to be returning. He mentioned the energetic neighbor and her suggestions. He said he had given the information to the Grand County Sheriff's Department and that they would be checking trailheads to see if the truck might be there. In the meantime, Moab police had put out an Attempt to Locate (ATL). In Moab, a magnet for the young, the adventurous, and the risk-seeking, an ATL is not exactly a red alert. "You just don't jump out and go look for every one of 'em," Shumway says.

Shumway nodded, plowed through some paperwork, then decided he would take a drive before lunch. No one was too alarmed about the missing woman — people took off for days without telling anyone all the time in Moab, and she was a world-class athlete. And it wasn't his job. It wasn't his jurisdiction, either. But he knew how big the desert was, how many trails crisscrossed the canyons and rivers of southern Utah. First he stopped at Ballengee's house, took a quick look. Then he drove ten miles north to the Sovereign Trail and checked the trailhead, and found nothing. Then he decided he would check out trailheads on the way back to town.

Law enforcement officers often talk about intuition and gut feelings, and how important it is to recognize them. On the way back to Moab, though, Shumway felt something unfamiliar.

He drove down Kane Creek, to the parking lot of the Amasa Back Trail. He's not sure why, but he passed it, kept going, to the top of the hill, to the little spot near the cliff. That's where he saw the white Ford Ranger. He wanted to document things in case there had been a crime. He pulled out his eight-megapixel Canon digital camera and took pictures. Later he would look at the receipt that the runner had left inside the car. It was from

Burger King, for a chicken sandwich and large fries and a large coffee. It was dated Wednesday, December 13, at 11:00 A.M. Now it was 1:30 in the afternoon, two days and two cold nights later. Shumway had another feeling, a bad one.

It was the effort she had expended crawling into and out of the little depression. It was her body shutting down. It was fear. She knew she needed to stop hyperventilating. She forced herself to breathe more slowly, and it worked. She breathed. She didn't know where her dog was, and soon it would be cold and dark, and she was broken and bleeding inside, and no one was coming but at least she was breathing. So she breathed. She breathed and she waited to die.

John Marshall moved to Moab five years ago so he could run and bike and kayak and do all the other things that people in Moab do. "Moab is a big person's Chuck E. Cheese's," he says. "If you run out of things to do here, it's your own damned fault."

He runs an off-road-adventure-tour business where he takes people into the desert on gigantic flatbed four-wheel-drive vehicles that he maintains. He is forty-seven years old, blond, five-foot-ten, 175 pounds, muscular, blue-eyed, broad-shouldered, and if ever the Grand County Search and Rescue team were going to publish an informational pamphlet seeking donations, they would want someone who looked like Marshall on its cover. On Friday afternoon, December 15, he was hanging out at a local auto store because it was customer appreciation day and the business was serving food. Lovers of the outdoors in Moab usually don't make a lot of money. They are keenly aware of the value of a free lunch.

He was wiping the remains of a pulled-pork sandwich from his face when his pager went off. Shumway had called his sergeant, who had called the county sheriff, who had paged the search and rescue team. It was 1:09 P.M. Forty-nine hours ago, Ballengee had fallen.

A dozen people met in a parking lot outside the search and rescue shed next to the police station. They listened as cops read aloud from notes. "We're looking for a female, a local, an adventure racer . . . she's been missing for two days . . . her name is Danelle . . ."

And one of the search and rescue members, a runner named Melissa Fletcher, who happens to be Marshall's girlfriend, yelled, "Ballengee!"

Marshall had met Ballengee once before, when he worked as a volunteer at the Primal Quest in Utah, in 2006. When he had first seen her then, she had just finished a forty-six-mile trek across the desert. The temperature had been 105 degrees. She had been without water for the past four hours when he first saw her. Her feet were more blisters than flesh. Marshall suggested an IV drip that day. Ballengee declined. She was in a hurry.

Today, according to the team's rotating calendar, it was Marshall's turn to lead. He supervised the gathering of medical supplies and two Polaris Ranger ATVs and trailers on which to haul them. A dozen search and rescue members headed to the Amasa Back trailhead. They discussed what type of person they were looking for, what the person was probably wearing, the supplies she was likely carrying. Lost hunters tend to generate relatively little concern. They wear plenty of warm clothing, carry food and water, and, because many of them are smokers, often have matches and lighters. An injured runner was something else. Especially a runner like Ballengee.

In a newspaper story that ran a week after Ballengee disappeared, the point was made that the search and rescue team had taken a body bag for the operation. That upset Marshall. He thought writing about the body bag was morbid and unnecessary. Which is not to say that Marshall wasn't prepared for the worst. As he supervised the team at the trailhead, he remembered the woman stumbling out of the desert, refusing fluids, trudging into the 105-degree heat. He thought about what it would take to slow her down.

"I'm thinking," Marshall says, "this was a world-class, I-eat-nails-for-breakfast person we're looking for. I'm thinking she's been out there for two nights. I'm thinking she didn't twist an ankle. I'm thinking there's something very, very serious going on."

As soon as Marshall and the others got near Ballengee's truck, they saw the dog. It was running in circles, "going a million miles an hour." Marshall suspected it was the runner's dog. He knew something about canine behavior, especially when humans were imperiled.

"Most dogs won't leave their master as long as their master has a pulse," he told a newspaper reporter. "To see that dog was a truly saddening sight."

He called Taz, tried to coax him over. But Taz wouldn't come. The dog circled Marshall and the others, then dashed toward town. Marshall thought they should try to grab it, but no one could. Then the dog stopped, looked back over his shoulder. Then the dog was gone.

The team tried to figure out which way Ballengee went. Where would an athlete like her go for a training run? Search and rescue team members in places like Moab tend to be extremely fit themselves, and, if not risk-seeking, at least adventurous. But as they were trying to decide where to look first, they realized she was in an entirely different category. "People like Danelle train at such a high level," one member said, "there isn't anybody around who does what she does."

Marshall sent Melissa Fletcher running up Jackson's Trail, a narrow, steep, single track, because it was the most difficult and she was the most fit member of the team. He stayed near the truck to coordinate the search. Though he wasn't a search and rescue team member, Craig Shumway had, after calling his discovery in, gone home, changed into hiking clothes, and trekked up the Cable Arch Trail to make sure Ballengee wasn't there. She wasn't. Marshall sent two men and a woman down the Amasa Back Trail in ATVs. Riding the second ATV were Mike Coronella and Barb Fincham. In the first ATV was a sixty-year-old commercial-heating-and-refrigeration installer named Bego.

Gerhart is five feet, eight inches tall, weighs 180 pounds. He has a full gray beard, piercing blue eyes, and a pot belly. He looks like he'd be more at home in front of a cheeseburger than driving an ATV through the backcountry looking for a woman about to die.

He hitchhiked to Moab in 1970, a California Eagle Scout with a college degree and no particular direction. A Moab cop asked him for identification and Gerhart asked if the cop knew anyone looking for work, and that's how he ended up as a trucker, "with guys who had two-hundred-word vocabularies, and one hundred of 'em were 'fuck.'"

He has worked for the Grand County Search and Rescue squad for eleven years. He rigged ropes in New Zealand for film makers shooting *Vertical Limit* in 1999. He served as a consultant to a television show called *I Shouldn't Be Alive* in 2006. In 2003 he hiked into Blue John Canyon, where he and a group of men winched a boulder and retrieved the hand of Aron Ralston, who had hacked it off in order to free himself. Others might have broader shoulders and younger legs, but of the ninety-one calls that went out to members of the Grand County Search and Rescue team in 2006, Gerhart responded to eighty-eight of them, more than anyone else.

A lot of men and women who run (and hike and bike) in wilderness-rich areas like Moab speak of the majesty of the outdoors, the intoxicating consequences of fresh air. Many submit that the majestic sweep of the sky and the exquisite desolation of the desert serve as prima facie evidence of a loving spirit. But those tend to be the younger, leaner runners. Gerhart sees things a little differently.

"What happened to someone like Danelle is pretty good evidence against the existence of a benevolent God," he says. Regarding the secret to survival, he says, "It's all about knowing how to suffer."

Gerhart was a mile down the Amasa Back Trail, puttering along in his ATV, when his two-way radio sputtered to life.

"The dog! The dog!" It was Marshall. Taz had come back. He had sprinted down the trail, passing Coronella and Fincham's ATV. Fincham had gotten out of the ATV to follow the dog on foot, and the dog had promptly disappeared.

The dog dashed by Gerhart's ATV and stopped. It looked at Gerhart, then it dashed off the trail, up to a little mesa. Gerhart clambered out of the ATV and walked up the mesa, where the dog was waiting. Gerhart stared at the dog. The dog stared at Gerhart. And the dog was gone again.

People journey into the desert without enough water or the proper clothing every year, and people die. People slip, and they never rise. People get lost, and they stay lost. Search and rescue team members do their best, but when someone is missing for three days and two nights, in winter, help often consists of a "recovery" mission. It often includes a body bag. Less than a month earlier two men had died near Moab. They had frozen to death. Both were wearing heavier clothes than Ballengee. Gerhart knew all that. But he had a feeling. Gerhart is not a sentimental man, nor prone to a lot of religio-mystical mumbo jumbo. This is about as close as he gets: "My mind said, *'Follow the dog.'*"

But the dog was gone. So Gerhart backtracked to where he had first spotted Taz. Just a few weeks earlier, he had taken a tracking course from U.S. Marshals, and now he studied the ground. He looked for dog tracks next to footprints of a woman runner. When he saw them, he followed them, away from the main road, down a little spur, toward a hidden canyon. He saw that the trail got rockier and rockier, more and more rugged. He hopped into his ATV, and he drove toward the hidden canyon, the sound of his engine echoing off the red rock walls. And he drove and drove some more. And then he stopped. He thought he heard something.

The dog had been disappearing all day, and this time, when he got back, he ran straight to the puddle and started drinking. And he drank and drank. And as much as the runner loved the dog, as inured to pain and loss as she was, she was still human. "Bad dog!" She yelled at Taz, "Can't you drink out of another sinkhole?"

And there they lay, a week before the shortest day of the year: a woman broken and bleeding inside, a dog lapping up her precious water. She cried. She thought again of the people to whom she had not said, "I love you." And then something shifted. It wasn't the dog's fault. It wasn't anyone's. Is this what acceptance felt like? She wasn't angry anymore. What was the use of regret? Now she was at peace. And then she heard a sound that didn't make sense. A motor.

Later a lot of people would invoke divine mysteries, seek answers in the supernatural. Shumway would reflect on the strange feelings that led him to search for the missing truck, the inexplicable and powerful urges that guided him up the Kane Creek Road and to the little patch of dirt on top the of the hill, beneath the cliff. "I'm a God-fearing person and I can't explain it," he says. "It was a sense of urgency. I had never felt it before. But I felt compelled to go." Marshall would ask out loud how someone with virtually no body fat could possibly live through two cold nights in the high desert, "how her internal metabolism defied the laws of physics." People referred to the entire episode as a "Christmas miracle." When it came to mythmaking, though, no one beat the dog lovers. In the news accounts and stories of the accident, Taz morphed into a furry genius, a four-legged phantasm, a kind of barking, galloping Gandalf. Some search and rescue team members talked about how, in hindsight, it looked like Taz had planned the rescue the whole time. "It was like he was trying to get us to pay attention to him, so when he showed up later, he could lead us to her," Marshall says. (Marshall is a dog lover.)

But that was all later.

First Gerhart had to hop off his ATV again and walk toward the sound. That's when he saw them. There, on a rock, in the little hidden canyon, was a woman on her back. And there, lying next to her, with his snout on her chest, the mutt.

"I'm so glad to see you," Ballengee said, weeping.

"I'm glad you're glad to see me, and that you can say so," Gerhart replied. At least that's the way he tells the story. The way he remembers, she was lucid but emotional. He was amazed she was so articulate, but he was concerned about keeping her core temperature from falling, so he fetched from his ATV a heavy sleeping bag with Velcro straps, what search and rescue team members call "Doctor Down." The way he remembers it, he kept her talking even as he was radioing for help, scanning the landscape for a place where a rescue helicopter might safely land, shoving her hands into heavy gloves. All of that, according to Ballengee, is accurate but incomplete. The way she remembers it, Gerhart was weeping, too.

Taz ran to Gerhart and licked him. Then the commercial-heating-and-refrigeration installer said something to the runner that people have said to other people as long as there have been pets. "You got one heck of a dog," Gerhart said.

*   *   *

She didn't sleep well last night. Every time she shut her eyes, she was tumbling down the slick rock, picking up speed. Every time she opened them, she was on her back, halfway down the steep wall, cold and alone, broken and bleeding inside. And if she did sleep, then what? She was afraid of the nightmares. She didn't want to find herself back in the hidden canyon, cold and alone and dying.

It was midafternoon, January 23, almost six weeks after she fell, and she was tired, and she hurt, and though she was lying on the couch in the basement of her parents' house in Evergreen, and they were upstairs, and she was safe, and though Taz was lying on the floor next to her, and even though she and her dog had been on the *Today Show*, even though she and Taz had ascended in the popular consciousness to Christmas Miracle and Wonderdog status, the reality was messier, more difficult.

She didn't have control of her left hand. She wasn't sure if she ever would. Her feet felt as if she was standing in an icy stream. She wasn't sure if they would ever feel differently. Both were consequences of frostbite.

She was taking six Neurontin pills a day to help reduce the pain. She was taking three 600-milligram tablets of ibuprofen for inflammation, four 30-milligram iron pills to help increase her red-blood-cell count, and Percocet for more pain. And antianxiety pills for the nights she had trouble sleeping, like last night. And stool softener. Until a few days ago, her father had been injecting her every day in her stomach with a drug to lessen the chances of blood clotting. After she complained about the pain, her doctor finally relented. Now she was taking 325 milligrams of aspirin daily.

Her pelvis had broken in four places. At one spot it splintered into too many pieces for doctors to count. She cracked three vertebrae. She lost a third of her blood. Doctors at Denver Health medical center had operated on her for six hours, inserting a titanium plate in her pelvis.

When the *Today Show* called afterward, she wasn't all that interested. Of course she was grateful to be alive, but in the hospital, she hurt, and she was tired and hungry and — truth be told — scared about what the injuries would mean. Then the *Today Show* people said they wanted Taz on the air, too. She hadn't seen the dog since the search and rescue helicopter had lifted her into the sky, right after she scratched him behind the ears and said, "It'll be OK, boy," and Taz had gone home with John Marshall, who couldn't live with himself if he let animal control take the dog. Taz had trotted into Marshall's house that Friday afternoon, where he had ignored the bowl of water Marshall set out for him and ignored Marshall's dog, a mutt named Hasbro, "the most fantastic dog on the face of the earth," who was barking and yelping and wanted to play. Taz had trotted to the toilet bowl, drunk greedily, walked into the living room, and passed out. If agreeing to be interviewed by the *Today Show* meant she'd be able to see Taz, Ballengee was on board.

Now she was talking about how freaked out the hospital public-relations people had been when Taz showed up, and how the television crew told the hospital PR people to shut up while the cameras were rolling, and how after the shooting was done, and after Taz had gone home with Ballengee's sister, Michelle, to her home in Denver a quarter mile from the hospital, the dog had escaped, and how her sister knew where he was going, so she walked to the hospital and there was Taz.

Cards came from all over. One day a box filled with dry ice arrived. It was from a woman in Michigan who had seen the *Today Show*. Inside were five pounds of hormone-free aged rib steaks and a red-and-white Christmas stocking with a stuffed Santa inside. On the top, embroidered in green, was the name of the intended recipient — Taz.

Ballengee had visitors — including the guy from Leadville — and heard from friends and relatives and strangers. They called and wrote and e-mailed, and she wouldn't make the same mistake again — this time she told everyone how much she loved them. There were a lot of them. And love was great, and maybe she *was* a Christmas miracle, but she was still human, and this was life.

She couldn't walk. She stayed in the hospital for fifteen days, and the first week her biggest accomplishment was forcing herself to sit up in bed without passing out. Ten seconds was a good day. Just a week ago, she tried to get out of bed to use a portable commode that was only a few feet away, and fainted. Now she could make it to the bathroom, using a wheelchair, by herself. That was a big deal. She couldn't afford all the medical bills. At the moment, the bill from Grand Junction, where she had been taken by the helicopter, totaled forty-five thousand dollars, and the insurance policy that had sounded so good when she bought it turned out to not be so good, and she hadn't even received her bill for surgery or her Denver hospital stay yet. She had managed a lap and a half around a West Denver mall in her wheelchair yesterday, and that had felt great, "just to get the blood flowing," and runners and endurance athletes she had competed with were holding fund-raising events for her, and that was great, too, but she knew she wouldn't be able to walk for at least two months, and after that it would be another few months before she could run, and then it would be "how to run fast, then how to run aggressively. On trails and up and down mountains. Whether I'll be able to do it at the levels I used to; I'm gonna try. But if I can run again at all, I'll be so happy."

She works hard at planning to be happy. But she is scared, too, and she has nightmares.

She talks about the nightmares, and about Bego Gerhart (whose name, when she first heard it in the canyon, she thought was "Bagel," "probably because I was so hungry"). She talks about Dorothy Rossignol who, unbeknownst to Ballengee, has promised that when the runner moves back to Moab, she will be watched with special vigilance — even for a nosy neighbor —

and nagged about where she's going, "even when it's just a trip to the mailbox." She talks about how much she misses being outside, "just being with Taz, running through the woods."

She talks a lot about Taz, how people ask if he gets extra treats now, or extra attention. He doesn't. "He's always been spoiled," she says. "I treated him pretty well before."

Mostly she talks about her days in the hidden canyon, and the cold, and how she was sure she was going to die, and about the way she saw the white stripes in the sky and heard the strange voice that commanded her to keep tapping her heels.

The most likely explanation is trauma. She knows that. She earned degrees in biology and kinesiology, after all, not philosophy and religion. But she's not sure. Her mother thinks that *her* mother came back to earth as a butterfly, that Danelle's paternal grandfather was reincarnated as an eagle. Peggy Ballengee thinks it was her father-in-law who flew over her daughter that Thursday morning, just nine days before Christmas, in the hidden canyon.

"Maybe there is something to it," Danelle Ballengee says. "I don't know. As far as I'm concerned I'm going to be the best person I can . . . I'm OK without an answer."

She is reading *The Audacity of Hope*. She has been watching movies at night. She recently watched *Touching the Void*, the story of a man who had to crawl his way off a mountain in the Peruvian Andes and through a crevasse with a broken leg, and *Eight Below*, the tale of eight sled dogs who face death by freezing in Antarctica. A visitor suggests a few comedies, considering the nightmares.

Then Taz starts barking. He sees a squirrel outside. Ballengee's father walks down the steps when he hears the barking and tells his daughter he'll take her mutt for a walk.

"He's kind of dumb," Gary Ballengee says, patting Taz on the head. "Brilliant at saving lives, but he'll go out and chase that squirrel all day. Just kind of dumb."

Her father and her dog are behind her, and it's not easy to

turn her head, but that's what Danelle Ballengee does. She's done more difficult things. She turns and looks first at her father, who doesn't notice, then at her dog, who tilts his head and looks back at her. He tilts his head first to the left, then to the right, side to side, just like he did that terrible afternoon when Danelle Ballengee lay dying. And then the runner smiles at her dog and she puts her head back on her pillow, and she rests.

9

THE TRAGEDY:
MARCO PANTANI, CYCLIST

THE MAN ON THE FIFTH FLOOR WANTED PIZZA. FOUR NIGHTS in a row, a clerk from Le Rose Hotel called, and, four nights in a row, the restaurant owner dispatched a waitress with a Margherita pie for the guy in 5-D. Why someone in a hotel room overlooking the Adriatic wanted delivery didn't concern the restaurant owner. Oliver Laghi was a businessman and this was Rimini, where businessmen didn't ask too many questions or make too many moral judgments. Two hours south of Venice, three hours northeast of Rome, a world away from any notion of office or deadline, Rimini beckons and teases with its cloudless summer skies and vast sandy beaches, but, at night, away from the T-shirt shops and gelato stands that line the main drag, there exists another resort of less innocent but no less potent allure and economic vigor — the one of all-night parties and easily accessible cocaine and prostitutes. So it was mid-February? So it was the resort's off-season? Some guy wants to hole up and look at waves and chew crust in the dark — who was Laghi to wonder? Business is business.

On a Friday evening, February 13, 2003, the clerk from Le Rose Hotel called again. The fifth night in a row, and this time the guy wanted an omelet. This time the clerk told Laghi who the guy on the fifth floor was.

Imagine Babe Ruth putting away a few hot dogs around the corner, and he calls and could you join him? Imagine Michael Jordan's car is stalled, and would you mind bringing some jumper cables? Imagine you're a businessman who doesn't ask too many questions or make too many moral judgments and you have just speed walked two blocks and you're holding the omelet you whipped up yourself — Fontina cheese and ham, two eggs, no toast, no potatoes — and your country's greatest and most-beloved athletic hero opens a door and stands in front of you, bloated, grayish, unkempt. Imagine he hasn't bathed in days. Imagine terror in his eyes, confusion. Imagine gazing at exhaustion so deep you think you might weep.

Imagine you start babbling. "I have followed your career!" Laghi exclaimed. "The Tour! The Giro d'Italia!" Imagine you can't help it. The businessman couldn't. He wept.

The hero had always confounded. The unthinkable acceleration, the perfect gesture at the most unlikely moment — that's what defined his greatness. That's one reason people loved him. He attacked when others retreated, fought when others quit. Even now — wrecked, malodorous, terribly sick — he did it again. The impossible. He smiled. A great, dazzling smile. A miracle, really. He patted Laghi on the back. There, there. No need to cry.

Laghi couldn't stop. "Please," he said, "accept the omelet for free." Then Marco Pantani, one of the greatest cyclists Italy has ever known, one of the greatest climbers in history, now disgraced, now dying, did something else miraculous. He laughed. He also insisted on paying.

Imagine you have a chance to ease the pain of a demigod, but you are a businessman, and your restaurant is busy. Laghi hated to go. Would it be OK, he asked, if he came back to visit tomorrow? Tomorrow was Valentine's Day. Laghi would bring more food. They could talk about cycling. They could talk about whatever Pantani wanted to talk about. Would that be OK?

The hero's smile was gone now. Huge efforts exact huge costs. They always had with Pantani. The exhaustion had returned. And sadness. Great sadness. Laghi remembers it: *"Molto triste."*

"Sure," the hero said, very quietly. "Sure. Come tomorrow and we'll talk some more."

Imagine you'll never see your hero alive again. Imagine no one will. Now, imagine a nation that can't stop chasing ghosts, that won't stop weaving reassuring little lies. Imagine an entire country that can't face a simple truth.

Cycling's greatest climbers are . . . different. The greatest climbers, the pure climbers — those who can ascend any given mountain faster than even the most accomplished all-around champions — these men are not just lighter and smaller and more sinewy than other cyclists, who are themselves lighter and smaller and more sinewy than most humans. The pure climbers are not just positively spidery in their ability to scale steep routes. No, these great climbers are different because they are so . . . odd.

They tend to be loners, like Charley "the Mountain Exterminator" Gaul, the dyspeptic Luxembourger who disliked journalists, avoided emotional displays of any kind, hated warm weather, performed best in icy rain and at high altitudes, and, shortly after winning the Tour de France in 1958, grew fat, grew a beard, and grew into a grumpy hermit who lived in the woods and refused all visitors. (When Gaul crested the punishing Col D'izohard in 1958, calm, expressionless, pedaling swiftly and with no apparent exertion, an observer remarked that "it was as if he were an angel . . ." Ever after, the summit has been known as *Sommet des anges*, or Summit of Angels, and those few who have grasped glory at high altitudes have been known as Angels of the Mountains.)

Angels tend to be dour, like Alejandro Federico Martin "the Eagle of Toledo" Bahamontes, who won the tour in 1959 (vanquishing Gaul) and who was once described as possessing a face "hollowed by suffering, the eyes widened by fear." They tend to be obsessive about the wrong things, like Lucien "Mr. Polka Dot" Van Impe, the Belgian climber who reportedly focused so ferociously and exclusively on winning the spotted jersey given to the Tour de France's best climber that he never even considered attempting to win the overall race until a coach suggested that it might be a good idea. (The next year, Van Impe won.)

Angels are fragile, exquisitely tuned creatures, acutely, painfully sensitive.

"Tell Lance Armstrong seconds before a race starts that he's a jerk, that he's arrogant, that he dumped his wife after she nursed him through cancer, that no one likes him, and he'll smile and wink and then go destroy the field," says a longtime biking fan who is obsessed with the Angels. (Angels tend to inspire obsession, even in a sport marked by obsessives and obsession.) But Armstrong, though a great climber, is not a climbing specialist. He is not an Angel. (His excellence in all phases of cycling is what makes him so great, and so freakish.) "But tell a climber, like Pantani, that his bandanna is on crooked and chances are he'll start sobbing, then drop out of the race."

Because of their misguided single-mindedness and their sensitivity, they tend to take tactical thrusts from competitors as personal affronts, then to seek immediate, thrilling revenge, in much the same way (and with approximately the same reward) as the small child who, grievously offended by his face, contemplates performing surgery on the innocent nose.

Angels are rarely champions, and champions are rarely Angels. It is the calm and the predatory and the brilliantly conniving and the consistent who win major races. But it is the Angels who make us forget the science of the sport — the computer-refined carbon frames and the diets calibrated to the tenth of an ounce and the wind-tunnel-tested, custom bodysuits — and force us to witness the art. It is the Angels who attack, absent any apparent regard for consequences, who find fearlessness on paths where others hang back, who pedal into arrogant climbs and desperate, primal pursuits. The great champions calculate and focus and hold something always in reserve. The Angels inspire and baffle and alarm.

Angels tend to be held in awe because, when they do win, the way they do it is so simple and primitive, as basic and easily comprehensible as going faster than anyone else where it's basically impossible to go fast. Consequently, they tend to be suspected of cheating, as in the case of Richard Virenque, the six-time winner of the Polka Dot jersey who belonged to the Festina team that was thrown out of the Tour in 1998 after the team's trainer was caught with four hundred flasks of performance-enhancing EPO. They tend to deny all charges against them, as Virenque did, and they tend to eventually be proven guilty, or to confess, as Virenque also did in 2000.

They tend to inspire worship and resignation and all kinds of knotted explanations and excuses from their fans. "Technological advances, the progress of science, and the demands of life sometimes lead us to cross the threshold between the acceptable and the inexcusable," a reporter wrote of Virenque.

They tend to come to bad ends. Even when the reclusive and cranky Gaul left his cabin in the woods and returned to public life, he did so with "great gaps in his memory . . . frequently . . . confused and distant," according to Leo Woodland of Cyclingnews.com. The Tour's very first climbing star, Rene Pottier, a "solemn, sad-faced man" who wore the yellow jersey in 1906, hanged himself the next year, from his own bike hook. In 1999 Thierry Claveyrolat, king of the mountains in 1990, shot and killed himself. Most recently Spain's Jose Maria "el Chaba" Jimenez died last December of an apparent heart at-tack at a psychiatric hospital in Madrid, where he had been suf-fering from depression. Jimenez was thirty-two years old.

"A rider in the old style," five-time Tour champion Migel "Big Man" Indurain said of Jimenez at the time. "When things went well, they went very well. When things didn't go well, they didn't go at all."

No one was ever more old style than Marco Pantani. Even among the other frail seraphs — a group prone to exposed nerve endings and thrilling, evanescent victories and unfortunate de-mises — he stood apart. No Angel ever ascended more swiftly. None ever fell so far, so fast.

"The best climber in the history of the sport," Lance Arm-strong said after his rival died.

"The cursed champion," said Mario Pugliese, a journalist and a friend of Pantani's since each was eleven years old.

For seven years Pantani seduced a cycling-mad country, vexed a sporting establishment as few cyclists ever have, and wounded legions of fans who refused to believe their hero was falling. In 1997 Pantani climbed the iconic and fearsome Alpe d'Huez faster than anyone in history. The next year he won the Giro d'Italia (the Tour of Italy, his homeland's biggest race and the second-biggest race in the world) and the Tour de France, one of only seven men to have ever achieved the double triumph in the same season, and the last to do so. With his Tour victory, he rescued the sport from irrelevance and destruction in its most scandal-plagued hour.

He was a cheater. He was an innocent victim. Sensitive and cruel. Loving and arrogant. A villain. A hero. He saved the Tour de France. He brought shame on cycling. He inspired others. He destroyed lives.

This is what people say, and it's all true.

*   *   *

In another time, in another country, a doctor might have prescribed Ritalin. But this was Cesenatico, Italy, 1976. The six-
year-old boy was clumsy, accident prone, always moving but
seldom with much grace. A skinny child with a fearsome sweet
tooth (he loved Nutella and the apricot jam his mother, Tonina,
made especially for him, and at night he sneaked down to the
kitchen and licked mascarpone from the bowl), a thumb-sucker
(as he would be until he was eight years old), a loner with big eyes
and big ears. A sweet little boy — a mama's boy, really. Tonina
Pantani bought her young son, Marco, a red two-wheeler because she thought it might calm him down.

It didn't. Three times as a child he was hit by cars while cycling. Tonina says she knew every time, even before she heard.
"I would say at work, 'I'm terrified Marco will fall today,'" she
says. "Then I'd come home and my husband would tell me,
'Marco fell today.'"

By the time he was twelve, he had traded in the little red
two-wheeler for a racing machine, and the rest of his life receded.
Every day he'd ride to the distant hills of Emilia-Romagna, and
every day upon his return he'd bring his bicycle inside to wash it
in the bathtub. Afterward he'd let it dry in the hallway on the
second floor. At night he'd bring it into his bedroom.

"It bothered me because it made the walls dirty," Tonina
remembers. "We had a garage. He could have kept it in the
garage." She fretted, and loved, but mostly she worried. Marco
hated that, she says. Marco promised that he would call if he
were in trouble. So that when she didn't hear from him, she
shouldn't worry. She worried anyway.

His father, a plumber, worried for different reasons. At the
end of Marco's first year on a racing bike, Paolo Pantani told his
son that, if he loved biking so, he should devote himself to it for
another year. At the end of the year, if cycling hadn't worked out,
Paolo would take Marco plumbing.

It worked out. At twenty, in 1990, Pantani won the amateur

version of the Giro d'Italia, including two stage victories in the jagged Dolomites. By the time he was twenty-four, he had turned professional, placed second in the Giro and third in the Tour de France. In the mountains, with his feral attacks and ridiculous, out-of-the-saddle surges, he was incomparable. He had a following and a nickname. Because of his youth and the size of his ears, which was exaggerated because he was prematurely balding, cycling fans called him "Elefantino," or Baby Elephant, which he hated. He was an Angel now, one with prodigious talent and horrible luck. In the October 1995 Milan-Turin race, a jeep drove onto the course and Pantani hit it head on, shattering his left leg. People said he would never race again.

His mother is crying, and who can blame her? Marco was her only son, and it hasn't even been five months since his death. Outside the locked front gates of the family villa in Cesenatico, Pantani's birthplace, fifteen miles up the coast from Rimini, a car full of fans from some far-flung province, or maybe from another country, stops so they can shoot videotape, then snap photographs, then just stare.

Tonina ignores the car. She's learned to do this. Behind her, inside the house built with her son's enormous cycling wealth, airing out, open for the first time since she heard the horrible news, is the wing where he stayed. There is his tanning booth, and his bedroom and bathroom with his Lion King cologne still on the counter of the sink, and the chamber that has become his shrine, filled with photos and keepsakes. There is the great champion sucking his thumb as an eight-year-old and peering over this shoulder with embarrassment; there is the hero standing with the pope; and a tiny, red plastic Volkswagen a little boy from England sent him. Children always adored him, even at the end. There's a framed yellow jersey from the Tour de France. A photo of the cyclist passing Lance Armstrong on a steep, narrow road.

It is a hot day, windless, cloudless. On the front lawn a grass-covered wire sculpture of a bicyclist. Behind the sprawling structure, a swimming pool. On one side of the villa, fields of corn. On the other side, a vineyard. Looming in the middistance, the hills into which he would disappear as a little boy, pedaling to places Tonina couldn't imagine, to places that always worried her.

She sits on the porch underneath a flat, tinny summer sun. She is not private in her grief. She never has been. In an interview shortly after he died, she said he had been murdered. She blamed members of his cycling team. She lashed out at officials in the cycling community. She said that she would name names. Since then, Marco's manager, who took him on in 1998 and stayed with him until he died, Manuela Ronchi, has been present to monitor Tonina's interviews. She is here now. The manager, it turns out, is measured and diplomatic only when compared with Tonina.

"There was no proof," Ronchi says. "Not even an idea of proof. In five years, he never, never tested positive. If not for that scandal, he would have won four Tours! And he would have won by four hours, not two minutes!"

Ronchi is grieving, too. And who can blame her? Pantani was more than a client. He was a friend, in some ways like a little boy to her, a little boy in desperate trouble. Someone crying for help. Pantani had that effect on people.

I ask if anyone could have saved him.

"A woman," Ronchi says, and at this Tonina nods. "A woman who really loved him." His mother weeps bitterly.

They blame Pantani's Danish girlfriend, Christine Johansonn, who, it should be noted, admitted to sharing cocaine with him for years and, after his death, gave — or sold — an article to *L'Hebdo*, a Swiss weekly, which was headlined, "We Did Drugs for Love." They blame the journalists who they say sensationalized the doping charges. They blame the cycling powers for making Pantani a scapegoat for the sport's woes. They blame themselves.

Others blame them, too. Mario Pugliese, the lifelong friend who, for the past seven years, has been a reporter for *La Voce di Romagna*, the regional paper of Cesenatico, says Tonina and Ronchi were more interested in Marco's lucrative cycling career than in protecting his life. Pugliese also blames his editor for not allowing him to write a story addressing Pantani's addiction. Michael Mengozzi, a friend who repeatedly tried to get Marco to quit drugs and who, just a few months before Pantani's death, journeyed to Cuba to retrieve him from a vacation gone horribly wrong, blames the staff at the hotel where he spent his last week. When he sees a piece of stationery I carry from Le Rose Hotel, he says, "These people aren't good. These are the ones who let Marco die."

Some of the people I talk to in Cesenatico and Rimini blame the local cops, for not arresting the national hero after a series of car accidents, when they knew or should have known he was using drugs, for not scaring him straight. Many blame, naturally, the drug dealers who supplied him.

Some fans say he was injected with drugs by jealous competitors while he slept. Or that Italian industrialists orchestrated his downfall because he'd participated in a Citroen advertising campaign. Some of his countrymen blame Cuba. A few Cubans blame Italy. And if people can't find someone to blame, they invent someone. Vittorio Savini, who managed the racer before Ronchi and now serves as president of Club Magico Pantani, a fan club, says Pantani was targeted by influential and unnamable cycling authorities.

But why? I ask. Why would they single him out?

Wide eyes, arms out, leaning forward. "That's the question!"

And who wanted him out?

"That's the question!"

Franco Corsini, a Cesenatico restaurateur who tried to save Pantani up till the end, says, "He was a thorn in someone's side.

There was a plot to get rid of him. A plot high up. I think maybe he was murdered. *Morto! Morto!*"

He weeps when he says this. "He died for cycling. His life was cycling." Loud sobbing. "He died for cycling."

There is only one person the friends and fans and competitors and family of Pantani don't blame for the hero's death. They can't. They can't blame their hero.

When bones shatter and flesh rips, what happens inside? As Pantani's body healed from his 1995 crash, did his soul twist in upon itself? Or was that the moment the mask slipped, when the ravenous monster inside the sweet little boy scrabbled out? Is this when the cyclist turned into a junkie?

No one thought to ask then — why would they? Certainly he was different when he returned to cycling. But dangerous? Marked for death? When he came back to the sport he rode with a shaved head and a goatee, a hoop earring and a bandana emblazoned with skull and crossbones. At the beginning of a steep, absurd mountain chase, he would tear off the bandanna and fling it to the ground. Elefantino was dead. Marco called himself "Il Pirata." So would everyone else.

He was different, but he was the same. Whereas other top racers rely on packs, use teammates as pacers and protection, Pantani rode as he always had, alone, often from behind, slashing, with no apparent strategy other than sacrificial velocity during the most astonishing climbs.

The prodigious talent, and horrible luck, held. In the 1997 Giro d'Italia, a black cat darted in front of Pantani and he crashed and dropped out. But, later that year, on his way to another third-place finish in the Tour de France, after a long and hard day on the road, he scaled the forbidding Alpe d'Huez in thirty-seven minutes, thirty-five seconds, a record that still stands even after last year's time trial up the mountain.

The next year, in 1998, Pantani won the Giro, then showed up for a Tour de France that was imploding after the entire French Festina team was disqualified for blood doping. A sport of cheaters — that's what skeptics had been whispering for years. Now they shouted. Il Pirata, dashing and explosive, quieted them by winning the Tour with spectacular ascents. Here was purity.

The sport needed a hero, and it could not have invented a more engaging one. He chatted with fans, played with children. He presented wonderfully thoughtful, wonderfully strange quotes to journalists. He helped those in need. When an earthquake damaged the town of Assisi, Pantani bought and loaded a truck with food to drive there. It was Pantani who coaxed the troubled Angel of the Mountain, Charly Gaul, into making some public appearances again and rekindling ties with his racing brethren. Pantani invited the hermit to rejoin the company of humankind. Was it just kindness, or had Il Pirata peered into the woods and seen himself?

For his victories, Il Pirata was cheered. For his good deeds, he was admired. For his exceeding and engaging oddness, he was beloved. In Italy, where he was the first paesano to win the Tour since 1965, he was something else altogether.

"He was like the pope," says Pugliese.

Yes. Just like the pope, except that Pantani was twenty-eight, a sensualist, delighted with the trappings of fame, intoxicated with his singularity. He shot marbles with fans after races, played the horses, hunted pigeons. Other athletes delivered homilies about sacrifice and effort and teamwork. Il Pirata waxed as only Il Pirata could.

"We are all imprisoned by rules," he told Matt Rendell of the *Observer* (UK) in one interview. "Everyone longs for freedom to behave in the way they see fit. I'm a nonconformist, and some feel inspired by the way I express freedom of thought.... There's chaos in everyday life, and I tune in to that chaos."

He could afford all the chaos he wanted. From his comeback until the year after his double victory, he made an estimated $10 to $15 million, much of it from endorsements and special appearances. A Spanish organizer paid him $30,000 just to show up for an event. Though he invested — much of it in property in and around Cesenatico and Rimini, including the capacious villa he built for his family — he didn't deprive himself. He bought his girlfriend, Johansonn, a metallic-blue A-Class Mercedes. He drove a BMW. He danced at Rimini's discos. He was said to enjoy the company of prostitutes. He drank and he used cocaine.

"Yes," says Pugliese. "But a normal amount for a star like him."

Cycling had never seen a disco-dancing, marble-shooting, philosophy-spouting Angel like Pantani. In 1999 he announced his intention to win the Giro-Tour double two years in a row, which no one had ever done. It actually seemed possible. With just two stages left in the Italian race, Il Pirata had built a lead of five minutes, thirty-eight seconds — insurmountable unless something terrible and bizarre happened. It did.

On June 5, shortly after dawn, at the mountain sanctuary of Madonna di Campiglio, cycling's drug inspectors knocked on Pantani's hotel door. Vittorio Savini, then his manager, was with him.

The inspectors told Pantani that his blood hematocrit level — at the time the most accurate indicator of the performance-enhancing drug EPO — was too high.

"We exchanged a look," Savini says, "and then Marco punched his dresser."

Pantani could have served a quiet, if embarrassing, two-week absence from competition, then simply begun racing again, as other cyclists have done. Because the test didn't detect EPO, just the abnormally high level of red blood cells, racers were technically barred from competition for their health until the hematocrit level returned to normal. It wasn't even officially a drug violation. Instead of sitting out quietly, Pantani claimed he was a victim of a plot, accused authorities of botching the test and fabricating results. He demanded DNA testing (which later proved the tests were accurate). He retreated to his villa. He lashed out. He began speaking of himself in the third person. His cocaine use escalated.

He gained weight, went days without sleeping. He always had driven fast, but now he drove into accidents, once speeding the wrong way down a one-way street and wrecking eight cars. There were long, inexplicable absences.

"He could have faced that problem like an adult, like a man," says Pugliese. "Or he could have faced it like a kid and tried to escape it like a kid. And he chose that."

Other cyclists accused of doping have admitted error, focused on recovery and saved their careers. But this was an Angel of the Mountains, a man of outsize, enormously fragile pride. Other cyclists found guilty of doping have focused on creating new lives outside the sport. But this was Pantani — man of miracles, patron saint of long odds and steep climbs. He got back on his bike.

In the summer of 2000, he helped teammate Stefano Garzelli win the Giro. Then he took on Lance Armstrong in the Tour de France. Piqued after Armstrong announced that he had allowed Pantani to win a mountain stage (which he in fact had), Il Pirata insulted Armstrong in the press. When Armstrong responded that "unfortunately, Il Elefantino has shown his true colors. I thought he had more class than that," Pantani was enraged, and he let his rage define his riding. He attacked as only a splenetic Angel could — or would.

First, on his way to a stage victory in the Alps, he dropped Armstrong. The next day, he opened up a one-minute gap on a climb early in the stage and so rattled the normally phlegmatic Texan that Armstrong forgot to eat at a crucial moment, bonked on the Joux Plane ascent, and lost two critical minutes to the only rival — Jan Ullrich — who actually posed a threat to Armstrong's Tour aspirations. Later, Armstrong described it as his worst day ever on a bike.

Pantani's attack was thrilling, vengeful, and enormously self-destructive. He eventually was caught, then lost fourteen minutes overall. The next morning, he dropped out of the Tour.

The following season, in 2001, police raiding the riders' hotels at the Giro found a syringe with traces of insulin in Pantani's room, and he was banned for another six months. Seven judicial inquiries would eventually be launched against Pantani, including one that charged him with sporting fraud for using performance-enhancing drugs while being a professional athlete.

Money wasn't enough. Adulation couldn't save him. The antidepressants he was taking didn't make him happy. What choice did he have? He would not quit, even as his cocaine addiction consumed him. He got back on his bike.

At the 2003 Giro he was mobbed every morning at the sign-in. This would have been the perfect moment for his fans to face the truth, to change the narrative they and their hero had conspired to create. But his fans — his country — wanted an Angel. Twice the number of fans surrounded Il Pirata as anyone else, including the leaders. Didn't they know how far he had fallen? Maybe they did. Maybe it drew them. Maybe they thought he could rise, against ridiculous odds, once again.

He couldn't. He might have been an Angel, but he was also just a man. On the eighteenth stage of the Giro, descending the Colle di Sampeyre in driving hail and rain, Pantani crashed. There is a photograph of him the moment after the fall, sitting on rain-slicked grass, clutching himself, crying. His fans screamed for him to continue.

Continue? Il Pirata, who perceived competitors' tactical maneuvers as grievous personal affronts, who, if he wasn't stalking a pack, was assaulting it, devouring it? Il Pirata, who had been hounded by racing authorities when he should have been honored? Now that he'd crashed out of contention in his homeland's biggest race, his fans wanted him to join the pack, to continue when he could not triumph?

Angels confound. They perform the impossible. They find the perfect gesture at the most unlikely moment. And now, Pantani did it again. He gave his fans their miracle. He got on his bike and he rode. Not for victory, not to mount one of his furious, quixotic charges. He rode when defeat was absolutely certain. Just so he could finish. Just because people were asking him to. It was perhaps his least-talked-about ascent, his most ordinary. It might have been his most heroic climb. It was his last.

In the fall of 2003, for reasons no one can agree on, Pantani traveled to Cuba. He went there to dry out. No, he flew to the island for a massive binge. He wanted to reconcile with a girlfriend he'd met at the beach on a previous trip. No, it was because Diego Maradona, the great Argentinian soccer star, invited him to the place he'd been treated for addiction.

For three days, my translator and I search for the rooming house where Pantani stayed in Havana, for hints about what happened. It is a strange trip. People avert their eyes and profess ignorance to the most innocent queries, and dark rumors mutate and fester in narrow, cramped alleyways thick with diesel fumes and the heavy scent of human waste. We are invited into tiled rooms no larger than small closets, greeted with warmth and wide smiles and strong, bitter coffee. We are told of a local doctor who has discovered the cure for cancer in the venom of giant blue scorpions; we listen to not one but two sordid and fantastic rumors of hushed-up prostitute murders. We see mounted upon doors crude representations of pierced tongues and covered eyes — both a religious caution against bearing false witness and a political reminder that sharing information here is dangerous. In Cuba truth is a slippery, elusive commodity.

Yes, a local man we meet on the street in Havana says after

a couple mojitos, Pantani was here. He came in 1999, 2000, and 2001. He led bike tours around the country. The children adored him. Fidel entertained him at one of his secret palaces. The cyclist knew that money meant nothing, that it could not buy happiness, and isn't such insight the very essence of living? And now could we please give the helpful man some American dollars, "for cooking oil, for my sick mother." Yes, another local whispers in a bar, Pantani was here and he was quite possibly involved in the untimely end of a young prostitute — the one in the taxi, involving ecstasy and a botched Santeria cure, not the one where a woman was flung from a window of a famous tourist hotel.

"Certainly not," the mother of Pantani's Cuban ex-girlfriend proclaims. Her daughter was not the cyclist's girlfriend, they were merely acquaintances, and she has no idea how anyone could have thought differently. As she says this, her teenage daughter rolls her eyes at the translator and me.

On the third day, guided by rumors, a Santeria witch, some mojito-fueled guesses from locals, an old man selling rolled paper filled with roasted peanuts, a relentless translator, gossip, a vague article from the Italian daily *La Nazione,* and dumb Caribbean luck, we find the boardinghouse where Pantani stayed.

"He wouldn't eat," says Lidia Dios Fernandez, the owner. "He was depressed. He took whatever pills he could get his hands on. He would open doors and just take pills. Blood pressure pills, for example. My blood pressure pills."

Franco Corsini, the Cesenatico restaurateur and one of Pantani's close friends, heard the Cuba rumors and tracked the cyclist to Havana. He and Michael Mengozzi flew from Italy to help their friend, bringing antidepressants obtained from Pantani's doctor back home.

Fernandez says that before Pantani left her boardinghouse, he gave away a twenty-thousand-dollar Rolex watch and his bicycle to the poor children of the city. Sebastion Urra Delgado, a Cuban hunting guide who extricated Pantani from Havana at

Corsini's request, says that when he arrived in the city the cyclist was barely conscious and, if anyone gave away — or, more likely, sold — Pantani's possessions, it was Fernandez. "People looked at Marco and they saw a pot of gold passed out on the couch," he says.

Before he left Havana, Pantani scribbled in the blank pages of his passport. This is what he wrote: "My life is already over. The thing that matters in life is to feel death. I'm left all alone. No one managed to understand me. Even the cycling world and even my own family. I want to break this addiction. I want to finish with that world and I want to get back on the bike."

Back in Italy, when Pantani drove to meetings with drug dealers, Michael Mengozzi followed on his motorcycle hoping to dissuade him. He rarely succeeded.

Pantani checked in to drug rehabilitation centers twice but lasted only days each time. At the second one, in Milan, he had cocaine smuggled in. In a published interview with Pugliese, his journalist friend, in September 2003, Pantani declared that he was done with cycling forever. Pugliese says he asked his editors if he could write another story. "Marco Pantani's going to die," he says he told his editors. "Can we help him? Can we run an article about his drug problems?" He thought a good headline would be "Silence Is Killing Pantani." His editors declined. At the beginning of February 2004, a week before his friend's death, Pugliese wrote Il Pirata's obituary. "And I could have written it six months earlier," he says.

At the end of what would be Pantani's last stay at the family villa, his mother emptied his wing. "What a thorough cleaning job you're doing," he said. She always knew when he was going to fall. She had a feeling.

On Monday, February 9, he checked in to room 5-D, a split-level room on the top floor of Le Rose with a view of the Adriatic. He wanted it for only one night. "He seemed very sad," says Silvia Deluigi, the hotel owner's daughter. *Una grande tristezza.* "It was clear he wanted to be alone."

He made five or six phone calls, came downstairs, then walked into the winter night. Twenty minutes later, he returned. He wouldn't leave the hotel again.

Every morning Deluigi took a brioche and coffee to Pantani, and every morning he asked if he might have the room another day. Every night a waitress from Oliver Laghi's restaurant showed up with a pizza.

On Saturday morning, Valentine's Day, some of the guests on the fifth floor came downstairs to complain.

"They said, 'Who is that bald guy upstairs?'" says Pietro Buccellato, the hotel clerk and a foreign-affairs student at the local college. "'He's acting weird.'"

Other guests complained. Pantani was screaming. There were loud banging noises. When Lorissa Boyko, the cleaning woman at Le Rose, knocked on the door, Pantani screamed at her until she went away. Buccellato went upstairs to investigate.

"I heard furniture moving around. I talked about it with the owner and he said, 'Let's say we have to change towels as an excuse.' I called, but the phone was always busy."

At 8:00 P.M., Buccellato went upstairs and knocked at the door to 5-D. There was no answer. At 9:30, he knocked again and, this time, opened the door with a manager's key. The lights were on, the furniture upturned. Pantani was on the top floor, next to the bed, facedown. There was swelling in his brain and lungs brought on by an overdose of cocaine. He was thirty-four years old. He'd been dead for four hours.

It could have been me. I didn't possess extraordinary athletic gifts, or fame, or money, and I was thirty pounds overweight. I lived in a cluttered, one-room apartment in a Midwestern suburb and binged on cheeseburgers and vanilla milk shakes and read detective novels until sunrise, but other than that I was exactly like one of the greatest climbers who ever lived.

At first it was just a few beers and occasional cocaine, not a lot, just a normal amount for a guy like me. And then it was more than a normal amount. I remember myself as a sweet kid, and I had a sweet tooth, too. But sometimes the mask slipped. Sometimes the monster scrabbled out. There were nosebleeds and vomiting and car wrecks and hurt feelings and lost jobs and liver disease and worried people who didn't know what to do. Bad things happened, and things got worse.

Can we learn from Pantani's end? And what is the lesson? That those who climb too fast, too far — like Icarus and all other mortals who dare to spread their wings toward bright, shining suns — must surely crash to Earth?

It's bullshit. Why can't his mother and managers and friends and fans see that? Why can't people see that? There is no cautionary tale about fame and greatness here, no lyrical saga of hubris and tragedy. I could have died like Pantani. I could have died exactly like him. There would have been nothing lyrical about it.

Of course, other cyclists have taken performance-enhancing drugs. Some have been caught; others, no doubt, haven't. Maybe Pantani was singled out by a cycling establishment terrified that the savior of the Tour might be exposed as a cocaine abuser. Maybe he was hounded. But others have been singled out. Others have been hounded. It hasn't killed them.

Other cyclists have used recreational drugs, too, including, no doubt, cocaine. In 2003 the great Jan Ullrich, Armstrong's archrival, was temporarily banned from cycling for testing positive for ecstasy. It didn't kill him.

Italy's great cyclist, one of the greatest climbers of all time, the doomed Angel of the Mountains, died not because of judges, or lawyers, or reporters, or the cycling community, or his parents, or the embarrassment of oversize ears, or an uncaring world, or mysterious, shadowy overlords hatching sinister plots. He didn't die because he was hounded. He didn't die because anyone failed him.

It's cruel and narrow-minded to reduce a man's life to a medical diagnosis. Pantani brought a bruised majesty to cycling, and it was a rare and precious and thrilling thing that should be acknowledged and remembered. But we shouldn't forget the sordid way Pantani left this world. He lived as an Angel. He died as a drug addict. He died *because* he was a drug addict.

That I managed — with a great deal of help — to quit drinking and taking drugs makes me feel enormously, stupendously, ridiculously lucky and grateful. Why couldn't Pantani quit? Here are better questions: When will the family and friends and fans and country that loved him, and those who merely loved the idea of him, stop making up fables? How can a country be so stupefied by grief that it can't admit the truth? That its hero's demise was neither mythical nor profound but merely stupid and sad and sick and utterly wasteful?

A woman crosses herself, kisses the medallion of the Madonna hanging from her neck, then pulls out a digital camera. She snaps a shot of the flowers arrayed in front of Pantani's memorial — the lilies, gladiolus, carnations, plastic roses and daffodils, the peonies, the black-eyed Susans, the sunflowers. She wears a shapeless, dark-blue dress and her face is heavily lined. She might be fifty-five. She might be seventy-five. Her husband wears shorts and Nike sandals, and he, too, crosses himself, then kisses the cross around his neck. A young man is with them, perhaps twenty, perhaps thirty, perhaps mentally disabled or palsied, and he moves with the unselfconscious clumsiness of a very small child. His head rocks from side to side and every half minute or so he exclaims, "Pantani! Pantani!" and gurgles.

It is late afternoon on a hot Wednesday in early July, another windless, cloudless day. For forty-five minutes couple after couple, family after family follow the path marked by signs the cemetery's management has taped to walls and posts — "Marco Pantani Viale No. 6" on heavy plastic paper with arrows. There are no other signs in the cemetery. All the visitors cross themselves. Most take out digital cameras or cell phones. Some leave notes, keepsakes. Once man rode his bike 150 miles here, then left his shirt, on which he wrote, "Certain summers days in Cesenatico seem to reflect light the way a pirate lit up his people." A note pinned to a spray of plastic roses reads, "Goodbye, pirate of Romaglia, with pain I mourn you like a son. I remember when we met."

"He seemed like a son," says Liliana Pessarelli, a visitor from Modena. "Last year we came to visit his house, but he wasn't there. So this year we've come to the cemetery."

"Nobody could have believed when he died," says Giovanni Minconi, from Carrara, in Tuscany. "If he would have lived, he would have been a champion again."

At his funeral, the mass of mourners stretched two miles in lines six across. There were reports that thirty thousand filed past his casket. Today, a typical day at the Cesenatico cemetery, a hundred people come to cross themselves and take pictures and telephone friends back home to tell them where they are. "I used to work in peace," says Ennio Bazocchi, the graveyard caretaker, with a deep sigh. "Before we could leave [tools] around. Now, there are just too many people." One couple leaves the memorial, another couple arrives. More crossing, more disposable cameras, more flowers. At this very moment, no doubt, families are packing their cars in Rome and Naples and Venice, preparing for a journey to the final resting place of the funny-looking little man who achieved so much and died so horribly wrong, so horribly alone.

It is cloudless and windless, oppressively hot, and a sheen of sweat covers the faces of every single one of the mourners, or fans, or deluded pilgrims, or vultures, or whatever they are. The older couple and their son, or grandson, are still here. She weeps; her husband stares at the flowers. The boy makes his sounds.

"Pantani!" he croons over and over, occasionally gurgling, rocking his head. Does he know whose name he sings? Does he understand why the great champion is gone? Is his dull, ragged mourning less profound than that of those who make a martyr of the fallen cyclist, or is this the sound of genuine sorrow, at perfect pitch?

A hot, still day, cloudless and windless, broken only by the sounds of cameras clicking and the man-child's sad, sad song. "Pantani! Pantani!"

10

SIXTEEN MINUTES FROM HOME:
WILLIE McCOOL, RUNNER

OST PEOPLE KNOW WHAT HAPPENED. THAT A PIECE OF foam broke off *Columbia*'s external fuel tank and hit the shuttle's left wing. That NASA officials on the ground gravely underestimated the severity of the damage. That, in fact, the damage caused the shuttle to burn and break into pieces in the skies over Texas, just sixteen minutes before its scheduled landing on a clear, bright Saturday morning in February nearly three years ago. What most people don't know is something NASA investigators found when they sifted through and analyzed the wrecked vessel on the ground. Among the recovered shuttle parts was an instrument panel where switches appear to have been engaged and manipulated in the final minutes of the doomed astronauts' lives by the person in the shuttle's right seat — the pilot. It was evidence that the pilot was making adjustments and maneuvers even as *Columbia* was pitching and spinning toward Earth. One person who knew the pilot well says that, even when death was certainly imminent and known to the crew, Willie McCool was trying to make sure that as much material as possible survived the crash — for investigators, for researchers, for future astronauts. Another person, a NASA investigator named John Clark, whose wife, Laurel, died along with McCool and five others in the crash, says that what McCool did in those final moments "was a big deal. A very big deal."

Willie McCool was forty-one years old when he died that morning, and his singular achievements are what the obituaries and eulogies focused on: eagle scout, exceptional runner, test pilot, astronaut. He died serving his country, was publicly mourned. Towns where he had lived erected statues in his honor. He was a hero in every conventional sense of the word, pronounced so at a memorial service by no less a person than the president of the United States.

But McCool was a son and father, too. A husband and friend, student and mentor. He was just like other men. And very different.

They met in Guam, where Willie's father, a navy pilot, was stationed. Willie was blond, blue-eyed, and pasty-skinned, lean and sinewy. Atilana Vallelos had black hair and dark eyes and brown skin. He sat behind her in their high school speech class, and for months neither spoke to each other. She went by Lani. He had changed the spelling of his name from Willy to Willie because he idolized Willie Mays. "Which is cute," Lani says, "because he's so white." When they finally spoke, they talked about sports. Lani Vallelos told Willie McCool that she was a sprinter. And that's when Willie, a swimmer, discovered running.

"Lani," he wrote to her after he had joined the track team, after he had set records in the fifteen-hundred- and five-thousand-meter races for Guam's John F. Kennedy High School track team, "of all the people to whom I owe thanks for getting me into track and influencing me to continue on, I think you deserve the most thanks. If it hadn't been for you . . . I never would have joined track. Because of your efforts I have finally found something that I enjoy doing and that I do, in all modesty, fairly well.

"Lots of times in a race when my whole body aches, my lungs are burning, my stomach hurts, I feel like stopping and quitting, just saying, 'The hell with this.' But then I think to myself, 'What would Lani think if I just stopped and quit? Finish the race for Lani!' Also lots of times, just to get my mind off the pain and off the race, I'll just kind of relax and 'run dream' about you and being together and of the times we had together in the past and the times I wish we could have in the future. Having you as my own sure makes my life an awful lot less painful (most of the time) and much more enjoyable."

He was fifteen years old. After his sophomore year Willie and his family moved to Lubbock, Texas, where Barent McCool had been transferred. Texas had many more, and swifter, teenagers than Guam did. Impressing people with his running wouldn't be easy. He found other ways. Willie was in a gym fooling around with a jump rope. His friend Dale Somers had told Willie that one minute of jumping rope expends the same amount of energy as running six minutes. So Willie jumped rope for five minutes. Then another five minutes. Dale yelled to him. Go another five and I'll buy you a Coke. Five minutes later, another high school pal joined in. Another five minutes, he yelled to Willie, and you're a quarter richer. Then one of the dads saw what was going on. Willie, the dad said, five more minutes and I'll buy you a steak dinner. He jumped rope for thirty-five minutes.

Somers was on the Coronado High School basketball team, and in the summers he and Willie would play one-on-one. Willie wasn't very good, but when he lost he would demand another game. And another. And another. Sometimes, the boys would still be playing — and Willie would still be losing — when day turned to Texas twilight.

He still wrote to Lani, and Lani wrote back. But after a while, what was there to say? Besides, Willie developed a crush on a girl named Becky. It took him three months to ask her to lunch. That first date, he spent most of it talking about his girlfriend on the island. But she wasn't his girlfriend anymore. How could she be, an ocean between them? Lani dated, got pregnant and married, had two children.

Adolescent crushes are heady things, but they don't last.

"My earliest, vivid memory of him?" Al Cantello asks. "I was screaming at him, something about a crappy workout. Now, most kids, they'd listen, then say, 'Yes, but, yes, but,' but not Willie. He just looked straight at me, with those big steely blue eyes, taking it all in."

It was 1979, McCool's first, or plebe, year at the Naval Academy in Annapolis, Maryland, and Cantello's fifteenth year as coach there. He knew "hardly anything" about the runner from Texas.

"Willie had a modest high school career. Which was fine by me. What we do here is we take an athlete, and we develop him."

Here's how: "We're in a meeting," Cantello remembers. "And I say, 'OK, Willie, what percent of you is devoted to running?' Willie says, 'I don't know, with graduation, service, maybe twenty percent?' And I say, 'Willie, you'll never be a friggin' runner!'"

Early in their relationship, Cantello told McCool that he was nothing but a baton. It's a standard Cantello trope, one in a series of fierce and ego-deflating lessons the coach imparts to virtually all his plebes. Maybe you won some high school races, maybe you're going to be a big-shot officer one day, he'd tell the boys. But really you're nothing special. Don't forget it. When it comes down to it, "You're nothing but a baton, carrying DNA from one generation to the next."

McCool became the most disciplined, dedicated baton Cantello had ever seen. He listened to the coach's instructions about technique, and he employed them. He listened to the coach's lessons about nutrition and rest, and he followed them. He was in bed by ten, asleep by eleven, every night of his college career. He listened to the coach's lectures about giving your all, and he gave his all. All that work made him a better runner but not a great one.

By the end of his navy career, he had the twenty-sixth-fastest time ever, 24:27, by a midshipman on the Naval Academy's five-mile cross-country course. Which means his name isn't on the plaque in the glass case of the athletic department building. That's reserved for the twenty-five fastest. His greatest accomplishment as a navy runner occurred when he medaled in the ten thousand meters in the league outdoor championships. Cantello can't remember much else.

Looking back, the coach wonders whether Willie could have been better had he been tougher, a bit more ruthless. "He was a little bit sheltered," Cantello says. "If someone stepped on his toes during a race, Willie would say" — here Cantello affects a high-pitched whine — "'That's poor sportsmanship.' Meanwhile, a guy from New Jersey is running next to him, getting ready to throw an elbow, saying, 'I'm gonna put that jerk in lane three.'"

But Willie was other things. He was relentlessly cheerful, given to striding up and down the hallways of his dorm exclaiming, "Five weeks till the meet. Beat Army!" He was elected captain of the cross-country team as a senior, the guy the team rallied around. "He was energetic, he was enthusiastic, he was smart," says Mark Donahue, the captain when McCool entered the academy. "When I look back on it, the word that comes to mind is 'innocent.'" McCool was the brainy runner that Cantello asked to help his son with algebra one Saturday night. For a midshipman, a Saturday night is a precious thing, one of the only times he is allowed off the academy grounds. McCool didn't hesitate.

When he graduated from the academy in 1983, he was ranked second in his class. "He made more of himself in four years than anyone I can remember," Cantello says. Then the coach pauses. "But is he the most inspirational? You gotta remember. I've been here forty-three years."

A couple of years later, when he was studying for his master's in computer science at the University of Maryland, Willie made a point of taking care of Cantello's newest group of batons. He drove the plebes to meets. He joined them in practice. He filled up the team cooler with water. Every night before a meet, he invited them to his condominium in Crofton, eight miles west of Annapolis. He cooked them spaghetti. ("Willie knew as much about making spaghetti sauce as . . ." Cantello says mournfully. "He used carrots! That's a misdemeanor. That's a no-no.") But the batons were grateful.

"He protected all of us," Ron Harris, a plebe in 1983, says.

The plebes called McCool's condominium the "Bat Cave" and treasured their time there. They didn't know what lay ahead for him, the greatness in store. They just knew the guy making funny spaghetti sauce.

"The amazing thing," Harris says, "was that he had so much time for us. He had time for everything."

It was about this time that Willie heard from another navy man that Lani was separated from her husband. Willie hadn't forgotten her. Sometimes when he ran with his navy teammates he talked about the girl he had been in love with in the South Pacific, the one with the black hair who got him into running in the first place. He wrote to her, and she wrote back. He flew out to see her in Tempe, Arizona, where she was finishing college, and they drove to a nearby football stadium. He handed her his watch, which she had used to time him while he ran quarter miles on Guam. She had always loved watching Willie run. She knew how happy it made him.

"Everything came back," Lani says. "The smells, the phone

calls. It was like we had never been apart. My heart . . . it jumped. You know the saying about seeing a rainbow? I was seeing double rainbows."

After her divorce, Lani and Willie were married, in 1986. Her sons were toddlers. Sean was then five, Christopher was three. "I asked him if he wanted kids," Lani says. "And he said, I already have kids. We have kids." Another son, Cameron, was born on September 15, 1987. The next day McCool, by then a navy pilot, left for a six-month tour of duty aboard an aircraft carrier.

Willie and Lani and the boys spent most of the next decade in Washington State, in the town of Anacortes, just a short drive from the naval base on Whidbey Island, where McCool flew the Prowler, a four-person aircraft used for jamming radar, and other electronic warfare tactics. Once, at the Patuxent River Naval Air Station in Maryland, he pulled a Prowler out of a spiral, or a "death spin." No one had ever done it before. Today, every Prowler pilot and would-be pilot studies what McCool did that day; it's the official navy procedure for pulling a Prowler out of a spiral.

His work meant Willie was gone from home a lot, but Lani had the children to take care of, and her passion for photography, and she played the harp that Willie had bought for her. Lani was a military man's daughter, so she knew the drill. When Willie was home they played chess together and went on backpacking trips with the kids. He wrote her poetry.

In 1996 NASA selected McCool for its space program. The family moved to Houston, where Willie joined forty-three others in a group of future shuttle astronauts — they called themselves "the sardines" because there were so many. It was the largest group of shuttle astronauts since the 1978 class. By then McCool, the navy pilot, had amassed more than twenty-eight hundred hours of flight experience in twenty-four aircraft and made more than four hundred landings on aircraft carriers, which even among pilots is a very big deal.

But the other sardines were big deals, too. They had been selected from a pool of twenty-four hundred applicants. McCool was surrounded by people just like him. There was a former circus gymnast who was also a fighter pilot and doctor. There was a flight surgeon who could name most birds — in Latin. Joining McCool on the shuttle *Columbia* would be an Israeli air force colonel, son of Holocaust survivors, who flew on the mission that had destroyed Iraq's nascent nuclear reactors in 1981. Top guns all, oozing competitive juju.

Steve MacLean was one of the sardines. What struck him most about McCool wasn't his intelligence, or his skills, or his competitive zeal (though MacLean says all were extraordinary, even by NASA standards). What MacLean remembers is watching McCool run.

"It was like he was on wheels," MacLean says. "It was a thing of beauty."

What he remembers even more is how he treated others, especially children. At weekly soccer games involving astronauts and their families, a goal couldn't be scored until the smallest kid playing had touched the ball at least once — a rule McCool pushed for.

As MacLean says, "When he was talking to somebody, no matter who it was, that person was very important."

Almost every day, at twilight, whether in Houston or in Anacortes, Willie would come home and find Lani cooking dinner for the kids. He loved his work, but he hated that he was gone so much. He would offer to help. Lani would decline. He'd insist. She'd tell him to go for a run. Sometimes she'd watch him take off.

"It looked like he ran on air," she says.

Half an hour or an hour later he would come in dripping with sweat, and he would slam a knight to a new position on their chessboard in the living room, or write a line of poetry. And then he would lie on the living room floor and stretch, and Lani would play her harp as the dinner cooked. And Willie would move closer to Lani. And closer. Until finally he was stretching his legs while he leaned against Lani.

"Our friends said we were the luckiest people in the world," Lani says. "And they were right."

One day McCool asked Cameron to join him on a run. But his son, then thirteen, didn't want to.

"I have too much homework," he said.

McCool promised to help him with the homework if he'd run.

"Well, then, I'm too sore."

McCool promised he'd feel better after a run. He'd run, but the teenager would whine about it. For Willie's forty-first birthday, a few months before the shuttle launch, Cameron gave his dad a card promising fifteen "complaint-free runs, to be used whenever you want."

Lani told her husband to entertain the boy, to make the running more fun. She told Willie to tell him stories, to take the boy's mind off how much he hurt.

But Willie was a natural listener, not a talker. Still, he tried. He began by retelling novels he thought a teenage boy would like. The first, told over weeks and weeks of running, was *The Worthing Saga*, by Orson Scott Card. By the end of the book, Cameron could talk and run without gasping. Then there were other novels — Cameron can't remember them all — and now that the boy could talk without gasping, they would discuss the works.

They'd talk about "the philosophy behind the stories or just ideas in general," says Cameron.

Willie ran out of new novels. He started telling his own stories. He talked about throwing berries at cars on Guam, getting in trouble. He talked about building model airplanes with his father. Those were fine, but Cameron wanted stories from the academy. He wanted to hear about his father's life as a plebe, how he had to tuck his chin in to his chest and recite dinner menus and jet parts while upperclassmen screamed at him. He wanted to hear about the ice-cream-eating contests his father participated in as a senior, how a plebe stood behind him and massaged his temples to prevent "freeze headaches." Willie wouldn't just tell the stories, he would act them out — as the frightened plebe, the screaming midshipman, the ice-cream-gulping senior. They would run out of the gates of the NASA center in Houston, along the sidewalk, counting telephone poles. By the time his father flew into space, Cameron had quit counting the poles. There were too many. They were running three and a half miles from the gates of NASA. Three and a half miles out, three and a half miles back.

Just a few weeks before McCool and the rest of the *Columbia* crew would head into space, in December 2002, he went for a run with a man named Andy Cline, whom he had met on a backpacking trip a year earlier. The men ran in Anacortes, where the McCools planned to return full-time after the *Columbia* mission. McCool wanted to show Cline a spot he had discovered. They ran through the Anacortes Community Forest Lands to Cranberry Lake. Cline told the astronaut how he wanted to run faster, how he would like, for once in his life, to break the three-hour mark in a marathon.

"And Willie said that was no problem, that he'd pace me and that he would help me get to that. And I believed him. When you were with him, you felt like you had his undivided attention. That life seemed pretty clear."

McCool and Cline always talked a lot on their runs, but on this run they talked even more than usual.

"About God and faith, and what that looks like and the variability of that," Cline says. "He said that every one of us has some sort of faith and the trick was in recognizing it, in seeing it.

"And I know it sounds odd to say this, but I couldn't help thinking as we talked. And what I thought was, 'This might be the last time I ever see Willie.'"

We like our heroes' lives to adhere to the simple and ascending trajectory we associate with great men. And in its public outlines Willie McCool's life did that. A disciplined and strong-willed distance runner from an early age, a little boy who built and flew model airplanes, an honors student who loved chemistry and poetry equally well.

But his life wasn't quite so simple. No one's is. Willie's biological father was a heavy drinker known to have a bad temper and quick to take it out on his wife, Audrey, his son, and Kirstie, Willie's little sister. After his parents divorced, Willie took it upon himself to be Kirstie's protector when they went to visit their dad.

Soon the visits stopped altogether. Audrey was a dietitian then, in Southern California, working full-time, doing her best to take care of her children and to keep her husband from finding them.

Can a hero come only from a crucible of agony? Did McCool watch out for others because he had a tough childhood? Did he run because he had discovered a place where his life was not so painful? Did his biological father — by most accounts a highly intelligent man — pass on some of his best genetic material to his son? Did Barent McCool, Willie's adoptive father — a navy pilot and by all accounts a loving if demanding and unsentimental teacher — mold the boy who became his son into such a perfectionist? Was it Audrey's drive and need that turned Willie into a man before he was even a teenager? There's a theory for every question. One sounds as good as another. None matters too much. "We had to grow up young and early," says Kirstie Chadwick.

Lani McCool is gazing at a hawk in a tree, his wings spread, drying. She has just hiked twenty minutes or so to Sares Bluff, a scenic outlook just a few minutes' drive from her home in Anacortes. It is cool, late summer in the Pacific Northwest, and she is happy. She wishes more people would understand that joy is something Willie would have wanted for her.

"I'll be out somewhere, maybe at a function involving NASA, and I'll be throwing my head back laughing, and people will stare and say, 'There's Willie McCool's widow.' What do people want? That we continue grieving forever?"

Late summer, two and a half years since the accident, and for the past two days she has been remembering the twenty-four years they knew each other, the seventeen and a half years they were married.

We have visited the naval station at Whidbey Island to pay respects at the memorial for Willie. There, engraved at the base of a replica of the Prowler, is "CDR William McCool STS-107 Columbia 1 Feb 2003." Lani traces a heart in the concrete with her finger. We have poked around her house, looked at the chessboard where he used to slam pieces after his run, at the harp Lani played while Willie leaned against her legs. She has shown poetry he wrote to her, photographs she took of him.

The past two and a half years haven't been easy. His work materials are in the garage. She managed to open one box but couldn't open any more. She thinks about the trip to Switzerland he'd been promising since she saw double rainbows. She thinks about the darkroom he was going to build for her in their house in the Pacific Northwest. She's tried to go to church, but every time she got close she started crying, "because the Eucharist is as close as we get to someone who's dead," and that's reminded her of the times she and Willie attended church together. Sometimes, because of terrible allergies, she couldn't walk to the front of the church to receive communion. So Willie would bring her back a wafer on his tongue, and people thought they were kissing and it scandalized the congregation, and it makes her laugh to think about it.

Soon she will drive Cameron to college in Seattle, and, after she drops him off and returns home, she will pass a theater and see on the marquee the name of the film *The Corpse Bride*, and she will break down sobbing.

She has five books on her bed, is reading all of them, but in the afternoon overlooking the Pacific Ocean she can't remember the name of a single one. Sometimes she looks at Willie's books. Books of Russian, which he was teaching himself. *The Odyssey*. *Macbeth*. Sometimes she leafs through them. In the margins of a biography of Einstein, she found something that made her smile.

Willie's delighted scrawl: "Light Bends!!!"

Life hasn't been easy, but it has been . . . life. It has been good. That was something Willie and Lani always agreed on. That it was good. That it should be good.

"There are so many gifts," she says.

The poems he wrote, the letters he sent. The memories she has of him. The future.

"I miss him horribly," she says. "It was a loss, but I realized it was OK, because we lived a good life. I have no regrets. I don't think I ever said he died too young. . . .

"People misinterpret it, because I'd give anything to have him back, but he's not here. I am OK. I miss Willie and I loved him. But I am OK."

She attended the most recent launch, on July 26, because she feels like her husband's death and the lessons NASA learned from it will help other astronauts. Still, she is much more at home in Birkenstocks and leggings than pearls and a dress. She makes jokes about how all the memorials for the *Columbia* crew were easier to take, because "I love wearing black." In the hotel rooms afterward, she says, "I'd get a plate of chocolates and I'd take a bite out of each — I didn't have to worry about being good."

She knows that some other naval wives view her with something other than love. She knows that she doesn't quite fit the image of a military spouse. She says that Willie adored that about her. Some of his friends say the same thing. She shows me a poem that he read to her from space; it was the last time she heard his voice.

"He said, 'Hold on, I've got something here.' And then he read this: 'I've witnessed the beauty of Earth from space, far, far above. What a treasure it is to behold. But I would trade this view for your embrace, my sweet love, for only you enrapture my soul.'

"That was the last two minutes I heard him. So, yeah," she says, "I feel lucky."

Andy Cline is running. Some days it's in the Anacortes forest, some days it's somewhere else near his new home in the Pacific Northwest. He still wants to do a marathon in less than three hours, but he doesn't know if he'll be able to.

Today the running isn't easy. It doesn't feel good.

"And I'm dying," Cline says. "And then I'm thinking, 'If Willie were here, he'd kick it up a notch.' So that's what I do."

Cameron stopped running as the launch date got closer, then his father went into quarantine, and then the *Columbia* accident. But after a while, he started again.

As he ran, he says, "I was thinking in the back of my head that I was doing it for him but always remembering that he had been doing it for me."

Then Sean, his oldest brother, said he wanted to run, too. But he wasn't in the greatest shape. So Cameron set up a schedule. He encouraged his brother to tune out his pain. And he told him stories.

"Like my dad did for me."

Al Cantello is sitting in his office at the Naval Academy. On his wall is a framed sweatshirt that Willie wore. In Cantello's file cabinet are the size-ten-and-a-half white Air Pegasus shoes that Lani mailed after the accident. In his drawer is a letter McCool wrote to the coach, inviting him to the launch:

"Your coaching laid a foundation of discipline, drive, and passion that has carried me across the many milestones of my life. With boundless appreciation, Willie."

The coach, former world record holder of the javelin throw, still burly and vigorous at seventy-four, leans forward across his desk.

"Look," he says of the boy whose presence seems to fill his office, "he wasn't the Second Coming. He didn't network very well. He wasn't a very good correspondent. Too much sensitivity."

This is my second day visiting with Cantello. During that time he has talked about the crushing demands of running at Navy, politics, coaching, life. He always returns to Willie McCool. To his naïveté. His love for Lani. His death.

"Afterward," Cantello says, "there was the initial bereavement, in Houston, when the president spoke. Then, shortly after that, the vice president spoke here and some admirals, too, and a couple dozen busloads of congressmen. But it was perfunctory grieving.

"And then a year goes by and they have a ceremony at the National Air and Space Museum. Candles, subdued lighting, all the appointments and trappings were there. It's supposed to be a night of solemn closure. We're supposed to be in the cathedral of this nation's highest aspirations. I look around and who's there? Lockheed Martin, Boeing, Grumman." People who didn't know Willie. People who wanted to trade on his symbolism. More perfunctory grieving.

"Here. You want to understand Willie? You should listen to this." Then Cantello pulls something from one of his desk drawers and slides it into his computer. It's a CD labeled "Willie McCool Wake Up Music 'Imagine' Aboard Space Shuttle Columbia Flight Day15 Jan 29, 2003." It's from three days before the accident.

We sit and listen to the melancholy, aching strains of "Imagine." Then, a female voice: "Good Morning, Blue Team. The song 'Imagine,' by John Lennon, was for Willie this morning." A few more bars of the music, subtle hissing that hints at the distance from Mission Control to the orbiting craft. Then the voice of Willie McCool. Cheerful. Enthusiastic. Still innocent.

"Good morning, Linda, that song makes us think that from our orbital vantage point we observe an Earth without borders, full of peace, beauty, and magnificence, and we pray that humanity as a whole can imagine a borderless world as we see it and strive to live as one, in peace. . . ."

The coach is looking away from the computer, away from me. In the short time I have known him, it's the first time I've seen him speechless. His eyes well up.

"OK, Willie and your team," says the voice from Houston, "we appreciate those words and we wish everyone down here could have the view you do."

Cantello leans forward, hits his keyboard, takes the CD from the computer. Then he leans back in his chair. "What's the right way to grieve?" he asks. "Do you go to a tree, rub some sand between your fingers? Hell, I don't know." More than a few cross-country runners have told me how hard Cantello took Willie's death. Not the coach, though. "How do you grieve?" he repeats. "I'm going to tell you how I'm going to do it."

He slides a letter across his desk to me. It's a memo: "subj: CDR Willie McCool, USS Memorial at Navy XC Course." In the memo, Cantello proposes a stone marker on the cross-country course, "placed just to the left of the current tee shack [so it] would not impede golfers, runners, or golf-course management . . .

"This simple monument would serve to inspire generations of Navy runners, who, like Willie, endured the resolute pursuit of being a Navy runner . . ." Cantello sent the letter in July 2003. Still, no marker. "Man, for all practical purposes," he says, "is a son of a bitch."

Then the coach complains about golf courses, and golfers, and buildings on golf courses, and the nature of man, and about why petty-minded bureaucrats and penny-pinchers are making it so damned hard to get a monument to the runner who wasn't the Second Coming but who made more of himself than anyone Cantello ever saw. Then he says that he doesn't care how long it takes, he's going to get a monument built to Willie McCool.

He and some of his runners walked off the distance on the cross-country course, factored in Willie's best time ever on the course, figured out Willie's pace. They want the monument to stand at the top of a grassy hill, a brief level stretch of the five-mile course, just before it descends to a narrow path through trees. It's 3.1 miles from the finish line. Willie would have covered the distance in sixteen minutes.

Cantello's cross-country record at Navy is 236–64–1. He has coached three all-American runners, has been named the NCAA Mid-Atlantic Regional Coach of the Year three times. He had a 67–9–1 dual-meet record when he coached navy's men's indoor and outdoor track teams. In 1997 the Naval Academy Alumni Association awarded Cantello the distinguished athletic leadership award for a coach or faculty member who did the most for the physical development of the midshipmen. He has coached at the U.S. Naval Academy for forty-three years.

This is how Cantello wants to be remembered: "My legacy," he says, "will be to preserve Willie's time in perpetuity for the five-mile course, so when I'm dead and gone people will know where he was, when he was sixteen minutes from home.

"I'm just carrying Willie's baton."

11

LOST IN AMERICA:
STEVE VAUGHT, HIKER

THE TRIP WAS NOT GOING ACCORDING TO PLAN. HE KNEW HE couldn't have prepared for everything — you don't get to be a 410-pound ex-Marine, clinically depressed and a quasi-Buddhist and halfway across North America on foot without accruing some wisdom about things like nasty surprises and the necessity of acceptance — but by the time he reached Dayton, Ohio, even for Steve Vaught, things were getting to be a little much. It wasn't the two rattlesnakes, or the three cases of poison oak, or the kidney stone. It wasn't the twenty blisters, or the heat, or even the guy who e-mailed him to proclaim that "he could absolutely not, under any circumstances let me pass Kingman Arizona, because it would bring on Armageddon." It wasn't that his wife had told him she wanted a divorce, or that his ghostwriter had complained that Vaught's journal entries were "boring" and "pedantic." It wasn't the clowns who jumped out of the car while he was still in California — real clowns, with the noses and the feet and everything — and danced around him, yelling, then jumped back in their car and drove off. "How many men can say they got bum rushed by a bunch of clowns?" he asks. It wasn't the other guy (at least he thinks it was a guy) who e-mailed him and wrote, "You vulgar maggot . . . you are a fiend and a sniveling backbone-less coward."

It wasn't the reporters — "Short and fat and drunk, they all say the same thing . . . they say, 'Oh, yeah, it'll be great to walk with you' and they end up sitting there talking for three hours for two inches in the paper." It wasn't the woman who showed up in three towns along his hike and said she wanted to "absorb" him. That was creepy, no doubt, but it didn't make him want to quit. It wasn't the heat of the desert or the cold of the mountains or the loneliness or the rage that came over him after he'd thrown his antidepressants down a sewer drain in Amarillo.

It was all of that and it was none of that. It was as shallow as vanity, as deep as the confusion that can steal into a man's soul at 3:00 A.M. when he looks in the mirror and doesn't recognize the sallow apparition staring back.

He thought about how he would appear the next time he was on television. He worried that he would look too fat. It was as simple as that. It was also much, much weirder than a lot of people might imagine, because even though he desperately wanted to lose weight, he knew that to focus on weight loss was to lose himself. That's the kind of Dr.-Freud-meets-Dr.-Phil puzzle that will present itself to a morbidly obese man as he trudges alone across the deserts and mountains of the American West. It's also the kind of insight carried by any man who as a child has ever been called fat boy or forced to pull on a pair of Husky jeans. It's the knowledge earned by every teenage girl who is assured by her worried mother, "You have such a beautiful face," then asked, "Do you really need that dessert?"

Everyone is special. In the United States, at the turn of the twenty-first century, that's a truth as self-evident as the ones about life and liberty. Here's another verity of our times: you can make yourself more special. You can get whiter teeth and a nicer car and a better job and firmer thighs — all in easy monthly payments. You are a wonderful person. Now, here's how to get more wonderful.

It was Steve Vaught's luck — or curse, or both — to captivate and inspire a sizeable segment of the sizeable segment of the U.S. population that has ever found itself pinned between those two shiny, grinding truths. It hadn't been his intention. He didn't hug and kiss his wife and two children and start a twenty-nine-hundred-mile hike in order to lug with him the hopes and dreams of every chubby — and depressed and lonely and lost and just generally dissatisfied and yearning — adult in the country and around the world. But by the time he had arrived in Dayton, that's what was happening.

What had started as a plan at once unadorned and profoundly unhinged — to walk across America in order to drop pounds and discover joy — had become a mega–book deal and a publicity scrum and a quasi-corporate enterprise. He wasn't just Steve Vaught anymore. Now he was "the Fat Man Walking." He had a Web site, thefatmanwalking.com. No wonder a mythology of the Fat Man Walking had taken hold. It was this: a man who suffered through things worse than most of us can imagine had eaten more than most of us can imagine until he was more gargantuan than most of us can imagine. Now he was undertaking an epic trek, and it would save him. A variation of an old story, more popular now than ever, two thousand years later: suffering and redemption, writ extra, extra, extra large.

A hike? Hardly. It was Paul Bunyan meets *Pilgrim's Progress*. People checked out his route on thefatmanwalking.com and e-mailed him to tell him, if he could lose weight, they could quit cigarettes. Or start exercising. Or lose weight themselves. They could change their lives. Naturally, Oprah's people called.

But how could he save anyone if he couldn't even save himself? By the time he got to St. Louis, right around Christmas, he had been stuck at 318 pounds for more than a month. That's when his wife told him she wanted a divorce. By the time he got to Dayton, he was 345 pounds. Once he had to use a truck weigh station to make sure. People e-mailed him, told him to avoid fast-food restaurants. Had those people ever walked along the highways of middle America? Had they ever seen anything *but* fast-food restaurants?

The Fat Man was getting fatter. And desperate. And when word got out that Vaught was calling timeout in the middle of his path to salvation — that the trail to happiness had hit a road-block in Dayton and he was returning to California for a month to work out with a personal trainer — the mythology of the Fat Man took a hit. Have gods with clay feet ever been treated kindly? Some of his would-be corporate backers were not happy. His HarperCollins ghostwriter was not happy. The television folks were not happy. Some of the visitors to his Web site were not happy. The truth is, Vaught was not happy.

"First, he's this big schlub," says David Mollering, one of two documentary film makers who would spend twenty weeks with Vaught on his journey. "And all of sudden he's Forrest Gump; that's a lot to handle for anybody."

No doubt the schlub-Gump metamorphosis was proving taxing, though Vaught handled it with at least some aplomb, referring to himself in the third person as "Forrest Lump." But there were other things, too. He hated being fat. He hated disappointing people. He hated the idea that he might fail. These were all problems that a lot of people could relate to. All challenges that any man — even a skinny man — could understand. But a man doesn't eat himself to the land of truck-stop scales because he's like the rest of us. Oprah's people aren't holding for you and me. We all have demons. Vaught had a fiend. Or maybe he was the fiend.

"He's been carrying a six-hundred-pound gorilla," says Pierre Bagley, the other documentary filmmaker. "I used to say, 'Steve, if there's a monster in this thing, then you're the Dr. Frankenstein.'"

*   *   *

He made the decision in a Target store. Friday night, March 23, 2005, in the pharmacy aisle. He was there with his wife, April, and his two children, Melanie, then eight, and Marc, then three. Vaught felt a stabbing pain in his back, a tightness in his chest. He struggled for breath. He thought he might be having a heart attack. By the time he had made it home and sat down and realized he wasn't about to die, he had come up with a plan.

It was a big plan, a bold plan. It was the kind of plan we all cook up from time to time — quit the job, ditch the wife, hit the road — but that only a few follow. Vaught had already followed a few.

He had dropped out of high school and joined the Marines at seventeen, was married at twenty, divorced at twenty-four. He was living in San Diego then, in Southern California, a muscled 250 pounds, an honorably discharged lance corporal with a girlfriend and a job as manager of a tow-truck company. It doesn't sound too bad. It probably looked good. But people didn't know that his father had left Vaught and his three younger siblings and their mother when Vaught was three. They didn't know his father had spent much of his life in prison for crimes Vaught doesn't want to discuss. Vaught applied for a job as a cop after the Marines, and they hooked him to a polygraph and asked if he'd ever thought of killing anyone, and he said no. The lie stopped the interview. "Not only had I thought about it," he says, "I'd worked it out." He was thinking of his father.

But other children survive abandonment. Other children endure less-than-ideal parents.

Vaught loved drawing. He wanted to be an artist. When he was thirteen, his stepfather told him drawing was for sissies.

"I could have sweated gold and it wouldn't have been good enough," Vaught says. "I could have been playing classical piano and he would have hated me. It wasn't what I was doing. It was who I was."

Before he became the Fat Man, Vaught was simply a very unlucky boy who became an unhappy grown-up. But that describes a lot of people. They get by. They don't decide that the answers to life's problems are a coast-to-coast stroll. Maybe Vaught would have gotten by, too, if not for the accident.

It happened late in the afternoon. He was on his way to pick up a birthday card for his girlfriend. The sun was in his eyes and he was going too fast. Even if he had seen the couple in the intersection, he might not have been able to avoid them. But he was going too fast, and he didn't see them until he was on them. The woman, Emily Vegzary, seventy-five, went through the windshield and died instantly. Zoltan Vegzary, eighty-one, lived for twenty-one days before he died. Vaught spent his first night in jail (he would serve thirteen days for vehicular manslaughter) with the dead woman's blood and pieces of her skin in his hair.

A year later he had gained sixty pounds. He and his girlfriend had split up. After a brief stint in Las Vegas with an uncle, he ended up in an attic apartment in Youngstown, Ohio (where he was born and which he hated), unemployed, barely paying the thirty-five-dollar-per-month rent.

One night he hears a noise — pop, pop, pop. There's a man outside his window shooting a pistol. Vaught leans his head out the window, sees the man, starts laughing. He can't stop laughing. The man looks up and sees the Fat Man leaning out the window.

"What are you laughing at?" the man with the gun yells. "I'll put a bullet through you."

The Fat Man keeps laughing, then stops.

"Go ahead," he says.

"I just didn't care," he says. "I knew that eventually something bad was going to happen to me, so why be concerned about it. Maybe I was hoping that would be the night it happened. Maybe that was my way of saying, 'Let someone else do it for me.'"

Are those the words of a mad scientist, or the monster he created? The Fat Man's not sure. How could he be? Imagine hating your father and your stepfather. Now imagine killing two people. Imagine being Steve Vaught. Would you have been able to leave the attic? Vaught speaks about fear and despair with eloquence; he quotes Lao Tzu and the *Tao Te Ching* and Alan Watts with passion and precision. When it comes to what saved him, though, when it comes to love, there's this: "I met a girl, and the girl sort of drug me out of it."

They moved to California, he got a job at an auto-repair company, and one day Vaught comes home and the girl says she's been sleeping with her boss. Time for another bold decision. He sold everything he owned, bought a one-way ticket to England, where his ex-wife was living, and, when he told customs agents he had never been married, they checked their records, saw that his ex-wife lived in England, then sent him back to the United States. He took a Greyhound Bus from Newark to Harrisburg, and from Harrisburg back to Youngstown, Ohio, and from there he managed to fly to Albuquerque, where he stayed with an old friend named Jeff for a few weeks, and from there to San Diego. It was a long, meandering trip undertaken by a man who had nothing better to do than to drift, and, as anyone who has ever drifted himself knows, salvation can bob up in the most unexpected place. In San Diego he stopped to say hello to Jeff's girlfriend. And there he saw a friend of hers who looked familiar.

Vaught knew her from a happier time in his life, when he was twenty years old, freshly discharged from the Marines, and life was filled with possibilities. She had been thirteen then. Now she was twenty-three and he was thirty. And three months later she was pregnant, and Steve and April were living in San Diego, expecting.

In the mythology of the Fat Man, April saved Steve. The love of a good woman and all that. And maybe there's some truth to that. Other men are saved by love, grounded by children.

Maybe Vaught was, too. Maybe without April, and without the births of Melanie and, four years later, Marc, things would have unraveled faster. Maybe things would have been worse. But they were bad enough.

He couldn't stop eating, for one thing. He couldn't stop thinking about how empty he felt, for another. Maybe they were the same thing.

"I said, 'If the next thirty-three years are as good as the last thirty-three, I got it, I don't need to hang on anymore.' I thought, 'What kind of father am I going to be?'"

When Melanie turned three, Vaught started to think more of his childhood. He remembered playing underneath a kitchen table and pulling on the tablecloth, a percolater full of coffee falling on him and scalding him, and how when he was in the hospital no one could find his father. He remembered how no one could ever find his father. He remembered his father leaving.

Your child turns three. You remember the horrors of being three. Some men would have vowed to be a better father.

"I thought, 'They're [April and Melanie] almost better off without me.' Once you think that, you're in a bad, bad place. I thought, 'I'm just polluting this child's environment by being around.' If I can't fix myself, and I was convinced I couldn't, then it's better if I'm not around."

His weight climbed from 300 pounds to 320, and from there to 350, and from there to 375. "Go see someone," April said. "Or just go." So he saw a therapist who put him on Paxil and Wellbutrin, antidepressants. He remembers the day they kicked in, how the smell of the pavement and the colors of flowers "almost knocked me out."

He had a beautiful wife and two great children. He had a therapist and antidepressants that allowed him to function. He'd found work managing an auto-repair shop. He had two exercise machines and two mountain bikes in the family garage, but he never used any of them. And he ate alone because he couldn't stand to have people see how much food he consumed. He couldn't stop eating.

"I'm killing myself," he thought, "and I don't know how to stop." The night he left the Target store, he was thirty-nine years old. He weighed 410 pounds. He had gained more than one hundred pounds in seven years.

After the children were asleep, April and he sat up for hours in bed talking about his plan and why it was necessary. "The kids don't get the father they deserve, I don't get the husband I deserve, and he doesn't get the life he deserves," April told Pierre Bagley.[1]

She told Steve he should hurry up, that he should get started as soon as possible.

On Monday he quit his job. The same day, he took a warm-up hike. He carried a pack with a fifty-pound plate from one of the weight machines.

"Almost killed me," he wrote in his journal. "The back and leg pain was unbelievable."

The next day he tried again. "Same route, much less pain." Over the next two weeks, he made it as far as four and a half miles, did a few local television interviews, and lined up two camping stores to donate equipment.

On April 10, 2005, he lumbered away from Oceanside. He carried with him four flashlights, ten D batteries, two sleeping bags, an electric fan, and no cell phone. He had two hundred dollars in his pocket. His pack weighed eighty-five pounds.

The plan was to get from the Oceanside Pier to New York City in six months. He walked nine miles the first day, ten the next. Drivers screamed obscenities at him. One threw a Big Gulp cup at him. He developed a blister on his left foot, so he took a day

---

[1]April Vaught declined to be interviewed.

off. Then another day. The fifth day, he made it five miles. Not what anyone would call a steady pace. But before he became the Fat Man, before legions of wounded seekers made him into their standard-bearer, no one had ever accused Vaught of being the steady sort. He thought about his feet. He thought about the rain. He thought about different ways of tying his shoes and about his "fancy hiking pants" that ripped twice and that he sewed twice, and then they ripped again, and he thought more about his feet, and how when he moved up from a size eleven to a size twelve shoe, his whole life improved, and how "it is funny how something that is normally a minor incident in one's life becomes epic when you are involved in something like this."

He thought about how his left knee hurt, and how nice the people were who stopped to walk a few miles with him along the way, who welcomed him into their houses, and he thought about all the reporters who were showing up and walking with him — from newspapers and radio stations and even a local television show. He thought some more about his knee, too. When he stopped at the Ontario Mills Mall in Riverside County, on April 27, he thought about how unhappy he still was. As any tortured soul knows who has ever decided that peace depends on the successful completion of a single task, it's a nerve-racking way to live. "Not because of the pain," he wrote in his online journal, "but because I cannot face the possibility that I may have a serious injury and this trip might very well have ended for me tonight. I absolutely cannot fail at this, because to do so means that I am going to fail at living, fail my kids and my wife."

April drove to the mall and picked him up, then took him to a doctor. He had strained a tendon, painful but not serious. A week later she drove him back to the mall and he started again.

He started, and he almost stopped.

"I got to the desert and I thought, 'Oh, my God, what have I done?'" It was 105 degrees, he was running low on water, and he didn't see a store anywhere. That was in Daggett, just east of

Barstow. "I'm hot and miserable and depressed and sitting in an abandoned Shell station, thinking, 'Why is this happening to me?'" He wasn't even halfway across California.

Another morning, still in the Mojave, short on water again, he came to a cool little creek under a bridge.

"It wasn't that hot yet, but I was tired. I see these little watermelons growing on the side of the road. Turns out they were gourds. I put my feet in the creek for a little while, then I fall asleep, under the bridge."

When he woke, ready to fill his two-gallon water bottles, he noticed something had changed. It was quieter now. The creek wasn't burbling. It wasn't running at all. "I just kicked myself in the butt," he says. "I felt like, that was my life. You find a beautiful creek in the middle of the desert, you wake up, it's gone. You've got to seize the moment."

By the time he made it to Arizona, he was more careful about water, more cautious about mapping his daily route. He had a cell phone courtesy of a California-based radio station, and a national following courtesy of all the press attention. The *Today Show* called. *Dateline* called. One day he had more than fifty-one thousand hits on his Web site. He had groupies. Still, with all that, he was just a man walking across a country. In the Arizona desert, he was daydreaming when he heard a strange noise. In front of him, almost underneath his foot, a diamondback rattlesnake about to strike. Vaught pulled out 9mm Ruger P89 and shot it. (Later a British newspaper would describe how Vaught had dispatched a cobra. What was weirder, shooting a snake in the desert, reading about it in a British newspaper on your Web site, or seeing it described it as cobra? Walk across the country by yourself, and "weirder" begins to lose some of its meaning.) By Winslow he had a book deal worth almost a quarter of a million dollars.

"When he got book money, he could afford hotels," Bagley says. "That became a problem. It was 'I got a bath, I got a toilet, I got running water.' It was hard to give that up."

About twenty miles east of Gallup, Vaught wrote in his journal, "I didn't feel like I was going to quit, I just wanted to sit in a comfortable chair, in a warm room, and relax. So I indulged myself and that turned into four days quite easily." In Gallup he stopped at a restaurant called Roadkill and tucked in to a chicken fried steak. A reporter and photographer were there, and the picture went up on his Web site. April knew how easy it was for Steve — who had already dropped to 346 pounds — to stumble so she told a group of middle-aged Albuquerque women who had contacted her online exactly where her husband was. They called themselves the "Kat Walkers." The Fat Man called them a "Dr. Phil weight-loss group."

From Vaught's online journal:

> Well, they came on like gang busters, snatching me up from my low point . . . and we hit the road. They eagerly listened to my complaints and excuses, agreed that they were valid, and then said "OK then! Let's get to the walking" and they have not let up yet. I would have hidden from them because facing the truth about my weakness and forcing myself to be responsible to myself, my family, and my journey is not what I was looking for. Comfort, sympathy, and macaroni & cheese is what was I was looking for . . . self indulgence in short. What I needed though was some good support, motivation, and a swift kick in the shorts, which is exactly what they provided.

People surprised him. People were nice. A fruit vendor gave him an orange. A couple offered him a bed and shower. A woman asked him to help her. Her mother was morbidly obese. She was dying. What could the woman do?

People were depending on him. People were helping him. He was losing weight. He was calming down (when he came upon another rattlesnake in New Mexico, he didn't shoot it). He should have been happy. Even the Frankenstein monster had moments of bliss, stretches of solidarity, uninterrupted, contented grunting.

But reporters kept calling. Bagley and Mollering wanted to spend more and more time with him. Before he arrived in Albuquerque, HarperCollins informed Vaught that he would be working with a ghostwriter and that the ghostwriter would need access. The ghostwriter called, and he demanded more access. The ghostwriter told Vaught what his journey meant. Vaught thought he already knew what his journey meant.

Was Vaught miserable because people were hounding him, or was it because he was afraid of failing, or was this the garden-variety despair of a man with too many miles to go, too many promises to keep? Or was it that, no matter how far he walked, he couldn't escape his childhood? Or was he just constitutionally predisposed to misery and self-destructive behavior, if not an ogre with bolts in his head, then at least a world-class head case? He wasn't sure. He needed to be sure. But how could he be sure of anything with antidepressants clouding his thinking? He decided that was the problem.

He needed to do something bold. Something drastic.

"Why does a four-hundred-pound guy not just go to the gym, not just eat right?" asks Bagley. "Why does he think he has to walk all the way across the country? He's not great at making life decisions."

In Amarillo he threw his antidepressants down a storm drain. Then he filled the empty bottle with Skittles. When Bagley or Mollering asked if he was still taking his pills — they worried about him — he would shake the Skittle-filled bottle and smile.

Over the next few weeks, through the Texas Panhandle, he would lock himself in his hotel room for days at a time. He would refuse to talk to anyone. He would cry. Once he threatened

Bagley's teenage son, who was working as a cameraman for the documentary filmmakers. Once he threw his phone against a hotel wall. Things didn't improve in Oklahoma. He was laid up while he waited to pass a kidney stone. He suffered three cases of poison oak.

By the end of August, he had been written about in the *New York Times* and the *Washington Post*, featured in Italy's *Gazzetta del Prione* and Germany's *Stern*, interviewed twice on the *Today Show*. And Oprah's people called. Then they sent a crew to meet Vaught in Weatherford, Oklahoma. She asked him about his diet and exercise and how he was losing weight.

"Oprah was like, 'Call me, it's a weight-loss story,'" says Bagley. "It's not a weight-loss story! He hasn't lost that much weight. I'm not sure what it is . . . but it's not a weight-loss story."

Was it a quest for clarity? If so, Vaught found it in Elk City, Oklahoma. "It was a day of awakening," he says. "I know it sounds corny, but one day I woke up and a lot of the nonsense seems to have evaporated. A lot of the noise inside me was gone. The sky was pretty, the people were nice. It seemed like the whole world had lightened up. I just felt like something had changed."

How? The isolation, for one. The hiking. And being drug free. "I don't say that medicine is bad for everybody who uses it," he says. "I know some people need it. But for me, it dumbed me up, I felt like I couldn't function on it."

The discomfiting thing about heightened awareness is you start noticing things that never made you miserable before. Even though he weighed less than 340 pounds now, and even though he had reduced his pack weight from eighty-five to fifty-five pounds (by getting rid of clothes and using lighter equipment, mostly), it was still a lot to carry. He had been talking to representatives from GoLite almost since the trip began, and they had been imploring him to reduce his load. "If you want to be an idiot," an employee had told him, "go ahead and keep on with what you've got."

In Oklahoma a GoLite employee named Kevin Volt flew out and met him. He spread out a tarp and placed all of Vaught's belongings on it. He looked at his two-pound first-aid kid. "Are you going to operate?" Volt asked. "Are you going to do surgery?" He replaced it with some antiseptic and Band-Aids in a Ziploc bag. He sneered at Vaught's three cannisters of cooking fuel. "Inviting people over for a barbecue, are you?" He threw two of the canisters in his rental car. The electric tent fan ("absolutely essential in the desert," according to Vaught)? Gone. Volt convinced Vaught to replace his three flashlights with one microflashlight, to replace his five-pound bag with one weighing one pound, his four-and-a-half-pound tent with a one-pounder, to get rid of his liner. Vaught also left his tape recorder and digital camera behind, because, as Volt pointed out, his video camera made them redundant. "He said," Vaught remembers, "'You gotta be smart out there. Everything should do two things or more. If something does only one thing, you should think about whether you need it.'"

Vaught had three sets of clothes. "Are you going to parties?" Volt asked. He had multiple notebooks for writing. "If you want to write stuff," Volt said, "buy notebooks on the way." When he left Oklahoma City, his pack weighed sixteen pounds. He kept his five-pound laptop computer. He got rid of the pistol.

By the time he left Oklahoma, at the beginning of November, he was down to 330 pounds. He got to 325, then 320. By the time he got to St. Louis at the end of 2005, he was down to 318, but he had been there for weeks. He could not break 318. And then he talked to April on the phone and she said she wanted a divorce. (Neither Vaught nor April will go in to detail about the divorce. But Vaught says both he and his wife are committed to being friends and good parents.)

His weight started to climb again. He tried sit-ups. He tried high-protein diets. He heard from eighteen personal trainers, scores of anonymous e-mailers (whose advice ranged from "Why are you eating a chicken fried steak, you fat pig?" to even more hostile stuff), and a host of self-professed experts. "One person said, 'You should eat nothing but egg whites.' Another guy kept sending me e-mails about diet. He's got a chemical equation. It would drive Einstein crazy. A lot of people say, 'Why don't you just start eating less and exercising more?' I say, 'Goddamnit, why don't you have your own fucking show, instead of Oprah?'"

Only one person made sense. His name was Eric Fleishman, though he's better known as Eric the Trainer. Fleishman is a Los Angeles–based trainer who, presumably like more than a few Los Angeles–based trainers, has a Web site and a vision that goes far beyond good cardiovascular health. One of his workout regimens is called the "Sleeping Giant." Another is called the "Sleeping Beauty." He offers, according to his Web site, "programs [that] provide a holistic approach to fitness that incorporates gender specific exercises, eastern philosophy, and diet to achieve a perfect version of you."

"Sign Up," he encourages visitors to his Web site. "Call in. Get Fit. Be Beautiful."

Like Vaught, Fleishman is a talker. Like Vaught, Fleishman likes to talk about happiness and the state of the world.

They talked on the phone about loneliness and despair, about exercise and eating, about running away from trouble and the search for self.

"He's a very quirky guy," Vaught says, "but a very genuine guy, concerned about mental and spiritual health."

Fleishman drove out to a truck stop in California, and walked around, trying to discover the dietary reality in which Vaught lived. He flew out to meet Vaught in Dayton, Ohio, and they talked some more. "And an hour later," Fleishman says, "I said, 'You're a great guy and a wonderful person and I respect the journey that you're on, but it's a much more complex situation both physically and emotionally than I'd anticipated.'"

To Fleishman's surprise, Vaught suggested returning to California to work together for a few weeks.

So eleven months into a trip that was supposed to be completed in six months, Vaught flew to Los Angeles. He spent twenty-one days in a hotel down the block from Fleishman's gym. Every day he would lift weights for an hour and do martial arts for an hour and walk backward for an hour. He accompanied Fleishman to local schools, where he talked about motivation. He talked about determination and how, even when you were feeling helpless and scared, you kept going. Is it any wonder that children loved the Fat Man?

He flew back to Dayton, started walking again on March 3. He weighed 282 pounds.

Some days he made it fifteen miles. On those days, likely as not, he'd walk into a restaurant and order a stromboli. Some days he stayed in town. He might have stromboli then, too. He started gaining weight. He got back to 300 quickly, then to 305, then to 310. He consulted with a doctor in Florida who suggested a diet of 70 percent protein, and he started losing again. He got down to 285, became obsessed with the idea of weighing 260 upon his arrival in New York City. That would represent a loss of 150 pounds. That would mean he was a success. How to do it, though? "I thought, if seventy percent protein is good, then eighty percent is even better. And ninety percent is better than that." Just over the Pennsylvania border, he developed another kidney stone (he would suffer two more cases of poison oak in the state as well). He called the doctor, who calmly explained the insanity of his dietary plan. And he started creeping back up up again in weight. To 290, to 295, to 300.

"One television producer calls and says, 'You've walked two-thirds of the way across America and you're still fat? Have you considered surgery?' Another one said, 'The story is a little too murky now.'"

Didn't they realize? The story had always been murky. But the saga of the Fat Man . . . the mythology of the Fat Man . . . there was nothing murky about that. Tragic, maybe, but ultimately redemptive. Not murky. That's what the public wanted. That's what the television producers wanted. That's certainly what the publisher wanted. Didn't they realize? He wanted it more than anyone.

The ghostwriter was calling regularly now. He had already written what he called the "backbone" of the book, sent it to Vaught. "Fill in the rest" is what Vaught says he was told. In the "backbone" Vaught breaks down sobbing eleven times in the first chapter, exclaims at one point, "Hey, I'm a big fat loser."

Vaught was not happy about that.

"You know," he says, "a guy who walks across the country is not a big fat loser."

Other long-distance hikers pay attention to landscape, to soft dawns, to the way the birds sound at dusk. Vaught spent much of his journey next to highways, listening to diesel trucks. At night he stayed in motels, plugged in his laptop, and worked miserably on the backbone of his book.

Now Vaught and his ghostwriter were arguing about tone, about structure, about almost everything.

It's doubtful that any ghostwriter would have an entirely easy time with someone as simultaneously driven and lost as Vaught. It's also a safe bet that no one but Vaught would proclaim to a visitor, "It's bad if you have a ghostwriter and you've said to him on more than one occasion, 'You're lucky you're not within choking distance.'"

He was rarely camping out now. He could afford motels. Plus, he had to keep in touch with the ghostwriter, and he had to work on the revisions, and there were endorsement deals to consider.

A shampoo manufacturer offered him fifty thousand dollars if he would hold up a bottle of their product every time he was interviewed on television. He declined. A company offered a phone, computer, and RV if he agreed to sing the praises of their wheatgrass, and "it sounded pretty good," but the company wanted to take over thefatmanwalking.com Web site, and he refused. A company that marketed patches to help people quit smoking asked him to wear its product. "But I had never smoked. The guy says, 'You don't have to say you smoked, you don't have to lie, just that you're wearing a patch, people will assume that's why you don't smoke.'" He turned them down. "Another company wanted me to sponsor their glucosamine product. Same kind of deal — I can't make it across the country without my blah blah. But I don't think you need supplements. So that was no deal."

Some vitamin company people made an offer, too. They would market "thefatmanwalking" vitamins. He said that sounded OK. And they wanted to sell "thefatmanwalking" cholesterol-reduction pills, too. He, oddly enough, had never had a problem with cholesterol levels, but OK, that was fine, too. High cholesterol was something a lot of people needed help with. And they would sell "thefatmanwalking" diet pills, too. That was a deal breaker. "I'm not going to accept ads that are exploitative of people who are overweight," he says. "They wanted me to prostitute myself."

"I had started to realize there were a lot of people getting a lot of inspiration from what I was doing, and I didn't want to jeopardize that." It's easy to mock a man who makes a grab for the moral high ground just after he admits how delicious it would be to throttle someone. But what would you do if someone offered you hundreds of thousands of dollars to expose your most terrible secrets, then hired someone else to make them prettier? And how many men would turn down endorsement deals worth millions?

It's doubtful he was ever a jolly fat man. By mid-April he is weary, eager for the trip to be over. He needs to hurry now. He is in rural Pennsylvania, almost four hundred miles from New York City, and, if he doesn't make it across the George Washington Bridge by May 15, HarperCollins might cancel the book.

"The first half of the trip was much better than the second half," he says. "Sometimes I think I should have turned around at the Mississippi River and just walked back. Since St. Louis I've had no time to walk around and meet people. I've been dealing with the fucking book. I'm on chapter nine now, and I still have four more chapters to go. A long time ago, this walk stopped being about weight loss and personal redemption. It's about business now."

He just passed his third kidney stone a week ago. He is in the midst of his fourth case of poison oak. He's worn fifteen pairs of shoes, lost four toenails, and suffered twenty blisters "before I got smart about it." It is pouring outside, so he's taking the day off. Maybe he'd be taking the day off anyway. He is back up to 310 pounds. He is seated at a Denny's off the highway in Bedford, Pennsylvania. He orders the pepperjack omelet, with no pancakes, and he eats it in front of a reporter, which is a very big deal to Vaught because he still doesn't like people to watch him eat.

"We need to medicate ourselves against the hollowness and pain," he says. "We think we can buy happiness, buy a cure or relief of our symptoms, but we can't. This has become crystal clear to me . . . the solitude of this walk has made this clear to me."

He has dark brown hair and bottle-green eyes. He flirts with waitresses, complains about being a prisoner of the people who love the Fat Man but don't know Steve Vaught.

He doesn't say much at first, but once he gets going he says a lot. He quotes from *Extraordinary Popular Delusions and the Madness of Crowds*, *The Three Pillars of Zen*, *The Best Buddhist Writing*

2005, Healing Anger, by the Dali Lama ("that was a big thing for me"), and references the *Girls Gone Wild* collection; he ponders the ubiquity of the Internet and the meaning of Taoism and proclaims that "the inevitably of life is failure." His is the trippy wisdom familiar to anyone who has spent more than a couple of days in the backcountry, or the desert, or even a weekend alone shuttling between a Motel 6 and Denny's, cut loose from the moorings of things like jobs and deadlines and family and friends.

The thing about such trippy wisdom is this: it might be trippy, but it's wise.

"Stop looking for the pill or the miracle cure," the Fat Man says. "You know what's going to cure me? Sausage and eggs.

"I tell people, 'You gotta stop watching TV, you gotta unplug.' The news would have you believe you walk out your door, there are gunfights and mayhem. But people are awesome. I've met some angry people, but no evil people. With the exception of a couple weird things here and there, it's been great.

"You can live in the past, you can live in the future, or you can live right now . . . this is your only true reality . . . tomorrow will happen . . ."

It's easy to smile indulgently at the philosophical musings of a man who left his job and family to find himself, at the proclamations of a guy who rails against the evils of consumerism while being defeated by chicken fried steaks and plates of stromboli. But can you imagine killing two people, gaining 160 pounds, losing 105, walking twenty-nine hundred miles?

On May 9 he walks across the George Washington Bridge, and the next day he appears for his third and probably final interview on the *Today Show*. He weighs 305 pounds, but he knows it's just a number. Soon the book will be out. After that? He's not sure. He might teach. Oprah might finally air his interview, might even have him in the studio. He might walk across England with Eric the Trainer. Fat Man Walking and Eric the Trainer together. That's a thought.

He will be forty-one on August 1. "My plans for the future? Attachment is one of the biggest problems we have as human beings. The stronger you hold something, the more attached you get. Consumerism is just destroying people. They worry about the future, they worry about the past. My only responsibility in life is to take care of my children. That's not a big deal. You feed them, you love them, you guide them. College funds and things like that? Worrying about that stuff doesn't make it happen."

Before he got held up by the rain and poison oak in Bedford, Pennsylvania, he received an e-mail from a girl named Kristin in Sioux Falls, South Dakota. She wanted to tell Vaught that on Easter Sunday her pastor had mentioned him in his sermon. "It was inspirational," she wrote.

"I get tons of those," he says. "I almost feel guilty for getting them."

Can you imagine what it's like to be famous for your girth, soon to be divorced, technically unemployed, to wonder what's coming next? Can you imagine the most successful thing you've ever done, or are likely to do, about to end? Can you imagine what it's like to be an inspiration to people you've never met, a disappointment to yourself?

It's easy to think Steve Vaught is different, that his story is singular. It's comforting to behold his awesome bulk and to decide that his torment and confusion and even his murky triumphs belong to a creature unlike the rest of us. But to do so is to miss what's most important about Vaught's struggle.

He's not a savior. Not a monster, nor a monstrous inventor. Those are myths. He's just a fat guy trying to lose weight. He's just a self-taught, hyper-articulate, sometimes very cranky person trying to navigate the distance between where he is and where he wants to be. When it comes to that never-ending, utterly human journey, we could do much, much worse than to heed the wisdom of the Fat Man.

"As far as worrying about next year," he says, "I think about it, sure. I don't want to say, next year I want to be a writer, next year I want to be this, or that. You set yourself up for failure. No matter what happens next year, I'm going to make it the best possible moment . . . because that's where I'm living, in my moment. You're going to have good and you're going to have bad . . . and they're both equally as important. Wherever the road takes me, that's where I'll go."

12

A MOMENT OF SILENCE:
JOHN MOYLAN, RUNNER

HE WILL WAKE AT 4:00 A.M., AS HE DOES EVERY WEEKDAY EX-
cept Monday. He'll wear shorts and a T-shirt, even in
the rain, unless it's winter, when he might pull on a
Gore-Tex jacket and pants. When it snows and the snow is heavy
enough, he'll stretch thin rubber sandals with metal spikes over
his running shoes. He'll grab a small canister of pepper spray.
Three seasons out of the year, he'll lace up one of his six pairs of
"active" size-thirteen Sauconys that he keeps in a closet underneath his hundred hanging T-shirts, and in the winter he'll wear
one of his half-dozen pairs of active Nikes from the same closet,
because the layer of air in them doesn't seem to compress in cold
weather as much as the foam in the Sauconys. He'll be out his
front door at 4:15, back inside at 5:05. Then he'll shower, eat a
bowl of instant oatmeal, make himself a lunch of a peanut-
butter-and-jelly sandwich or pack a cup of yogurt, and leave his
house in Warwick, New York, at 6:10 to drive to the train station
in Harriman for the 6:42 train to Hoboken, New Jersey. The trip
will take a little over an hour, and in Hoboken he'll board a 7:55
underground train bound for Manhattan. Once there he'll walk
fifteen minutes to his office at an insurance company at Madison
Avenue and Thirty-sixth Street.

John Moylan is a man of habit and routine and caution, and

for much of his life attention to detail has served him well. Some mornings, when he's feeling adventurous or wild, he'll make a little extra noise between 4:00 and 4:15 A.M., just to see if his wife of thirty years, Holly, will wake up. She hasn't yet.

His running route starts outside his front door and it hasn't varied for six years, since he and Holly and their two daughters moved from Crystal Lake, Illinois, when his then-employer, Kemper Insurance, transferred him to New York City. Down Kings Highway, through the small village, up a small hill, and, by the time he passes the Mobil gasoline station at the end of the first mile, he'll know if the run will be easy or hard, and if it's hard, he'll remind himself to eat healthier that day, to make sure to get to sleep by 9:00 P.M. At one and a half miles he might pass a gaggle of geese that like to waddle near the black granite memorial to the seven people from Warwick who died on September 11, 2001. He'll run past one dairy farm and its herd of cows, and he'll make mooing sounds and wonder why they never moo back. Later he'll pass another dairy farm and moo at those cows, who always moo back. One of life's mysteries. He'll run past what's really no more than a giant puddle next to the road that he thinks of as the turtle pond because he once saw a turtle waddling across the concrete toward the water. He'll run four to five miles, ten or twelve on Saturday, and on Sunday anywhere from ten to sixteen. Mondays he rests.

Moylan is by nature conservative, by profession cautious. He has been in the insurance business for thirty-three years and has spent much of his life calculating risk, calibrating the costs of bad planning and devastating whim. Men who worry about the future can guard against the worst sorts of accidents. Men who look ahead can avoid life's greatest dangers. Even when running, even during the time of his life that is devoted to release and escape from daily tallies and concerns, he can't quite escape the principles that have guided him for so long.

"What do I think about?" he says. "God, just about every-thing. Am I on target for my marathon goal? How am I going to pay my daughters' college tuition? Do I have good retirement plans?"

Some days — one of life's mysteries — he thinks of that terrible morning five years ago.

He and one of his coworkers, Jill Steidel, had just arrived at their office on the thirty-sixth floor of the north tower of the World Trade Center in downtown Manhattan. They were carrying coffee they had picked up from the Starbucks in the building's atrium. He had his usual — a grande-size cup of the breakfast blend, black. It was 8:46 A.M., and Moylan was standing at his window looking west, gazing at the ferries on the Hudson River. It was one of his great pleasures, what he called "one of the simple things in life." That's when he felt the building shake and heard a loud *thwaaang*. He had heard longtime employees talk about the 1993 bombing in the building's parking garage, and now he thought the building might be collapsing as a result of residual structural damage. Then he heard screaming. He was one of the fire marshals on his floor, so he rounded up his employees — there were about twenty-five of them — and herded them to the stairs. As a longtime runner, he checked his watch as the group entered the stairwell. It was 8:48 A.M.

The stairwell was packed but orderly. He remembers two "nice, neat rows" of people, scared but polite. He remembers many breathing hard and sweating, wide-eyed. He remembers thinking that his experience as a runner helped him stay calm. "What was it?" someone asked. "It wasn't a bomb," someone else said.

The people in front of his group would sometimes stop suddenly, which made his group stop. That didn't make sense. Neither did the smell. Moylan had been in the air force as a young man, and it was a familiar odor. I thought, "What the hell is jet fuel doing here?"

It took twenty-eight minutes to get to the ground floor. Moylan left the building at 9:16 A.M. He turned to his right and looked east just as two bodies hit the ground. He saw other bodies on the ground, realized that's why fire fighters had kept people from exiting the doors in a constant flow. He saw greasy puddles of blazing jet fuel, huge chunks of twisted metal. He saw more bodies falling. (It's estimated that of the more than twenty-five hundred people who died in the twin towers, two hundred had jumped.) He and the others were marshaled to the overpass that stretched over the Westside Highway and to the marina next to the Hudson River. At the marina he looked back. People on the higher floors were waving pieces of clothing and curtains from the windows. There were helicopters — he thought there were eight or ten — circling. He could see that the helicopters couldn't get through the fire and smoke, and he knew that the people in the windows could see it, too. He was used to synthesizing facts quickly, and it didn't take long to comprehend the horrible calculus confronting the people in the windows: be burned alive or jump. He wondered what he would have done.

Thousands of people were on the marina. Some stared upward. Others walked north, toward Midtown. The Kemper employees for whom Moylan was responsible had all gotten out safely; now Moylan needed to get home. The subway was shut down, as was the underground train to New Jersey, so he boarded a ferry to Hoboken. When he got to Hoboken at 9:59, he looked back, and, as he did so, the south tower, which had been hit at 9:02 A.M., crumbled. The north tower, his tower, would fall at 10:28 A.M.

In Hoboken he boarded a train for home, but first he tried to call Holly and his daughters, Meredith and Erin. He had left his cell phone in his office, so he borrowed one, but it wasn't working. Neither, he remembers, were the landlines.

He remembers the hour-long train ride to Harriman, and from there the drive to Warwick. He remembers with absolute clarity walking through his door at 4:00 P.M., covered in soot, smelling of fire and death. Five years later, the memory still troubles him.

"The home office had called looking for me, which just scared my wife even more. My suit was ruined. I was reeking. I scared the living daylights out of them. My daughters especially were emotionally ruined, or disturbed. . . . When your family thinks you're dead and you walk in your house and surprise them . . ."

He stayed up all night watching television. In the morning he knew what he had to do. He rose from the bed where he had failed to sleep. "I wanted desperately to go out running," he says. He gathered his running gear and dressed. He looked at his running shoes. He couldn't put them on.

Moylan knows better than most men how accidents can shape a life. He had been working in the East Norwich, Long Island, post office in the summer of 1970 when he learned he had drawn the eleventh spot in one of this country's last drafts. He had always thought how neat it would be to fly planes, so he enrolled in the U.S. Air Force. And that's how he got to Iceland. There he was, in the summer of 1971, a cop's son from East Norwich, playing softball at midnight, soaking afterward in thermal hot springs, gorging on fresh salmon, drinking beer with pretty girls who spoke another language. Forget planning. He couldn't have dreamed that summer — "one of the best years of my life." Pure chance. Then another one of life's mysteries. Late one night in April 1972, there was a knock on his barrack's door. It was the chaplain. Moylan's father had died; he was only forty-six. After the funeral, Moylan asked his mother how she was going to hold on to the house. She told him not to worry, but he pressed. Did she need his help?

The air force gave him an honorable hardship discharge, and he went back to the post office, and he might still be there if his mother hadn't insisted that he go talk to one of the leaders of the church she attended. He was an insurance executive, and he was always looking for bright young men.

So in 1973 Moylan became a company man, a trainee for Crum & Forster, a salaried student of chance and fate. Every morning he waited for the 7:00 A.M. Manhattan-bound train from the station in Syosset, Long Island, and every morning he stood in the same spot and walked through the same door and sat in the same seat. And every afternoon he did the same thing at Pennsylvania Station, when the 5:06 eastbound train pulled in. Then, one afternoon, the train stopped twenty feet short of its usual spot and people pushed and shoved and Moylan's seat was taken and he had no choice, there was only one empty seat left. He found himself sitting next to a pretty brunette dress designer from Huntington. Her name was Holly.

Accidents happen, and it's one of life's mysteries the effect they'll have, and all you can do is try to control what's controllable. And that's how a young, married company man started running. It was 1979, and Moylan had gone from a lean, 180-pound military man to a 220-pound twenty-eight-year-old pudgy, listless suit. He needed to do something. He had read an article about Bill Rodgers, and the New York City Marathon, and he decided that running sounded like fun.

Moylan is not a man to make a big deal out of things, and he doesn't make a big deal about that decision. But two years later, in the spring of 1981, he ran the Long Island Marathon. He ran it in just under four hours. In the fall, he ran the New York City Marathon and did even better, finishing in 3:51.

He cut out junk food, started eating lean meats. He woke early, ran before the sun rose. He experimented with equipment and distance and learned "to not let my mind get in front of my body. I learned that patience is a virtue."

He wore his running shoes when he walked from the train to his office building, and he wore them when he took his midday forty-five-minute walks around Manhattan. He always worried that people thought he looked funny. By 2001, by the time he was fifty, he had run fourteen marathons, many half-marathons, countless 10Ks and 5Ks. Running helped him reduce his blood pressure from 120/90 to 110/60, helped him reduce his weight from 220 pounds to anywhere from 180 to 195, depending on where he was in his training cycle. His resting pulse is fifty now, and when he gives blood Red Cross officials routinely question him to make sure he's not a fainter. Running helped him cope when his mother died in 1985 at age fifty-nine, with the birth of his daughters in 1982 and 1985, with the demands of being a middle-aged father and husband and provider and company man. He ran because he didn't want to die young, as his parents had, and because it relaxed him and was part of his life. Accidents would happen, and there were some things a man couldn't do anything about, terrible things. But with discipline and attention and will, a man could carve out a safe place, a part of life that was predictable, calming in its sameness. Half an hour or so in the early morning stillness could help a man deal with almost anything.

It was Tuesday five years ago, the week after Labor Day, and warm for that time of year in that part of the country. A morning like this was rare and precious. It would be a good run. It felt like it would be a good day. At the Mobil station, Moylan picked up his pace.

He ran past the cows and the geese and the turtle pond. He thought about his retirement fund, even though he had many years to go before needing it. He worried about his daughters' college tuition, even though he had been saving for years. He wondered if he would run as swiftly as he wanted to in the New York City Marathon, even though it was still two months away. He was back at home at 5:05 A.M., and he showered and had his instant oatmeal and caught his train and met Jill Steidel at Starbucks, and they rode the elevator up to the thirty-sixth floor, and, less than a minute later, he felt the building shake. And the next day he couldn't get his running shoes on. He couldn't put them on the next day, either. He woke at four each day, got out of bed, thought about running, got his shoes out of the closet, then put them back. Then he would sit on the couch and watch television and his mind would drift. He thought about a framed photograph he had left on his office desk. Holly had taken it, and it showed Moylan and Meredith and Erin at a Yankees game in July. It was cap day, and they were all wearing Yankees caps. He doubted he could ever find the negative. Then he thought about all the people who didn't get to say good-bye to their families.

Friday, September 14, was his twenty-sixth wedding anniversary, and on that morning he got dressed and he laced up his Sauconys, and he opened up his front door. He looked outside into the darkness. Then he closed the door and went back inside.

It is late spring, nearly five years later, and he is looking at the space where the World Trade Center once stood. It is the first time he has been back here. He says he's surprised that the footprints of the two towers aren't more clearly marked. He's disappointed that the twisted cross of metal that became the focus of so many Christians is no longer on the site.

He gazes into the sky. "When I came out," he says, "it was on this level. I had a view — right in this area, the bodies were already falling. I could look up and see the people hanging out the windows. The news footage, you just saw smoke. From down here, it was like looking up from the bottom of a grill. I remember seeing how ungodly hot it was — there was an orange glow."

Moylan is a handsome man, square-jawed, grey-haired, hazel-eyed. He is six feet tall, a solid 190 pounds, on his way, he says, back to 180. He wears a blue suit and a pin of the Twin Towers and an American flag, and he looks like a soap-opera actor or the air force pilot he might have been. If this were a different place, he might appear to be just a tourist searching the New York City skyline for wonders.

He turns from the ghost buildings and looks toward the bank of the river, at the benches where he used to unpack his peanut-butter-and-jelly sandwiches or his yogurt cup. "This place was my luxury suite for lunch in the summertime. . . . I used to come out here on the bench and just dream."

In the weeks after the attack, Moylan studied a *New York Times* article about the sequence of events and realized that had he taken two or three minutes longer to get his coffee with Steidel at Starbucks, he still would have been in the elevator on the way to his office when the plane hit, and he wouldn't have survived.

Moylan turns back east, away from the water. Reflection can be healing, but he has work to do. He needs to get back to his office, five miles north, in Midtown. "The funny sense that I get being here," he says, "is life goes on. It's continuing."

It is early spring, dusk in Orange County, New York, and Moylan and Holly and their oldest daughter, Meredith, are driving the back roads of Warwick. Holly points out a place where George Washington slept. Meredith points out a dairy farm and creamery. We drive through the gaggle of geese and past the granite memorial to the people from Warwick who died on 9/11.

At dinner we talk about past races, about what running

meant to Moylan before 9/11. Meredith talks about watching her father finish one marathon on an ocean boardwalk, yelling, "That's my Daddy and he loves me," and years later joining him in center field of San Francisco's Candlestick Park for the end of a 5K run. Holly and Meredith talk about how they enjoy staying up watching *The Gilmore Girls* and chatting when John goes to sleep. Holly wonders aloud why her husband — or any man — needs a hundred T-shirts, and Moylan speaks mournfully of the "boxes and boxes" of his T-shirts she donated to charity.

I ask Holly and Meredith how long it took for them to get over the shock of seeing Moylan walk in the door, how they dealt with the hours of uncertainty.

"I wasn't uncertain," Holly says. "When we were watching the coverage on television, I told Meredith, 'Dad will be fine. He's a runner and he'll run right out of there. Besides, he called us from Hoboken, before he got on the train.'"

Moylan blinks, shakes his head.

"No, I didn't call you. I didn't have my phone."

"You definitely called us," Holly says. "You borrowed a phone and called us to let us know you were coming home."

Moylan blinks again. "I don't remember that," he says.

"Yeah, Dad," Meredith says, "you called from Hoboken. To let us know you were all right."

Harold Kudler, M.D., is an associate clinical professor of psychiatry at Duke University and a nationally recognized expert on post-traumatic stress disorder (PTSD). He hears part of John Moylan's post 9/11 story and says, "It's quite common for people in the middle of an acute stress response to have disassociative phenomena."

To Dr. Kudler, Moylan's elaborate memory of his family being traumatized as a result of not hearing from him makes psychological sense. "Sometimes," Dr. Kudler says, "the effort to create meaning and to create a meaningful narrative about what has happened to you actually becomes more important than the actual memory and might replace it. This story about coming home as a ghost and having everyone else scared might be a way to say, 'Boy, was I scared. I felt like a ghost in my own life. I wasn't even sure when I got home if I had survived that.'"

Moylan's responses during and after the attacks — his vivid recollection of details, his construction of false memories, his nightmares, his long avoidance of the WTC site, his difficulty running afterward — are entirely consistent with symptoms exhibited by people facing extreme trauma, even the most resilient people, according to Dr. Kudler.

"There's a tendency to medicalize or pathologize responses," Dr. Kudler says. "It might be better to think that here's someone who is faced with a new challenge that's so radically different than the one he faced a few days earlier.

"Think of it like mourning. When you're bereaved, you wouldn't be able to invest in yourself, because you'd feel overwhelmed, and you'd sort of lose your center. For a while you wouldn't be able to do the things that reminded you of who you were, of the thing you did for yourself."

And Moylan's inability to go for his normal run? "Running for him was something he did for himself, was important to him, and he made a point of always doing this regardless of anything else. Great exercise, recreational, self-affirming. But in the context of the disaster, when people are overwhelmed and filled with doubt, it's easy to see why someone wouldn't do those self-affirming things.

"And if he was angry, that anger may have drowned out his capacity to enjoy a simple pleasure like running, and take that simple time for himself. That anger could have drowned out a lot of those normal, good impulses."

When I tell Moylan what Dr. Kudler said, he is silent for a few seconds.

"He nailed me," he says.

He would wake in the middle of the night certain that his house was under attack. He would dream that he was trapped in a tower and flames were licking at him. He would dream of having to make a terrible choice but not knowing what to do. He would dream of dying, "that I went through what those people went through." Noises startled him. "He was restless and jumpy and things would frighten him," Holly says. "If we were out somewhere and a child cried out, he'd jump, he'd be scared."

During the day he thought of the people who had died. "I couldn't rationalize what had happened. People in the normal course of living, going to work, murdered. I thought about how they never got to say good-bye to anyone. I thought about my family, and about facing a decision to burn to death or to jump."

Every morning in the weeks after 9/11, he would get up and he would plan to run. But he never made it outside. He would make coffee, and sit on the couch, and sometimes watch television, and have his oatmeal, and when it was time to take his shower and catch his train, that's what he would do.

He couldn't stop thinking about chance and fate, and wondering why he had survived.

At his company's insistence, he had two conversations with Red Cross officials, once in a group, once alone. He talked about how angry he was that there had been an attack. He talked about how angry he was that he had survived while others had died. He talked about how angry he was that he couldn't run. "And that about covers it," he says. He reported for work on September 13 in Kemper's New Jersey office. The company assured Moylan and his coworkers that they would be reassigned to a building in

Midtown Manhattan, on a lower floor. The morning they reported for work there, on the tenth floor of Rockefeller Center, was the day authorities discovered an envelope filled with anthrax addressed to Tom Brokaw in the same building. Some of the Kemper employees left and never came back. Moylan stayed.

The nightmares continued. He kept jumping at the slightest noise. But Holly didn't say anything. "We had talked about counseling," she says, "and he just said, 'Let me see how things go.'" He knew that running would help him get over all his problems. So he got up every day ready to run. But he couldn't do it.

Then one day, he could. Just like that. One of life's mysteries.

There were no grand pronouncements before he went to bed the night before, no stirring speeches at dinner. He was still angry. He was still scared. He still thought about the falling bodies. But on Columbus Day, almost exactly a month after the attack, he managed to get his shoes on and to get out the door. He made it four miles, and every step was difficult. His legs were heavy. He had trouble breathing. But he made it.

His first race was a half-marathon in Pennsylvania the next April. It was a clear day, warm, "almost like September eleven," he says. "I remember that for the first time in a long time, I smelled grass, could smell flowers."

A few months later, in October, at a half-marathon not far from his home, he happened to overhear one of the runners mention that he was a firefighter. Moylan approached him. "He said he wasn't there, but he knew people who were. I told him I was in tower one. We both had similar feelings . . . about losing people. It was the first time I had verification that I wasn't the only person who felt like I did."

He ran the New York City Marathon in 2002 and 2003. He ran more marathons, more half-marathons. The nightmares faded away, as did his preoccupation with death and the randomness of fate. (He still jumps at the slightest noise, something he never did before 9/11.) Three years ago, Todd Jennings, who lived near Moylan and who had just started running, spotted Moylan on the train "in his gray flannel suit and running shoes." Eventually they started talking. About training regimens, and race strategy, and running in general. "No," Jennings says, "we never talked about nine-eleven."

There are things you can't control, no matter how much you worry and plan. Terrible things happen, and there's nothing you can do to stop them. Those are lessons that will change a man. For better or for worse.

Moylan left Kemper Insurance in 2002, after eighteen years, to go to work for Greater New York Insurance. He doesn't worry about what others think about his blue-suit-white-running-shoes combination in Midtown anymore. He ran a 3:22 marathon in 1982 and a 4:50 marathon in 2003, and he still wants to get back to a four-hour time, "but I don't worry so much about time anymore." He is training for this fall's New York City Marathon. He still thinks about retirement and paying for his daughters' education, but it doesn't eat at him quite as much as it used to. He still calculates risk and calibrates the likelihood of disaster and does his best to protect himself and his family, but he knows there are some things beyond a man's control, and to worry about them is to waste precious energy.

When he finds himself irritated or impatient, he thinks of a terrible choice he never had to make, and he is grateful. Every morning as he steps out his door, he is grateful.

"I told my wife I should have a new birthday," Moylan says. "My new life started on nine-eleven. The fact that I survived is a gift. I know quite a few people who didn't. I made a promise to myself. I was going to live differently." He tries not to dwell on the past, or to look too very far into the future. But he has made one promise to himself. "Yeah, I'm going to go back to Iceland sometime. That's a plan now."

Weekends he treats himself. Friday and Saturday nights he soaks a pot of steel-cut oats in water so he can have homemade oatmeal after his runs. He sleeps till 5:30, has a cup of coffee, "my luxury," and dawdles for a full hour before he heads out the door. September 11 falls on a Monday this year, so he won't run. But the day before, he'll step out of his front door just as the sun rises above Warwick. He'll pass the Mobil station and the silent cows and the mooing cows, but that day he'll go at least fifteen miles, so there will be other sights, too. He'll run by the VFW hall where the old men always wave and the fire station in town where the guys always have a nice word to say. He might see a deer, or a porcupine, or even a bear. At mile seven he'll run by a house where a snarling Rottweiler is tied to a tree, and he'll grip his pepper spray a little more tightly.

Just past that house, Moylan will ascend a gentle hill, heading east, and no matter how hard the run, no matter how he slept the night before or how he's feeling, as he crests the little hill, he'll slow down. It's his favorite spot on the weekend run — his favorite spot of any of his runs. It's just a little hummock, but, when a man reaches it, he can turn to the right and look south, and he can see an entire valley stretching before him and, beyond that valley, forests and hills all the way to the horizon. He will still have another seven miles to go, and then his homemade oatmeal, with the apples and bananas and raisins and cinnamon he allows himself on weekends. Then on Monday he'll think again about the day that changed his life, and on the day after that he'll catch the 6:42 train to Hoboken, and on the day after that he'll do it again. Or not. Who can really predict what will happen to a man, even a careful man, a man who takes precautions? That's another of life's mysteries.

Moylan will allow himself to walk a little bit on Sunday at the top of the gentle rise, to linger, to look at the valley and the forests and the looming hills beyond. He loves this spot.

"It's a nice place to get perspective," he says.

13

G-D IN HIS CORNER:
DMITRIY SALITA, BOXER

THE CONTENDER IS IN TROUBLE.

"No!" his trainer shouts. "No! Don't punch like that. What're you backing up for?"

Isn't it obvious? Charging him is a skinny, bug-eyed young sparring partner, panting and swinging at the contender's face with all the violent energy of a man out to prove something.

Dmitriy Salita sidesteps, ducks.

"No!" Salita's trainer shouts again. "Don't back up. Stand your ground!"

Salita wants to please his trainer, a hulking man named Harry Keitt, who once sparred with Muhammad Ali. But he also wants to protect his face.

Those are just two of the conflicting demands any successful fighter must balance. Relax but be vigilant. Attack but stay guarded. Listen to your advisers but watch out for yourself.

"Don't back up!" Keitt shouts again. "What're you backing up for? What're you backing up for?"

Salita is five-feet-nine, a muscled 155 pounds. He has a bristle of reddish hair, brown eyes, and a nose that looks as if it has been broken, though it has not. It is said that in their primes, even in repose, Muhammad Ali radiated joy, Mike Tyson menace. Dmitriy Salita exudes the sad dignity of a melancholy accountant or a very good, very anonymous, slightly troubled hit man.

"Don't cross your legs," Keitt yells. "Don't bend in front of him. . . . No! Don't punch like that. What're you backing up for? What're you backing up for?"

Even among fighters, an ambitious and conflicted bunch, Salita's ambitions and conflicts are more outsize than most. In a sport whose participants often thank Jesus or praise Allah before bowing to Mammon and doing their best to separate opponents from earthly consciousness, Salita is not just a Jew but a deeply observant Jew, involved with one of the world's most ultra-Orthodox branches of the religion, the Brooklyn-based Chabad-Lubavitch. He wants to be a champion, but he yearns to be pious. He lectures schoolchildren about the rewards of prayer, but he wants to hit someone so hard that those who say he isn't mean enough will shut up once and for all. He wants to inspire others to be better Jews, but he earns his living by pummeling opponents into submission.

It's a lot to ask of any man. But Salita is only twenty-four, a motherless immigrant fending off failure and expulsion from the only activity at which he has ever distinguished himself. He is undefeated, the seventh-ranked superlightweight in the world, according to the World Boxing Association, but after a near-disastrous performance in Atlantic City in March, he's facing a professional and existential crisis of sorts. On July 20 he will step into a ring in Midtown's Hammerstein Ballroom for what is shaping up to be a make-or-break fight. Win, and his career and dreams of financial independence will be back on track. Lose, and not only will his professional future be threatened but so will the hopes of all those who see in Salita a gritty and stirring example of Jewish strength. His fans say he has God on his side. His critics say he's better as a symbol than as a puncher.

What can he do?

He does what he can. He slides. He ducks. He jabs.

"No!" Keitt shouts. "Stand your ground! Slip and stand your ground!"

*   *   *

Tribal identity and ethnic politics have always played a major role in boxing. African Americans had Joe Louis and Ali, Irish Americans Jack Dempsey and Jim "Cinderella Man" Braddock, Italian Americans the two Rockys (Marciano and Graziano). To-day the connection still holds. Mexican Americans have lifted Oscar De La Hoya to iconic status. The biggest local draw in New York is "Ireland's John Duddy," whose fans plaster news of upcoming bouts on the walls of Celtic pubs all over the city.

Dmitriy Salita is different. He's Jewish, for one thing, in an era when "professional Jewish athlete" is most likely to serve as a punch line or trivia answer. And unlike great Jewish boxers of the past, who heard the bell as a clarion call to assimilation, not spirituality, Salita is openly devout. Orthodox tenement-tough Benjamin Leiner changed his name to Benny Leonard so his mother wouldn't discover he had taken up prizefighting. When she did learn his secret, she is said to have declared, "A prize-fighter you want to be? Is that a life for a respectable man? For a Jew?"

More recent Jewish boxers have strayed even further from religious practice. Or they had far shorter to stray in the first place. Max Baer, the sneering villain of Cinderella Man, fought with a Star of David on his shorts but in fact was raised Catholic (Baer's Jewish manager apparently encouraged the display for marketing reasons). Mike "the Jewish Bomber" Rossman, the 1978 light-heavyweight champion, was born Michael Albert De-Piano and tattooed the Star of David onto the calf of his right leg, in direct violation of the Jewish prohibition against self-mutilation. And for sheer sacrilegious chutzpa, few will ever outdo Vincent Morris Scheer, a New York City Jew who appar-ently decided he'd be a bigger draw as "Mushy Callahan — the Fighting Newsboy." Role models? True believers? *Feh!*

Salita is now the only ranked boxer in the world (and, quite possibly, in history) who keeps kosher, attends shul almost daily, refuses to fight on the Sabbath, wears a fringed garment, or zizith, and covers his head when he's not beating people senseless. He has three nicknames — Dima, the Star of David, and Kid Kosher — and a hard-core fan base of Orthodox Jews who travel to his bouts from Brooklyn and Long Island. They have a nickname too: the Kosher Nostra, naturally. Among Salita's corporate sponsors are Ecko Unlimited, the urban clothing and accessories company (it donates a percentage of its profits to orphans in Salita's native Odessa), and Kosher Zone Chefs (which is what it sounds like). After a White House employee read about him, Salita was invited to join George and Laura Bush at the 2004 White House Hanukkah party. There is a photo of the trio on Salita's Web site, which, if you search for it on Google, comes up thusly: "famous Jew boxer . . . !" Salita's life story is the subject of *Golden Boy,* a feature film being developed by Jerry Bruckheimer ("Mouse, Bruck Plan Ring-ding," *Variety* reported in 2004). Eminem is said to be interested in the starring role.

At least he was said to be interested before the Atlantic City fight in March. That's when the Star of David was knocked down twice in the first round. That's when the Kosher Nostra's idea of a holy warrior and Salita's hopes for a title shot started to look like unanswered prayers.

That's why Salita will be fighting for his professional life on Thursday night. His opponent will be a twenty-seven-year-old Minnesotan named James "Gentleman Jim" Wayka. Unranked at fourteen wins and four losses, Wayka is what an earlier generation of sportswriters might have referred to derisively as a "tomato can" or a "ham-and-egger." Unfortunately for Salita, so was his Atlantic City opponent. What's at stake in the match Thursday night isn't just Salita's personal ambition or possible climb out of poverty. There's also the issue of whether the next great Jewish hope is mostly hype. There's a larger, spiritual question, too. What kind of an Orthodox Jew makes a living trying to rip people's heads off?

He walks with his legs a little farther apart than most people. His cheekbones are high, almost Asiatic, and might have been inherited from a warrior who swept through his native Ukraine centuries ago. He speaks in a slow, almost funereal manner, except when the subject is boxing or Judaism, when his voice rises slightly and speeds up. He regularly interacts with a mix of uneducated athletes, corporate CEOs, religious leaders, and advertisers who want to use him to reach other people. Consequently, he has mastered at least three handshakes — the conventional grip and release; the more complicated grip, twist, snap, and release; and the grip, half hug, and shoulder bump. *Rocky* is his favorite boxing movie. He quotes Jim Carrey. He loves to eat. Sushi. Pasta. "And ice cream. I really like ice cream." Ungloved, his hands look surprisingly small and soft.

When he's not training, he'll wake up at 9:00 A.M., make himself a cup of coffee, and check his e-mail. Most mornings he'll find ten to thirty messages — notes from friends, questions about boxing, interview requests. Then he'll put on his zizith underneath a T-shirt or sweatshirt, throw on some jeans and running shoes, and a baseball cap in lieu of a yarmulke. Then he'll drive his Lexus — leased with his boxing earnings — to a rundown brick building on Ocean Avenue. This is the Chabad House, where he'll say morning prayers. He usually doesn't stay longer than twenty minutes or so. Later he might pay bills. "I make a good living today," he says, "but I haven't made close to what I want."

He lives in Midwood, a predominantly Jewish section of Brooklyn, in a three-bedroom house with his older brother, Misha. At night, after dinner, he'll see a movie with a friend, take a stroll on the boardwalk at Brighton Beach with Misha or a cousin. He likes music, everything from hip-hop to Russian music to pop. Eminem is one of his favorite artists. And Jay-Z. And Matisyahu, aka "the Hasidic Rapper." And Sade. "'Smooth Operator,' I really like that." He likes the beach. He likes looking at pretty girls. He likes to go online to check his investments. "On Ameritrade. Lately I haven't been looking because the market's down." Once a month he'll visit a yeshiva and talk to students — little boys to young adults — about how he became religious.

As for a conflict between piety and professional boxing, Salita doesn't see one. (Nor, when it comes to religions other than Judaism, do many others; Muhammad Ali was a devout Muslim, Evander Holyfield and George Foreman very public Christians. "They seemed to do OK.") "Most people are not going to be Torah scholars," Salita says. "It's no different if I'm a boxer or a writer or a waiter. You do your job — you do as much as you can. Reaching your capabilities and becoming a productive member of society, that's part of being religious." He says being religious also means focusing on the task at hand. "And that's made me a better boxer."

He knows that some people will never understand what an observant Jew is doing in his line of work, and he's a little weary of explaining. Besides, it's not like he took up boxing because he was a Jew or started praying more because he was a boxer. "I love Judaism," he says. "I love the culture of Judaism, the zizith, the tefillin, observing Shabbas, but you have to understand, we had nothing. My parents would buy the bags of fruit. You know the bags — the bananas and oranges and apples no one else wanted, in the sixty-nine-cent bag? That's what we ate. You've got to understand where I came from to understand why I'm boxing. Some kids get an education, and that's beautiful. But this is what happened to me."

People like to take things out of context, he says. "'You're religious,' they ask. 'How can that be?' What do they want me to do, quit boxing? If not for boxing, I wouldn't be able to talk to schools, to talk to kids. I wouldn't be talking to you."

He says he knows he's a role model. "Athletes, especially in boxing, great athletes take on social responsibility. That's the way the cookie crumbles, as Jim Carrey said in *Bruce Almighty*."

Salita couldn't possibly have imagined this life fifteen years ago. That's when Aleksander Lekhtman and his wife, Lyudmila Salita, left the port city of Odessa just as Ukraine declared its independence from a collapsing Soviet Union. They took their two boys, Dmitriy, then nine, and Misha, then eighteen, and Lyudmila's mother and left behind a tidy house with a large cherry tree in the backyard, careers as an engineer (Aleksander) and accountant (Lyudmila), and a lifetime's worth of casual but persistent anti-Semitism. Once, when a rumor of a pogrom filtered through the neighborhood, Aleksander bought a pistol. When a classmate called Dmitriy a *zhid*, (the Russian equivalent of "kike") and Dmitriy kicked the kid in the groin, Lekhtman told his youngest son he had done the right thing.

The five moved into a one-bedroom apartment in Midwood, a quintessentially American neighborhood, which is to say, a place where immigrants worked long hours at jobs far beneath their skills and children who had arrived a month ago tormented those who showed up last week. "Yeah, I got picked on," Salita says. "But it was because I had three-dollar sneakers and two-dollar slacks. You know, I'd get the other kids yelling, 'Payless shoes, Payless shoes,' and throwing food at me. I was the new kid on the block. It's something all kids go through."

Four years later, when he was thirteen, according to the lore that has sprung up around Salita, the boy who would be Kid Kosher ended up at Starrett City Boxing Club in East New York, Brooklyn, because his parents and older brother were determined that the child learn to fight back. "That makes a good story," Salita says. "But boxing was never for the purpose of defending myself."

In school, Salita says, he was shy. "I wasn't a cool kid, I wasn't with the in crowd. Let's put it this way: the prettiest girls in school didn't know who I was. In the boxing gym, I felt comfortable." There was also money, or the lack of it. "You know, people come from nothing, and they're hungry. Some people channel that into going to Harvard. Some people get a car dealership, become successful businessmen. I wanted to prove myself to myself and to other people. I channeled it into boxing. And it so happened I was talented at it."

Salita was one of the only white people at the gym. The other boys loved to spar with him, though "spar" probably isn't the right word. He made a game punching bag. "He had that European style," says Jimmy O'Pharrow, Starrett's founder and Salita's longtime trainer. "Stand up straight, that 'art of self-defense' stuff. But this is a ferocious country. It's always been a ferocious country. And I taught him to fight ferocious." O'Pharrow, who is Catholic, black, and eighty years old, is perhaps the young fighter's closest friend in the world and a man who rarely utters a sentence that doesn't seem destined for bold-faced type. Their relationship serves as the emotional linchpin of *Golden Boy*.

At Starrett's the radio was always tuned to Hot 97. Salita shadowboxed to hip-hop — Tupac Shakur, the Fugees, the Notorious B.I.G. "He didn't fight white boys," O'Pharrow says. "I had him fighting black boys, Spanish boys, kids who were out to kick his ass. And I taught him how to kick their ass, how to slip and slide, how to fight their way." Today, as O'Pharrow will tell just about anyone with a notebook, "Kid looks Russian, prays Jewish, and fights black."

His parents were happy their boy had found something he liked. "They thought it was an after-school activity, like tennis,"

Salita says. But, when he started arriving home with black eyes, they weren't so happy. Each of Salita's parents had a master's degree. A prizefighter their boy wanted to be?

Over the next few years, "Jimmy O" would drive Salita to tournaments around the country, often paying the entry fee. Salita remembers the T-shirts each entrant received. "A free T-shirt! That made my day."

O'Pharrow bought Salita a raincoat when the boy complained about running in the rain. He bought him an air conditioner during one sweltering summer. He told the boy he could be great.

His mother woke Salita at six every morning. He would run to the school yard, then run around the school yard, then run home to shower, then attend school, then back home for some homework and a nap, then the gym, then back home and more homework. One afternoon, when he came home after school, he found his mother on the living-room floor, shaking from a seizure. She had breast cancer, and it had spread. Salita was fourteen.

The next couple of years, he woke himself. He still ran, still worked hard in school, still followed Jimmy O's every bit of advice. But now to his daily itinerary he added trips to Sloan-Kettering Cancer Center, where his mother was spending more and more time. Sometimes he slept there, in his mother's room.

Jimmy O remembers the day she arrived outside the gym in her car. Soon she would be back in the hospital for good. Times before, when she wanted to say something to Jimmy O, she had left the car. Today she waved. It hurt too much to walk. She called Jimmy O to the car window.

"I want you to take care of my boy," she said.

She shared a hospital room in the last months of her life. Her roommate was an Orthodox Jewish woman. It was that woman's husband who called another woman, and that woman called a rabbi to speak of the young boy who had one afternoon in the hospital room proclaimed his plan to be a world-champion boxer. The rabbi called Salita. Did he want to talk?

Salita's family, like many Soviet Jews, was not observant. There were no weekly trips to the synagogue, no Friday-night candles, no Passover seders. He had a "Russian style" bar mitzvah. It was held in a Russian restaurant, now closed, in Brooklyn. There was a cake with thirteen candles. There were no prayers. Salita wore a yarmulke and a band played "the mazel tov song."

"The mazel tov song?" I ask.

"You know. 'Da-dum-da. Mazel tov, mazel tov, mazel tov.'"

Still, Dmitriy met the rabbi. Why? Because he was a lonely immigrant who didn't fit in at school? Because his mother was dying? Because even though he'd never been religious, he'd always thought himself a Jew, had been so enamored of the religious freedom he saw in his adopted country that he'd had himself circumcised a few months before his bar mitzvah? (His uncle did the same thing at age fifty-five). Because, he says, "I always believed in God, and had a personal spiritual relationship with Him."

In 1998 Salita won a bronze medal in the national Junior Olympics, "to show my mother I could do this at the highest level." Shortly afterward, Lyudmila died. Every day for the next eleven months, Dmitriy went to shul to say Kaddish, the Jewish prayer for the dead. Not just any shul, but the Chabad House on Ocean Avenue. Chabad-Lubavitch is a sect of Hasidism, a populist Jewish movement emphasizing spiritual revival that began in Eastern Europe during the eighteenth century. Based in Crown Heights, the Chabad-Lubavitch utilize telethons, the Internet, and loudspeaker-equipped vans ("Mitzvah Tanks") in the quest to save Jewish souls. Salita didn't go because he thought his soul needed saving. He went because his mother was dead and the Chabad House is where the rabbi who had called him taught.

After eleven months Salita continued to go to the Chabad House, sometimes for just a few minutes. He wrapped tefillin around his arm and forehead, then said morning prayers. Much of the time, he had no idea what was being said.

"It wasn't crazy," he says. "I don't want you to paint a picture that I was crazy religious from the beginning. I ate French fries and cheeseburgers. It was very step-by-step. If it felt uncomfortable, I took a step back."

He made deals with himself. After one boxing tournament, he went to both Friday-night and Saturday-morning Sabbath services. After another he shut off his computer Friday at sundown and kept it off until Saturday night. One weekend he kept the television off. A few weeks later, he avoided talking on the telephone.

The better he fought, the more observant he became. The more observant he became, the better he fought. When he was seventeen, he won a silver medal in the U.S. Nationals, and the next year, a gold.

In 2001, the day after he turned nineteen, he won New York's Golden Gloves title as a junior welterweight (the same as superlightweight — up to 140 pounds), along with the Sugar Ray Robinson Award for outstanding fighter of the tournament.

He turned professional in June 2001, signing with Bob Arum, and, with Jimmy O's blessing, left Starrett's and started working out at Brooklyn's fabled Gleason's Gym so he could train under the tutelage of Hector Roca, who has taught thirteen world champions.

From sundown Friday until sundown Saturday he refused to work or turn on the lights or even punch an elevator button. He attended Friday-night services and chose not to fight on the Sabbath. Friday-night fights are a staple of the boxing world, and if he hadn't been so observant, Salita certainly would have landed more televised matches and made more money.

There were other problems, too. When Salita signed with Arum in 2001, he expected big arenas and big fights in New York City, where his fan base was. Instead he found himself trading punches in Nevada, in Arizona, once even in Puerto Rico. He had hoped for exposure on HBO but ended up on regional stations "geared to the Hispanic market. A few times at the press conference, I had to speak Spanish."

He fought nineteen times for Arum and won nineteen times. "And I was able to support myself, but things didn't work out like we expected."

Kid Kosher was ready for a change, and, when his contract expired three years ago, Salita signed with Lou DiBella, a former executive at HBO Boxing and the creator of Broadway Boxing, a venture dedicated to presenting New York–based fights.

Salita knows that his commercial success is owed in part to his novelty. "It was a combination of being good and being the white, Jewish guy. But I won the nationals, I won the Golden Gloves, I won the Sugar Ray Robinson Award. I've won inner-city tournaments for as long as I've been fighting. I've been through the mill."

Last August he scored a technical knockout over Shawn Gallegos, and Salita thought he was poised for the success he had anticipated. "The plan for after that was to fight on a big pay-per-view card," Salita told me last winter. "But that didn't happen. And there was talk of a Madison Square Garden fight, but that didn't happen."

Some of Salita's fans said Salita was too good, that top fighters were ducking matches against him. Others said he wasn't good enough. "The people in his corner, they believe in him," says Bert Sugar, the former editor of the *Ring* magazine ("the Bible of Boxing") and Boxing Hall of Fame historian. "They're rabid. But they're cheering more from their heart than their

heads. I don't think he'll ever be an exceptional fighter. But boxing needs its heroes, and right now, there aren't many. He can be
a hero."

In December Salita earned a unanimous decision over junior
welterweight journeyman Robert Frankel, but Salita fought in
desultory fashion, even got knocked down in the first round. "It
was like I was just showing up at the office," he says. "I was going through the motions. I just didn't step it up." People who
said he didn't hit hard enough said it again.

"Yeah, it irritated me," Salita says. He says that because he's
a technically proficient boxer, people think he lacks the requisite
hostility. Yes, he would like to shut those people up with some
more knockouts. "But I wasn't as aggressive as I should have
been in my past two fights. I need to get back to my old style. I
know there will always be critics, and I have to accept that. All I
can do is the best I can, to pray and do the best I can."

The Frankel performance didn't help his career, but it
didn't derail it, either. On March 18 he fought in Atlantic City at
the top of the undercard for the James Toney–Hasim Rahman
heavyweight title bout. A victory, and the exposure it would
bring, would get him that much closer to a title shot for the junior welterweight championship — and a healthy payday. "Half
a million if it were televised, and in a place like Madison Square
Garden," Salita says. "Or at least a quarter of a million."

At Atlantic City's Boardwalk Hall, on March 18, 2006, the
Kosher Nostra — about a hundred strong and many bearded and
wearing yarmulkes — gathered in section 213, rows K, M, and
N. Nosebleed seats, which was probably a good thing, as they
couldn't have been farther away from the enthusiastically profane spectacle that is an Atlantic City heavyweight bout — the
bleached blonds in faux-satin boxers' robes making change and
offering beer to meaty men with expensive haircuts, other guys

with diamond rings asking the women in spike heels and fur if they wanted a "date" for the night, the hoop earrings and tuxedoed television announcers and tinted glasses and everything that has always accompanied crowds waiting to witness violent combat for entertainment. The Kosher Nostra had left Brooklyn and Long Island at sundown so they could make it here without violating the commandment to keep the Sabbath holy.

The Star of David followed a gigantic Israeli flag into the ring.

"Dee-ma," the Kosher Nostra chanted as Salita removed his blue robe, which has the Star of David emblazoned on its back. He had lost almost twenty pounds in two months to make weight, was now a pale slab of Ukranian-born, Brooklyn-raised sinew and muscle. Across the ring Salita's opponent — a ropy Mexican American from Las Vegas named Ramon Montano — knelt in his corner and crossed himself.

At the bell Salita circled counterclockwise, flicked a few jabs, circled some more, and then — before many in the audience were even seated — Montano was swarming and lunging, and Salita looked confused, and when Montano launched a nasty right cross and hit Salita flush on the chin and he dropped to the seat of his pants, confusion gave way to something like profound befuddlement. He was immediately up, circling again, still looking like he was analyzing what just happened when Montano, an apparently far less reflective athlete, lunged and charged and threw another right at Salita's bewildered mug. Now the crowd was befuddled, too. Montano had never knocked a fighter out in his career. And at that bizarre instant, in front of the whores and the announcers and the Kosher Nostra and the rest of the prizefight crowd, on the seat of his pants for the second time in less than a minute, was the kid they're going to make a movie about?

In his corner, between rounds, Salita continued to look confused, but when the bell called the fighters out to begin the second round, he was a different boxer. Still circling, still flicking jabs, but with purpose. When Montano lunged and attacked, Salita answered with hissing combinations, distinctly uncharitable hooks and jabs and uppercuts.

In the third round, Montano closed again, whipped his right hand toward Kid Kosher's bruised and bleeding face. When Salita sidestepped and rattled a left, then a right, to Montano's skull, a cheer descended from the nosebleed seats. "Dee-ma," the Kosher Nostra screamed. The sounds of fear and relief and hope, all in two fierce syllables. A prayer. "Dee-ma, Dee-ma!"

Salita fought cautiously and effectively the rest of the match, and, except for a moment when he was backed up against the ropes and Montano rocked him with another hard right in the fifth round, he seemed far from danger. Still, for a boxer whose success has reportedly derived from hand speed and clever footwork, he seemed curiously stationary, clumsy almost. But he hung on, and every time Montano charged, Salita responded with authoritative and accurate combinations.

When the judges announced a draw (one scored Salita the winner, another Montano, and the third called it a tie), the crowd jeered and booed. "That was a robbery," a woman in the front row said to her girlfriend. "That Dmitriy guy not losing! That other guy knocked him down!"

He wore sunglasses at the press conference. Later, in his hotel room, he rose slowly and stiffly to greet the stream of well-wishers and gawkers, speaking softly and politely to each. His face was swollen and bruised and lumpy.

"You scared me in the first round," a visitor said.

"Hey," Salita replied, "I scared me."

Four days later Salita and I met for lunch in Brooklyn. Beneath each of his eyes were purpling bruises. On each cheek, healing cuts. His right ear was still swollen and crimson. He wore a baseball cap, and a blue-and-white-striped sweatshirt over a gray T-shirt, and baggy jeans and blue-and-white running shoes. Peeking from beneath his sweatshirt were the fringes of his zizith.

He said he was discouraged. He said he wasn't sure what to do. He thought maybe he should move up a weight class to welterweight. He said he thought he might have gotten knocked down twice because he was weak from such rapid weight loss. ("I don't think it had anything to do with weight," O'Pharrow told me later. "It had to do with stupidity. He got caught with two good shots. But he showed he had some balls.")

Salita said Jimmy O had advised him to take some time off, to think, take a trip to Israel. Instead, he thought he'd head down to Miami Beach. "There's great food there," he said. "And pretty girls."

After fighters get knocked down, Salita told me as he dug in to his sushi, "they're either never the same or they're better. I ask and pray to God that I'm headed in the right direction."

We ate in silence for a while. To break the quiet, I asked him about a horrible boxing story I had just read in the newspaper.

The same night Salita boxed his way to a draw, a welterweight named Kevin Payne endured a brutal eight-round pummeling in Evansville, Indiana, on his way to a victory in a split decision over Ryan Maraldo. The next morning, Payne died after surgery to relieve swelling in his brain. His neck was also broken.

"Yeah, I knocked out the guy who killed Payne," Salita says in his quiet, respectful way. "Knocked him out in the third round."

After lunch he drove me to a subway station, and along the way we talked again about the odd intersection of professional violence and personal piety.

Salita said he would rather inspire a child to be religious than to fight. "One hundred percent," he said. "It's not even a question."

He asked if I would mind stopping for a minute at the Chabad House, and when we got there he asked if I wanted to come inside. There, one of the yeshiva students asked if I would put on the phylacteries and recite the Shema with him.

Later, in the car, I mentioned to Salita that I hadn't spoken Hebrew in a while.

"That's the first time you've put on the tefillin?" he asked.

"Uh, yeah."

"Then that's a good thing for you." For a Lubavitcher to lead a nonobservant Jew to be more Jewish is considered a mitzvah. "And a good thing for me, too."

Four months later we're driving in Salita's Lexus to a kosher restaurant in Brooklyn. The workout with Keitt is over. The July 20 fight, which will be televised on FSNY ("The network that doesn't pay me anything," Salita says), is still a month away. Tonight, before he goes to sleep, Salita will take a walk. He'll call Jimmy O, as he does every day. Next week he'll drive up to training camp in the Poconos.

After Atlantic City, Salita left Gleason's and returned to Starrett's, "to get hungry again, to remember who I was — like Rocky when he went back to the Philadelphia gym in *Rocky III*."

He has decided to fight as a welterweight. He began training again with Jimmy O and the old man's surrogates, like Harry Keitt. His friends say he hasn't been this happy or focused since he and Jimmy O were driving around the country to tournaments, collecting victories and T-shirts.

His cell phone rings. Salita answers, speaks in Russian. It's his father, who is at Sears. He has some questions about the pots and pans he is buying for his son to take with him to the Poconos. Salita will do his own cooking. There aren't many kosher restaurants near Bushkill, Pennsylvania. (Once, when he was putting on tefillin in his room at training camp, another boxer looked in and asked what Salita was doing. Salita told him. "Oh," the other boxer said, "I thought you were hooking up to the Internet.")

Salita says he'd like to be able to afford a chef for future training camps. He would like to buy a house in Brooklyn and an apartment in Miami Beach "with a water view." He would like to be featured as the main event at Madison Square Garden. "My long-term goal in boxing is, if I choose, I'll never have to work again. And I'd like to be able to help my brother and my father. And there are a lot of unaffiliated Russian Jews around here. There are a lot of things that could be done."

He says that after this fight he'll go back to junior welter-weight, because now that he's training with Jimmy O again, he's confident he can keep his strength. Plus he's looked at that division and says he can win it.

But first he's got to win Thursday night.

"I'm on the verge of a breakout fight," Salita says as we pull up to the restaurant. "You know what I mean? You pass the test or you don't."

His most fervent fans say he has already passed. "Dmitriy has been a champion since the day he laced up and said he wouldn't fight on Shabbat," Salita's publicist and fellow Lubavitcher told me. "He fights for a higher power."

Jimmy O sees things a different way. "You go to shul to pray to God," he says. "But in the ring you're alone. And if God gets in the ring with you, you kick His ass."

14

DRIVING LESSONS:
BARRY FRIEDMAN, GOLFER

M Y FATHER TELLS ME TO GRIP THE SEVEN IRON "LIKE you're holding a bird in your hands and you don't want to crush it," and I say, "OK," which is what I always say to my father when I think he is criticizing me, or when I have absolutely no idea what he's talking about, or when I'm filled with a vague and guilty rage toward him, or when all three are happening at once. I say OK when he talks about investment strategies and tax shelters and the enduring value of discipline and why I should buckle down and write a best seller and when he tells me the story of the ant and the grasshopper, which he started telling me when I was two years old. I'm forty-nine now, and I've been saying OK for forty-seven years.

"You want to sit, not bend," he says after I slice one.

"OK," I say.

"Both hands working together now," he says. "Belly-button focus."

I hook one. "Uh-huh. OK."

"Keep your lower body still."

I swing with savage intent, and miss. "OK."

"But not completely still."

Another whiff. "Oh, I see now. OK. Yeah. OK."

We face each other, holding clubs, alone together on a weekday afternoon at a driving range. It is a brilliant, sunny spring day in St. Louis, home of my father, and of my father's father, and — after he'd emigrated from Hungary — my father's father's father. I have come here from New York City, where I moved twelve years ago, because my father has agreed to teach me to play golf.

I asked because I wanted to understand his life better, because I wanted to find out what he was doing all those Wednesday afternoons and Saturday mornings and Sunday summer evenings, whether golf was a cause or a symptom of his failed marriage to my mother. I asked because I wanted to learn what my father found in the fairways and on the greens that he didn't find at home or at work, and whether he was still looking for it.

After he'd agreed I'd put off the trip for five years. Because I was busy. Because I wasn't sure I wanted to know the answers to my questions. Because neither my father nor I had ever discovered much joy in our teacher-pupil sessions, whether they involved cutting grass or changing oil or polishing shoes. And then my father had emergency bypass surgery and a subsequent bout of mild depression, and shortly after that his parents got ill and died. I helped write the eulogies that my father delivered. And so, filled with a sense of loss and impending mortality — his and mine — I called to finalize the details of the golf lessons.

There would be three days of lessons, he said, at least a few hours a day and maybe more, culminating in a nine-hole match, for which we would be joined by my older brother, who was flying in for business. OK, I said.

He told me to read *Harvey Penick's Little Red Book*. He told me to buy or borrow a couple of irons and go to the driving range and work on my swing. He told me to practice, especially the short game, "because if you really want to play golf, if you're serious about this, that's what you do, you practice the short game."

What I heard was, "You don't really want to play golf. You're not serious. You're not serious about the short game, not serious about making money, not serious about getting married and having children and not serious about making a success of yourself."

"OK," I'd said, half a country away. "OK, OK, OK."

And now, hour four of day one, I'm hooking and slicing and whiffing and topping in St. Louis. If I'd read a solitary page of Penick's book, would I be wiser? If I'd made a single trip to a driving range in New York, would I be better? If I'd done my homework, would either of us be happier? Does my father sense how I have already failed him?

"We're going to work on the fundamentals this week," my father says. "Stance, grip, putting, the short game and the basic swing."

"OK," I hiss, and when I look up, he is frowning, in pain, as if he knows what my OKs really mean. I think he does know. I hate when he worries about me. I like it, too. I think he has been worrying about me for a long time.

"But most important," he says, "is that we're going to teach you to have fun. That's the most important thing."

He tries so hard. He worries so much. I want to reassure him. I want to make him proud. I want to promise that I will practice the short game and hold my club like an endangered bird, that we will stride down lush fairways together for many years to come.

But I don't, of course. I can't.

"OK," I say.

My father and I are walking in a parking lot, and from time to time I reach out to feel his thigh. I'm nine years old. This is my earliest memory that involves golf. My father tells me that next month he is going on a weekend trip with some of his friends to Illinois to play golf, and he says I'm a big boy now and I can keep a secret and not to tell Mommy, he's going to surprise her. OK, I say, and I touch his thigh again, which is knotty with muscles. It's a big parking lot. I'm a worried child and I blow saliva bubbles to pass the time and to calm myself, and I am fiercely concentrating on blowing a big one as we walk, and I reach out again to touch my father's thigh and then I hear a strange voice and something is wrong and I look up and it's a strange man and then I'm sobbing, and here comes my father, laughing, rubbing my head, picking me up in his arms. Somehow I have wandered off, lost in my head, but never out of sight of my father, who has watched his dreamy boy with — what? amusement? bafflement? fear for the future? I bury my face in his neck and his hand covers my entire head.

When we get home I run into the kitchen. "Mommy," I sing, "Daddy's going to Illinois to play golf with his friends." Betrayal as casual and effortless as sneaking a cookie before dinner. I don't know why I did it.

Our second day at the range, I hit one straight and true.

"That's great!" my father says. "That's really, really great."

It's as if I've announced plans to marry, get a business degree, and move back to the Midwest, all at once.

"Now try it again. Just do the same thing again."

A capital idea, except that I, of course, have no idea what I just did. Consequently, I slice one, then hook two, then whiff, then slice four in a row.

"You're getting it," my father says with transparent dishonesty. "Let your hands move from eleven o'clock to one o'clock." I've never understood the clock designations for direction. "And swing from the inside out." He might as well be speaking Uzbek.

"Yep, OK," I say.

I'm a good athlete, but I've never been a quick study at sports that require balance. What I possess is a dumb, mulish capacity to absorb pain and humiliation until I master a physical movement. And once I master it my appetite and skill grow exponentially. I remember the moment on my snowboard when I felt balanced, when a mountain of certain doom morphed into my own snowy playground; the instant that the eighteen discrete mechanical parts of a jump shot merged into one fluid motion; the chilly afternoon when I realized I could rock from one foot to another on my Rollerblades without falling. With golf, though, my straight shot seems to have nothing to do with any choices I have made. It precedes only hours of anguish.

The afternoon drags on, with me screwing up nine of every ten shots and my father offering encouragement that I'm sure is criticism. He mentions every few minutes that people "who are serious" about learning to play golf work on their short games. He says that people who "really want to play golf" practice a lot. If you're "serious" and "really want to play golf," you visualize great shots, you believe in yourself, you learn to play as a kid. He actually says this. "The great players, the ones who are really serious, who really want to become the best, they learn to play as kids."

What does that make me?

"OK," I mutter through clenched teeth, slicing and hooking and whiffing. "OK, OK, OK."

Then I hit another one straight and true. I can't believe it.

"You're a natural, Steve!" my father exclaims. "You're really getting this."

On the way home from the range, my father suggests we stop for coffee. I think he senses how miserable I am. "How about Starbocks?" he says, which makes me grind my teeth. Does he mispronounce words intentionally? Where did he ever come up with "bocks"? Why am I such a bad son?

We roll onto one of the superhighways that roam the hills and floodplains of suburban St. Louis, the endless swaths of pavement that stretch to the horizon every way you look. I have always possessed a terrible sense of direction, and in the past decade St. Louis has become more confusing than ever to me. I ask how far we will be going.

"Ten minutes," he says, which makes me clench and unclench my fists. Ever since I was a child, prone to car sickness and embarrassing vomiting episodes, I would ask my father how long before we arrived at our destination. I wanted facts, exact times. I longed for the reassurance of certitude. But he offered me the same demonstrably dishonest pap. Two blocks, fifty miles, three state lines, it mattered not: "We'll be there in ten minutes."

He had been so looking forward to my visit. His wife — he was recently remarried — is off seeing her children and grandchildren in California. She is a kind woman, acutely aware of how my father yearns to connect with his grown children, and I suspect she arranged the trip for that reason. "So it'll be just you and me," he told me on the phone one evening (after suggesting reading lists and practice regimens). "We'll golf and see some movies and go out to dinner. We'll catch up. We'll have a good time."

And here I am, rocking myself in the passenger seat of his car, grinding my teeth and clenching my fists, a carsick seven-year-old in a forty-nine-year-old body. A body that isn't serious. A body that doesn't really want to learn his father's game.

Here are some reasons I never took up golf:

I'm twenty-one, a college senior, and there is a fat brown envelope in the mailbox of the house where I live in California. I share the place with five others, and we cook together and smoke marijuana and listen to the Grateful Dead and play Frisbee and talk about how empty our parents' lives are. I had recently announced to my parents my plan to become a newspaper reporter. In the envelope is an article about the glut of journalists immediately post–Woodward and Bernstein. It is the midseventies, and I'm part of the glut. The article talks about saturation in the field, declining salaries, and shrinking profits at newspapers. At the top, in my father's scrawl, is a short note: "Maybe you should consider business. At least take some accounting courses."

I'm almost thirty, have been fired from a newspaper job for my dissolute habits, and am now writing speeches for the Southwestern Bell Telephone Company. I wear a suit and tie every day and take naps every Saturday afternoon. I suffer from insomnia and chronic stomachaches. When I receive an offer to work on a magazine, I can't recall ever being so happy. I call my father to share my joy.

"You're taking a thirty percent pay cut?" he asks.

"Uh-huh," I say.

"And there's no 401(k) at the magazine?"

"Right," I say.

"And no dental?"

"Yes, but . . ."

"I don't understand," he says. "I don't understand why you're doing this."

I'm forty-five, and my father and I are sitting in a café in Colorado. For the past five years, I've been scraping together a life as a freelance writer. A tongue-in-cheek advice book, a collaboration with a professional athlete, some newspaper articles, a fairly steady string of magazine assignments. I recently finished a dark first-person account of a long winter in the mountains and a near emotional breakdown. It's the most personal thing I've ever written, my favorite story, and I just found out that a small literary magazine will publish it.

"You have a lot of talent," my father says.

"Thanks, Dad," I say. "That means a lot to me."

"No, really, I mean it. You should write a *real* book with all your talent."

"Thanks, Dad," I repeat. One thing we agree on is that my first two efforts weren't *real* books. "Thank you."

"No, really," he repeats. "You should really write a book. A real book. Have you thought about a book? It just seems a waste, with all your talent, not to write a book."

He is trying so hard. Was any father ever more encouraging to a son?

"Well, you know that piece I just sold to the literary magazine, about the winter and all that?"

He nods. I know he read it.

"Well, I'm thinking about expanding that into a book."

He looks at me, confused.

"Who would want to read that?" he says.

At our first practice session, I spotted the bulbous oblong poking out of my father's golf bag and asked about it. That was one of his drivers, he said, the Cleveland Launcher, but it would be awhile before it came out of the bag because people who were serious about golf worked on their short games.

I have always been something of a magpie, attracted to shiny things and quick fixes.

"OK," I said, then added that I thought I understood the short game. I told him that I had a strong feeling that I could really hit it straight with the Launcher.

"I know a guy who changes clubs like I change underwear," my father told me. "It doesn't help his game any."

Well, sure, I said. OK. Nevertheless, I told him I thought the graphite technology might suit my stroke. I have no idea what graphite technology is, but I would have said anything to get my hands on the Launcher.

"It's not the driver," he said. "It's the guy hitting it."

Yeah, I understood. OK. But what about all *his* gadgets, I said. What about the time we were watching television together and an ad came on for Callaway's first Big Bertha and he called the eight-hundred number and bought one?

"It's not the arrow," my father told me. "It's the Indian."

I have been whining for three days.

"Today," my father tells me on our third day of practice, as we stand at the driving range of Meadowbrook Country Club, "we are going to work on putting and chipping, we'll review your swing, and" — dramatic pause — "maybe we'll let you use the Launcher a few times."

I nearly yelp with joy. Because of the Launcher. And because the instruction is almost over. This is the last day of practice before our match tomorrow, and my older brother has flown in from Oregon to join us. Don is two years older, a lawyer and businessman with a wife and child, college funds that have been gaining interest since before his wife was pregnant, and an aggressive but not-too-risky retirement strategy. He is as calculating and shrewd in his approach to golf as to life. Don, it should probably go without saying, has an excellent short game.

Don takes a wedge and two irons and starts hitting.

Before I can swing the Launcher, my father wants to try something new with me today. He wants to introduce me to his "Inside Out machine." It is another of the gadgets he buys in direct violation of his arrow/Indian philosophy. Then again, he has always been a man of contradictions. He tells me to keep my feet still, to do the bird grip, to focus on my navel, then he adds, "But when you get up to hit the ball, trust your body. Don't think of anything." He stresses the supremacy of man over tools but later says, "If you're really serious about golf, you'll get fitted clubs." He emphasizes that lessons help any golfer, even the professional, that any golfer who "really wants to play" should be open to learning. Does he take lessons? "No, because it always screws up my game for weeks afterward."

So I shouldn't be surprised when Mr. It's Not the Arrow now places a thing that looks like a cross between an automatic sprinkler and a mechanical shoeshine machine in front of me, sticks a ball underneath it, and tells me to swing.

"Inside Out," he says.

Would it do either of us any good if I asked what in the world he was talking about?

I slice the ball.

"Try again," he says.

And I do. And I slice again. I try seven times and slice seven times.

"The ad says that on the seventh swing you'll be going straight and long," my father says. "Here, let me try."

While he works with the Inside Out, I slip the Launcher from the bag and smack one. I adore the heft, the soft little ping, the distance. I smack another. Meanwhile, Don experiments with irons and wedges, asks for exact distances to various flags, makes inquiries about how fast the greens are. And there we stand, a man and his two grown boys. My father mutters and curses at the Inside Out until, like magic, on the seventh try, he hits a towering drive 260 yards, and then another and another. Don squints, adjusts his grip, chips, drives, toys with his swing, chips some more, asks people driving by in golf carts about the greens. I whale away with the Launcher, spraying balls every-where, with lots of energy and very little direction.

Day four: on the first tee the Launcher fails me, and I whiff. Maybe I fail myself. It's different here on the course. There are trees to worry about, and middle-aged women waiting to play behind us, and a scorecard, and my shirt keeps coming out of my shorts, which, my father tells me, is a violation of Meadowbrook Country Club policy. I try again and dribble one about ten feet and he tells me to remember about my grip and to swing from the inside out, and to relax, to have fun, to let my body take over. I whiff again. Finally I ground one about eighty feet.

"That's all right," my father says. "You're on the fairway. You're in good position."

"No matter how bad you are," my pragmatic older brother tells me, "if you're fast, no one will refuse to play with you."

I sprint after my ball.

It goes this way for three holes, my father and brother playing slightly above par, me hacking and whiffing and slicing and sprinting.

On the fourth hole, I find myself three feet from a water hazard, then dribble three balls into the water. My father reaches into his bag for his folding, snap-jawed mechanical ball retriever to snatch the balls from the pond. "Best investment I ever made," he says.

Once, Don, eyeing the green, asks whether it's 135 or 140 yards away. I tell him that even good players are a pain in the ass when they're so sluggish, and does he have to be so calculating about everything? Can't he just hurry up and smack the ball? He tells me to shut up.

Once, I seven putt. Once, I lose a ball in the woods. My father offers advice for a while but eventually sees how it's adding to my misery.

On the seventh hole, he pulls me aside.

"You know, the score doesn't matter," he says. "This is just your first time. The thing that would make me happy is if you get to like this enough that when you go back to New York you decide to go out and play by yourself."

In the last years of my paternal grandparents' lives, they told me a story about my father. It's a golf story. It doesn't start out that way, but trust me.

My father is four years old and his baby brother, a two-year-old whom everyone calls Sonny, is sleeping in his stroller one morning when he stops breathing. That afternoon, his mother makes my father noodles and milk — his favorite — and she cries, but she doesn't say anything about why Sonny is gone, or where he is, or if he'll ever come back.

She cries for the next two years, and she doesn't mention Sonny for almost seventy years after that. But my father doesn't cry.

He is sixteen years old, a high school student, a letterman, a star in football and basketball and track. He works hard. He practices. He wants to be a doctor. He is serious and really wants to do well.

He is eighteen years old, a college freshman at the University of Michigan, and it is winter break and his parents are driving him to Union Station in St. Louis, where he will board a train to return for his second semester, but he has a stomachache, he feels sick. "Let's take him home, Herman," his mother, my grandmother, says, and they do, so he can sleep and get over his stomach flu.

The next day they drive him back to the train station. But he feels sick again, so they return home. On the third day, in the car on the way to Union Station, my father feels sick once more, and his mother tells him he doesn't have to go to Michigan, he can stay home and go to school at Washington University. So he does. He goes to school in St. Louis, and he gets married to his high school sweetheart and has two sons and thinks he's too old to go to medical school. He needs to support his family, so he works as a manager in the same drugstore chain as his father.

He is twenty-six, and he needs more money to support his family. He tells the president of the company that if he doesn't get a raise, he will have to look for work elsewhere. The president wishes him well.

He answers a blind ad in the newspaper, an ad that calls for "smart, hardworking young men." He has a wife and two boys — the youngest of whom tends to get lost and blow bubbles when he's daydreaming and throws up in the car — and a mortgage, and now he is a life-insurance salesman. He makes cold calls. Sometimes he doesn't come home until nine or ten o'clock at night. At breakfast he pores over thick booklets so he can take the test that will allow him to become a chartered life underwriter. He has pens and calendars made with his name on them.

He is thirty-five years old, and now there's a third child — a little girl — and sometimes he clenches his jaw when he's getting ready to go to work in the morning, and one night when his sons can't sleep they hear him in the kitchen cussing to their mother about the people in the head office. Sunday nights he takes his children to Steak 'n Shake for hamburgers, "to give your mom a break," and, on the evenings when it's the second son's turn to ride in the front seat, there is a serious speech about enjoying oneself, how it's important to relax, that there's no need to hurry into marriage, that "you have the rest of your life to be responsible." The boy is eleven years old.

At night the boy's father goes to sleep before anyone else in the house because he's so tired. On Saturday mornings, though, he wakes whistling, beaming. On Saturday mornings he plays golf. He comes home in the early evening smelling of grass, and grinning. He has his Saturdays, and sometimes Wednesday afternoons, and the occasional summer Sunday evening, and his annual trip to Illinois with his friends.

He returns from those trips expansive, talking about honor and how in golf "there's no referees, you have to trust yourself and the people you're playing with," and how "I've never met a man who cheats on the golf course who I like in life," and how "if a man plays square, you can trust him with anything." A few times he brings home a first-place trophy. "Bigger than the one in the U.S. Open," he says, laughing.

He is sixty-one, divorced and remarried for ten years. He is more relaxed now, less worried, less tired. He plays golf a lot, sometimes with his new wife. His children have never seen him so happy. When she is diagnosed with inoperable brain cancer, she insists that he keep playing golf, and he does, until her last two months, when he stays at home with her, feeding her and taking care of her in the bedroom, which she doesn't leave. When she dies he grieves, of course, and he has some fainting spells. And then he thinks of Sonny — he hasn't thought of Sonny in decades — and for the first time he cries for his little brother and he can't stop.

Ten years pass, and he has chest pains and emergency by-pass surgery and a bout with depression and a few girlfriends who don't work out. And then he meets someone who doesn't golf but says that if it's important to him, she'll learn.

And now he is seventy-four, married for the third time. He tells his children he loves them, often, spoils his thirteen grand-children and step-grandchildren with bicycles and computer games and toy trucks and trips to the zoo and sleepovers and ice cream sundaes in the middle of the day. Not one of them knows what a step-grandchild is. The word would mystify them. He is a lifetime member of the Million Dollar Round Table, which, in the life-insurance business, is as good as it gets. He is one of the most successful salesmen in the country, an innovator who sold the first group tax-sheltered annuity in the world.

(I know what a group tax-sheltered annuity is now. I know that it has earned his company many billions of dollars. "Your company should name a building after you," I say one afternoon between a slice and a hook.

"They don't even know my name," he replies.)

He paid for his three children's college education, offered them choices and career opportunities he might have dreamed about but could never pursue. He skis, owns property in a resort town, winters in Palm Springs, works when he wants, travels when he wants. All of that came to him because he was serious, because he really wanted it. Hard work and thrift and serious-ness of purpose have formed the bulwark for him against pain and loss, but they haven't been enough. Still, what else is there?

Isn't it obvious?

There are Saturdays and Wednesdays and summer Sunday evenings and a place where he can breathe fresh air and stretch and play, where honor means something and where people don't cheat.

I want to tell him how proud I am of him, how I wish I could live up to the example he set, how I envy him his discipline and success and self-sacrifice and generosity. I want to tell him how much he means to me. But I can't. So I vow to do the next best thing. I will hit a good shot in our match. If I need to be serious, I will be serious. If I need to really want it, I will really want it. Whatever it takes, I will do it.

Anything to hit a good shot.

I don't, of course. I don't hit a good shot. If it were that easy, if striking the ball cleanly and with strength and purpose and something approaching artistry were as simple as just distilling all the resentment and misunderstanding and rage and wounded feelings and guilt and gratitude and love a son holds toward his father into a smooth and honest and powerful swing, there would be legions of scratch golfers launching millions of elegant drives all over the world. There would be so many multitudes of white dimpled balls arcing across empty skies that no one would be able to see the sun.

But it's not that easy. So I whiff and hack and sprint and goad my brother, who plays with grim cunning. I kid my father about the ball retriever and ask him to tell me stories of the trips to Illinois, and I beg for tales from his early days in the insurance business and of his best shots and his favorite afternoons on the golf course.

I give up, and I relax, and I cheer my father on, and, if you're a golfer, or a father, or a son, of course you know what happens next.

I can still see it leaving the Launcher, flying away, a blur of white against the deep green of the trees, the baby blue of the Midwestern afternoon. A white smudge, low to the ground, a vector bending toward the distant green.

A mystery.

"Great shot!" my father yells. He applauds. "That's a great shot!" he yells again and applauds some more.

"I don't know how I did it," I say as he comes over to pat me on the back.

It doesn't matter, he tells me. What's important is that I did it and that I'm having fun. I may not play golf when I return to New York City. I'm not sure if I'll go to the driving range with friends. I don't know if I'll ever pick up a club again.

It doesn't matter. It truly doesn't matter.

We walk together up the fairway, my father and I, playing golf. He will shoot a forty-two for the nine holes. I will finish at eighty-six.

We are blessed.

"That's the great thing about this game," he tells me, his arm around my shoulder. It is a mild, sunny day, and the grass is soft and springy and the Emerald City of the final hole beckons. This is the lush fairway I imagined. "Even if you have a bunch of bad shots," my father says, "you never know when you're going to hit a good one. And that good one can save you."

AFTERWORD

GOING NOWHERE FAST

Graeme Obree lives with his wife and two sons in Irvine, Scotland, where he rides his bicycle and races in local and national events. His three-man team won the Scottish ten-mile time trial championship last year.

KINGPIN

Pete Weber joined his father, Dick, in the Professional Bowlers Association Hall of Fame in 1998, and in 2002 was elected to the United States Bowling Congress Hall of Fame. He has won thirty-four PBA tour events, including four U.S. Open titles, more than anyone else in the history of the event. He is one of only two bowlers to earn more than $3 million. Weber lives with his wife and three children in St. Louis, Missouri. He has adopted the nickname "PDW" and, after strikes, still often performs his signature move, a professional-wrestling-inspired two-handed crotch chop. He is one of the most popular bowlers in the sport.

"IT'S GONNA SUCK TO BE YOU"

Kirk Apt finished his thirteenth Hard Rock Hundred Mile Endurance Run in July 2007, more than any other person. Though he hasn't won since the 2000 race, he has finished out of the top ten only twice. He says he is still having fun.

Todd Burgess entered the race again in 2001 and completed the course an hour faster than the previous year. Whether he hallucinated is uncertain.

Carolyn Erdman never entered another Hard Rock, though she has paced many Hard Rockers and is one of the event's most diligent and popular volunteers. She runs every day.

LOST AND FOUND

In 2004 Gerry Lindgren was inducted into the National Track & Field Hall of Fame, and the next year he took a job as an assistant track coach at the University of Hawaii. He has talked to his former wife twice, but not to his children.

THE UNBEARABLE LIGHTNESS OF BEING SCOTT WILLIAMSON

Scott Williamson lives in Truckee, California, where he leads workshops on long-distance hiking and occasionally travels to Santa Cruz to do the tree climbing and cutting that supports his hiking habit. In 2006 he walked from Mexico to Canada and back on the Pacific Crest Trail. It was his second round trip. No one else has done it once.

In June 2007 Scott Williamson married Michelle Turley.

FALLING STAR

Marshall Rogers lives in a long-term-care facility in St. Louis, Missouri. He suffers from diabetes, and last winter both his legs were amputated.

UP FROM THE GUTTER

Rudy Kasimakis lives in Tupelo, Mississippi, where he manages a bowling shop and, in the summer, teaches children to bowl. His most profitable year on the PBA tour was the 2005–2006 season, when he earned $39,750. How much he makes bowling action games is uncertain.

TOUGH

Danelle Ballengee began walking in March 2007. In May, she entered and won the female division of a 60-mile adventure race. It took her twelve hours.

THE TRAGEDY

Since his death, three monuments have been erected in Italy to honor Marco Pantani. One is in Cesenatico, his hometown. The others sit in lonely mountain passes, where he so often rode alone.

SIXTEEN MINUTES FROM HOME

Lani McCool lives in Anacortes, where she works on her photography and has recently started writing songs based on her late husband's messages from space. Cameron McCool, nineteen, is in his second year at the University of Washington. Christopher McCool, twenty-three, is coaching debate at a Seattle high school and studying photography. Sean McCool, twenty-seven, was commissioned into the United States Marine Corps in 2005 and was sent to Iraq in the spring of 2007. He has a wife and a son, William Maxwell McCool.

The following have been named for Willie McCool: a lecture hall in Florida; a track in Lubbock, Texas; a science center in Las Vegas; an elementary school in Guam; a village in the Philippines; a hill on Mars; and an asteroid in outer space. This fall the long awaited and long delayed stone memorial to McCool was dedicated on a grassy hilltop of the cross-country course at the United States Naval Academy, where McCool ran as a young man.

LOST IN AMERICA

Steve Vaught is living in San Diego, where he works as a tow-truck driver.

After he finished his walk across the United States, Vaught's wife divorced him, his book contract was cancelled, and he gained back most of his lost weight. The filmmakers who followed him on his journey from California to New York have completed their documentary, *The Fat Man Walking*, and are looking for distributors, but they say that Hollywood studios want something with a happier ending.

A MOMENT OF SILENCE

John Moylan completed the New York City Marathon in 2006 and plans to run the same event in 2007. Last spring Moylan flew to London for business. It was his first overseas flight since September 11, 2001. He hopes to visit Iceland within a year. He runs every day except Monday.

G-D IN HIS CORNER

Dmitry Salita was 27-0-1 in the spring of 2007, an observant Jew praying for a title shot.

DRIVING LESSONS

Barry Friedman plays eighteen holes of golf at least twice a week. He turned seventy-six in April 2007. His family helped him celebrate.

PUBLICATION HISTORY

The chapters of this book have been previously published, some in slightly different form.

"Going Nowhere Fast" appeared in *Bicycling* (June 2003).

"Kingpin" appeared in *GQ* (November 1998).

"'It's Gonna Suck to Be You'" appeared in *Outside* (July 2001).

"Lost and Found" appeared in *Runner's World* (July 2004).

"The Unbearable Lightness of Being Scott Williamson" appeared in *Backpacker* (May 2005).

"Falling Star" appeared in *St. Louis* magazine (November 1987).

"Up from the Gutter" appeared in *Esquire* (April 1999).

"Tough" appeared in *Runner's World* (July 2007).

"The Tragedy" appeared in *Bicycling* (December 2004).

"Sixteen Minutes from Home" appeared in *Runner's World* (December 2005).

"Lost in America" appeared in *Backpacker* (August 2006).

"A Moment of Silence" appeared in *Runner's World* (September 2006).

"G-D in His Corner" appeared in *New York* magazine (July 24, 2006).

"Driving Lessons" appeared in *Travel & Leisure Golf* (May/June 2005).